Angels

OF A *Lower Flight*

ONE WOMAN'S MISSION TO SAVE A
COUNTRY . . . ONE CHILD AT A TIME

Susie Scott Krabacher

A TOUCHSTONE BOOK
Published by Simon & Schuster
New York * London * Toronto * Sydney

 Touchstone
A Division of Simon & Schuster, Inc.
1230 Avenue of the Americas
New York, NY 10020

This work is a memoir. It reflects the author's present recollections of her experiences over a period of years. Certain names and identifying characteristics have been changed, and some dialogue has been re-created.

First Touchstone hardcover edition October 2007

TOUCHSTONE and colophon are registered trademarks of Simon & Schuster, Inc.

For information about special discounts for bulk purchases, please contact Simon & Schuster Special Sales at 1-800-456-6798 or business@simonandschuster.com.

Designed by Jamie Kerner-Scott

Manufactured in the United States of America

10 9 8 7 6 5 4 3 2 1

Library of Congress Cataloging-in-Publication Data is available.

ISBN-13: 978-1-4165-3514-0
ISBN-10:   1-4165-3514-4

So rare and wonderful is it when two people stay together for so long that there are thousands of "Remember when . . ." moments that only the two of you share, only the two of you know about, and only the two of you share secret smiles over when you say it.

Like, remember when . . .

the puppies were born on Christmas night and we stayed up all night thinking of names for them . . .

we caught the little field mouse in the "catch and release" mousetrap and you took him a mile away so he wouldn't come back into the house (per instructions on the box), but you brought him back and let him go in the backyard because, you said, "he might have a family here."

we went skydiving (my first time) and you didn't tell me I had to jump first. Do you remember that I let you live?

when we almost didn't get married . . .

when I almost left you . . . but we stayed together.

Do you remember when we realized we were still in love after eighteen years, and I finally believed you wouldn't leave me?

Do you wanna make some more . . . memories with me? I can't wait. . . .

Joe—I love you. This book is for you.

"You don't think—not possibly—not as a mere hundredth of a chance—there might be things that are real though we can't see them?"

—ORUAL, TO THE FOX, IN *TILL WE HAVE FACES,*

BY C. S. LEWIS

Contents

Angels

OF A *Lower Flight*

Overture

As I stand in knee-deep Colorado snow and watch the waters of the Roaring Fork River sparkle and wink, I realize I am finally happy. My gloveless hands are stuffed, deep and warm, in the pockets of my old ski parka. The breeze lifts the snowflakes like glitter from the tree branches. The flakes twirl in a cheerful dance before becoming part of the river below. It is a fine day near the town of Aspen, where I live with my husband, Joe.

Soon I'll leave again for my other home, Haiti. I don't know what awaits me on this next trip. If what I've encountered so far in my lifetime is any indication of what I'll face next, I may wish I had stayed home.

But my travels are about my calling, not about fate. At age forty-three, I feel that strange paradox of being young and old at the same time. No longer do I search for a finish line. I know it's there, unseen. I'm just taking each small decisive step toward that invisible finish and toward those who I know await my arrival and cheer me from the other side. Sometimes I hear them in my moments of despair. And I think about what we might say when we meet again. I'll tell them again that in this world they were loved. This I know, because I loved them.

I hear others too. Their voices are still here, still now. They send shafts of hope through my dark times:

Patricia, an elfin seven-year-old, now adopted by a family in Ft. Meyers. When she came to us, her smile was marred only by a cleft palate. We were able to secure an operation for her in the United States. Today she enjoys total health.

We found Sanon at age nine, hiding in an empty building with his two younger siblings. His parents had both died. His grandmother tried to care for him until she no longer could. Sanon was spread thin in his desperation, one part wedged in responsibility, the other immovable in grief. Today Sanon is seventeen, a muscled, astute young man who interns for our foundation. His computer skills shine, and he is being trained in management. He has never lost the drive to provide a better life for himself and his siblings.

Marty was never expected to live, much less walk. We found him at age three, abandoned, his skull enlarged from hydrocephalic syndrome. Whenever he tried to walk, he toppled over because of the extra weight. Today he jokes with the rest of the children at the orphanage that he's the smartest because his head, though healed, remains the largest. His progress is astounding: now six, Marty blazes through his ABCs; he sings with aplomb; and he doesn't just attempt to walk on his spindly legs anymore—he runs, he skips, he sprints, he dances.

Those are the mental pictures I hold closest. Once, in a lapse of judgment, I took my dog Flo-Dell to the grocery store in Aspen, where I promptly lost her. Panicked, I called my husband: "See— *this* is why we have no children," I said.

"What do you mean we don't have any children?" Joe retorted. "We have *thousands* of them."

Flo-Dell was soon found.

And, yes, Joe was right.

In my life, I have known both opulence and squalor. I have dined with celebrities, and shoveled hell with demons. What motivates me today is a faith that compels action, a vision to look upon each of the world's children as valuable and loved, and a belief that the unexplainable and miraculous happen on a daily basis. My platform—what I stand on—is courage, action, survival, and dignity, both for the desperate children of Haiti and for people anywhere who need help.

This is the story of how I journeyed from a world of hurt to a world of hope. The hope I found is seldom seen in huge successes but rather in a song murmured in a hospital, a bottle of water bought for a child, a note tucked in a dark place. These small flickers combine into enormous rays of light.

Chapter 1

Coffin Notes

I N THE WINTER OF 1995, I toured the pediatric and maternity wards of the government hospital in Port-au-Prince for the first time. Nearing the hospital, I could see dozens of women in the entryway, some clearly in advanced stages of pregnancy, others already holding tiny babies or toddlers against their breasts. A few were lying on straw mats or leaning against the concrete building, sweltering in the tropical heat. It seemed that each woman I passed either mumbled incoherently or wept, hands pressed to her face, her tears running between crooked callused knuckles. I had brought a few Haitian *gourdes* and American dollars to purchase water and medicine for the patients. I didn't yet know what else I could do.

An elderly gentleman dozed in the entryway with a shotgun balanced on his thighs. I gently tapped on the metal door frame beside him, and he started from his nap. Grasping his shotgun with one hand and the waistband of his britches with the other, he fumbled to keep his pants from falling down over his protruding hip bones.

"State your beezness," he said irritably, his English thickly accented with Creole.*

"She eez missionary." My companion, Viximar, a Haitian national, family man, and trusted friend, answered for me, although I disliked that description of myself and considered it inaccurate. I had come to Haiti without a Christian agenda or connection to an organization, only the desire to make good on a promise I made to God when I was little.

The elderly security guard waved us through. Once inside, I thumped Viximar on the arm.

"Don't lie!" I said.

He grinned. The word *missionary* always seemed to facilitate entry when needed.

If nothing else, I had come to Haiti hoping to leave my demons behind me, but soon after I arrived I realized that I had, in fact, fled to their native land. I had first come to this small country—a mere five hundred miles south of Florida—more than a year earlier, and in the twelve months that followed, I had witnessed more pain, suffering, and death than I could have possibly previously imagined. Though I had no earlier training or experience as a relief worker—my last job was owner of an antique shop in Aspen, Colorado—I somehow was able to start a small school and feeding program in Cité Soleil, a ravished district in the Haitian capital, arguably the worst slum in the Western Hemisphere. Viximar lived there with his family and was guardian of my school.

---

*Haiti has two official languages—French and Creole (sometimes spelled Kreyòl). The majority of Haitians (about 90 percent) speak only Creole, a hybrid of French that includes some Spanish, African, and Taino dialects. English and Spanish are also spoken on a limited basis, particularly in the business community.

The hospital I was visiting with Viximar was the government hospital, and while it's not the only one in Haiti, it is the cheapest, and meant for the poorest of the poor. When Viximar and I went inside we found three large wards, each measuring around twenty by twenty feet. About a hundred children and infants lay in the three rooms. Most of them were covered with flies and ants, and though they must have ranged in age from a few months to several years, it was difficult to tell, given the distortions of illness and malnutrition. Some of the children appeared to be there alone; others had an adult holding vigil nearby; many of them were crying. But the ones who immediately caught and held my attention were the children who simply stared. They seemed oblivious to the swarms of flies and ants feasting on their excrement. They were alone with no adult to watch over them, their tiny faces sculpted only by bones, hunger, and fear.

Words penned by Elie Wiesel, Nobel Prize–winning journalist and Nazi-concentration-camp survivor, have haunted me since I first read them. Wiesel spoke of an old man who could no longer fight and would soon be a victim of the "selection." In the concentration camps during the Holocaust it was a frequently used term for those weakened and no longer able to perform labor. They were *selected* for extermination. It was only now, as I looked into the eyes of these children, that the meaning truly penetrated my soul: "Suddenly his eyes would become blank, nothing but two open wounds, two pits of horror."

These children in the Haitian hospital had also been selected. For them it would only be a matter of time.

As I stood in the pediatric ward of the government hospital, I wanted to cry. *No*, I wanted to scream. But during the past year that I had worked in Haiti I had learned to do the opposite of what I would normally do back home in Aspen. So I stood there and thought through the situation: If I had been one of these children or mothers lying here, wondering if I was going to die, and I had seen a white woman, maybe for the first time, I would have been terrified. And if any woman would have looked at me and started crying, let alone screaming, I would have thought something horrible was happening to me.

So there was my answer. I wouldn't cry. I wouldn't turn away. I would do the opposite. Or something close to it, anyway: I would sing. And so I began to hum very lightly and smile at each person I passed, reaching out to touch tiny hands and feet.

I was afraid I would hurt the patients as I touched them; they had so many sores and bandages. I had never witnessed such agony. I wondered how many foreigners heard about this place and came, saw, cried, and left, never to forget it, yet leaving everything just as it was, as if they were never here at all. For several hours I walked through the maze of iron cribs and stained cots, in and out of the rooms, observing every kind of deformity, handicap, and disease that could be imagined.

I had spent the twenty years before I came to Haiti focused inward, on myself. My ambition had been to transform myself into someone who would be loved. Not satisfied with my natural state, I spent days at the hair salon and gym, manicuring, pedicuring, soaking, dyeing, running, tanning, waxing, and dieting. I read dozens of self-help books: *Dianetics. Psycho-Cybernetics. The Road Less Traveled. Think and Grow Rich. Transcendental Meditation. The Celestine Prophecy. The Seven Habits of Highly Effective People.* From the moment I left my parents' home, at age fifteen, my sole purpose in life had been "self" improvement. I walked out the door with no money and only a tenth-grade education. But I knew a few things. I knew that the only way I would ever make it through my remaining seventy years—what I figured I had left—

would be on my own. Not that I hadn't heard of God; I knew all about God. First, that He was slow. And second, that He seemed to have a mean streak, at least when it came to me.

Over the years, as part of my "self improvement," I had carefully buried my childhood memories, putting them safely in the ground, one by one, where I could keep track of them and keep them from contaminating my improved self. In the hospital in Haiti, as I walked on through each of the rooms, still singing quietly, I knew that for these children, growing up in this lonely place would result in the same sort of personal graveyard. If they ever got to grow up.

For years, I had scarcely touched a Bible, although I had gone to church every Sunday during my childhood in Alabama. I had spent most of each sermon watching the clock and hoping the preacher really meant it when he said ". . . and in conclusion . . ." for the seventh or eighth time. But the thousands of hours spent in a church pew had burned a complete set of hymns and Bible verses into my brain. Sometimes, when in trouble or depressed, I would hear the Psalms or other verses—not as if they came from memory, but from an invisible presence between my shoulders. That presence returned to me while I was in the hospital ward, and I began to put words to my humming, quietly singing the comforting parts of hymns I remembered: "Oh Lord my God, when I in awesome wonder / consider all the works Thy hands have made . . ."

Through the rooms I sang, I hummed, I smiled, and I touched. So many sick people. So much despair.

INSIDE A RUSTED CRIB lay a bundle of rags with a skeletal face nestled inside. A woman, the mother, I assumed, leaned over the rail. She wept, seemingly inconsolable, and clutched a small square piece of paper. I avoided going near her when I first walked by because I didn't want to disturb her privacy and obvious grief. I later learned to recognize that reaction as a peculiarly American one.

With my tour nearly over, I was ready to leave the bundle of diapers we had brought for whoever needed them and go back to the hotel. I was finished with watching people suffer. But something inside me made me turn and walk back to the woman by the rusted crib. For a minute or so, I simply stood near her. I watched her as, through her tears, she followed the tiny spiral of her baby's rib cage, heaving up and down. The baby stared at the mother, sluggish but awake. As with so many of the other babies, ants scuttled around and within her badly dirtied diaper.

Gently, I laid my hand on the woman's shoulder. She lifted her head for a second and then collapsed under my touch. Viximar, who was at my side, rushed to catch her before she hit the floor. She was frail and gaunt, not more than eighty pounds. I asked Viximar to take some of my gourdes, buy water from one of the vendors on the street, and quickly get her something to eat, if he could find it. He helped me settle the woman near a wall beside the crib.

"Ti-Judith," the woman whispered, gazing weakly up to where her tiny daughter lay. That was the child's name: Ti-Judith.

I removed my fanny pack from around my waist and placed it under the mother's head so that her cheek did not rest on the filthy concrete floor. I returned to the baby, Ti-Judith, and peeled away the diaper that stuck between her teeny legs. It was laden with thick yellow liquid. I changed her diaper and cleaned her the best I could without water. The little girl's lips were cracked, and her long narrow feet and hands were skin-covered bones.

The mother had fallen asleep. I reached down and read the piece of paper she clutched between her bony fingers. She looked a hundred years old, though she couldn't have been more than twenty-five. The paper appeared to be a prescription, dated days earlier. I recognized the French word for *saline*, barely legible, as the paper was soaked with either tears or sweat. The other word I recognized was an antibiotic.

When Viximar returned he knelt beside the mother and put a plastic pouch of water to her lips. She stirred, and almost immediately started to plead and cry again. I felt wetness forming in the corners of my own eyes but blinked it back. I thought of all the times that I made myself stop crying on demand when, with a stick in her hand, my mother said to "Dry it up!" After that, it was easier.

I tried to calm the mother, holding her hand, smoothing her hair, but she was crying for her daughter and wouldn't be consoled. I had never seen anyone bear another human being's pain with such desperate agony. I silently wished my mother had cherished me like that. I asked Viximar to try to get her to eat the *griot* (fried goat meat) he had brought back in a grease-stained paper bag. The women initially refused, but after Viximar placed a bit in her hand, she put the small bite inside her mouth and chewed. A small glimmer awoke in her eyes. She reached out and gobbled up the meal with abandon.

While she ate I asked Viximar to tell me where we could buy the prescriptions on the piece of paper. The only doctor Viximar could find on the compound was an intern, but he confirmed that what was prescribed was in fact a saline solution and a common antibiotic. The intern did not know where to purchase the prescription at this late hour and went on to explain that to administer the medicine we would need to buy a syringe and some gauze, because the hospital did not have any left. I gave Viximar all the money I had in my fanny pack and instructed him not to come back until he found everything on the list.

While the mother dozed again, I picked up the baby girl and held her. She didn't cry at all. Her gaze seemed focused on something invisible in the distance between us. I lifted her to my lips and kissed her nose. She didn't look like a baby, really, except for her smallness. I wondered if she would ever smell like the babies I had held in the United States. I had always loved the smell of baby powder, baby lotion, baby shampoo, and baby clothes drenched in fabric softeners. Ti-Judith's little blanket was tattered and badly stained; the pink and yellow flowers on it were faded and barely visible. Her tiny fingernails were long and jagged. It seemed as if I were holding an incredibly old woman, wizened and decrepit. I wondered if this child would ever get to be any older than she was now. I took a deep breath and watched, staring at her until she closed her eyes, hesitantly, as if the greatest battle of her life was to stay awake.

When Viximar returned two hours later he had all of the items requested except the syringe, which could not be purchased until one of the official pharmacies opened the following morning. I asked Viximar to explain to the mother that we would be back tomorrow. He gave the woman the antibiotics, gauze, and five plastic pouches of saline solution. We stayed until she drifted into sleep again. I changed Ti-Judith's diaper once more, and asked Viximar to place the remaining part of the bundle of diapers under the woman's head. We left her in peace.

The mother didn't stir.

I SLEPT THAT NIGHT at the El Rancho Hotel in a small room with faded red carpet on the floor and a bright red clawfoot bathtub, in which I washed and rinsed my clothes for the next day. My room was near the hotel casino, a decaying 1970s remnant of one of the few periods when Haiti had rallied itself enough to lure a few cruise ships into its tropical ports. I turned the rickety air conditioner on high to drown out the noise below from the UN soldiers and their Haitian prostitutes, laughing and cheering from inside the casino.

My plan was to leave early in the morning, buy the syringes, and get to the hospital before the Port-au-Prince traffic became impenetrable. Thoroughfares in the Haitian capital are seldom dependable and usually jammed with rickety *tap-taps* (the colorfully painted passenger buses used by locals, notorious for their ill-maintained brakes) or barricaded with burning tires planted by political activists or entrepreneurial protesters who will agitate against anything for a meal or a weapon or a few gourdes.

But when I awoke, it was to a pounding at the door and an angry sun beating through a gap in the partially drawn drapes. I looked at the clock on the nightstand—9:04 a.m. I had slept twelve hours. In an instant, I was completely awake. Racing around the room, I searched for my robe. "Hold on, I'm coming!" I eased the door open, leaving the chain intact.

"Madam, we must go! It is late!" Viximar said.

"My alarm must not have been set—give me two minutes!" I said. Then, thinking more rationally, I took the chain off and opened the door. "Viximar, please go to the front desk and ask if there is a pharmacy nearby where you can get some syringes. By the time you get back, I'll be ready—twenty minutes, tops!" Viximar nodded and then went running down the red-carpeted hallway.

Twenty minutes later I was ready, but it took us more than two hours to reach the hospital. Burning barricades manned by gun-toting gangs made us turn back four times to seek other routes, but of course every other street had already been clogged by hundreds of other vehicles seeking to avoid the same obstacles. When we arrived it was already 11:30.

I went straight toward the back room and crib where Ti-Judith lay. Someone had attached an IV tube to her, but instead of embedding the IV into her forearm, someone had inserted the tube into a vein on the side of her head. The tube led to one of the plastic bags of saline solution we had bought the day before. Ti-Judith's face was less taut and seemed to be a shade darker than when I left her many hours ago. Her diaper, new when I had left her the day before, had not been changed since. I went about the business of wiping her red, irritated bottom and cleaning the plastic sheeting beneath her.

Where was her mother? Deciding that perhaps she had gone to relieve herself or was sleeping outside with the other women camped around the hospital's entrance, I picked Ti-Judith up, careful of her IV, and walked to an area of the building where everyone seemed to be resting. I sat down against the wall and propped the infant against my thighs with her head at the top of my knees. I took the small mirror from my fanny pack and held it closely in front of Ti-Judith's face. She seemed transfixed by her own eyes. I moved the mirror slightly to the right, then to the left. Her eyes followed. I couldn't think of any baby songs, so I sang "Jesus Loves Me," a song I had learned as a child. For the first time, I saw Ti-Judith smile.

We sat there for maybe fifteen minutes before Ti-Judith started to cry and strain a bit. I was afraid I had dislodged the IV, so I placed the bag on her belly and played with her lips with my finger. She poked a little pink tongue out, then pursed her lips. Her fingers wrapped around my forefinger, and she tried to force it into her mouth. I stood up with her and went in search of a doctor or nurse. I found someone who looked like a medic. In broken Creole I tried to tell him the baby was hungry and that I wanted to feed her. He just smiled. *Okay.* I surmised that since they had no gauze, no diapers, no syringes, no medicine, and hardly any doctors or nurses, they probably had no food. Cuddling the baby against my breast, I walked back to the crib assigned to her, in search of baby food.

Viximar was waiting near the crib. He was leaning with his head against the wall where we had left Ti-Judith's mother sleeping the night before.

"She is *morte*," Viximar said, in a mix of Creole and English, looking at me with his head still against the wall. "She took the antibiotics, but they did not help her."

I stared at Viximar. It had not occurred to me that the antibiotics were for the mother.

"She had the bad blood," Viximar said. I looked at him, not understanding. "The AIDS; she had the AIDS." He shook his head sadly.

I looked down at the baby I held in my arms. I had put my finger in her mouth, not thinking that she also might have contracted the disease. She had sucked my finger and stopped crying.

"Who will take care of her now?" I asked, my voice wavering. "Where is her father?"

Viximar only shook his head. He did not know. We both looked at the baby in my arms.

THE TRAFFIC HAD ABATED somewhat, so it did not take long to reach the only market I knew of that sold Enfamil and baby bottles and return to the hospital. I spent the rest of the day holding Ti-Judith and talking to any doctor who made a rare appearance in the pediatric section. Around 6 p.m. I decided we should head back to the hotel before dark. There had been talk around the hospital that tonight in the downtown area there would be more shooting. I had learned not to second-guess this kind of gossip.

I changed Ti-Judith one more time, then left the Enfamil and a prepared bottle with a woman who was there with her twelve-year-old son, a burn victim. He had fallen into a kettle of hot oil that was used to fry griot and plantains. I gave her a few gourdes to buy the salve the doctor had told her to use to ease the child's pain, and she agreed to feed Ti-Judith a little of the formula every few hours until I returned the next morning.

After making arrangements to be picked up at 7 a.m. the next day, I gave Viximar a hug at the entrance of the hotel and said good night. Inside the lobby, a young woman with large inquisitive eyes sat behind the reception desk. "Madam Susie?" she asked. "I have a message." She handed it to me. It read, "Caller: Mr. Joe. Time: 8:53 p.m. Message: 'I love you.'" The woman smiled, revealing a large space between her bright white front teeth. "He said to make sure I tell you he loves you!" she said.

"That's my husband. I can't believe I missed him." I had tried to call him several times over the past few nights after returning to the hotel, but no luck. The phone lines worked sporadically, and when they did, all the hotel guests rushed to make calls, tying up the lines.

"Would you try to get a line out for me to make an international call?"

"Yes, I will try." And she did, each time pushing the receiver button down with her chubby forefinger. "The lines are down right now. We can try for you later."

I thanked her, went to my room, fell onto my bed, and prayed for the children at the hospital. I prayed they wouldn't suffer tonight, and that God would let them see their guardian angels so they wouldn't feel alone.

◆　◆　◆

TI-JUDITH WAS DEAD.

Viximar and I stood behind a toothless man whose only clothes were a torn pair of boxer shorts and gray rubber fishing boots. As he pulled back a gigantic steel sliding door, I felt my head jerk back involuntarily and my eyes begin to sting. The stench that rushed out at us was so powerful it seemed to have texture. The man reached above the door and yanked a string to illuminate the room. I tucked my nose into the inside of my elbow and walked into what was surely the nearest place on earth to hell.

All around us were stacks of dead bodies, their limbs crumpled and askew. Blood seeped from the stacks, many of which towered above me, and all the corpses showed obvious signs of decay. Viximar took one look and then fled toward daylight and fresh air. From somewhere ahead of me came the unhurried exhalations of the morgue caretaker, who was somehow able to breathe normally. In my horror, I was only dimly aware of the sound, at least until I could no longer hear it. *Where did he go? What if he closes the steel door and locks me in here?* I was alone in the morgue behind the government hospital. I choked the thought from my mind and began to pray. *Come back if You have left me, God! Oh, help me! You said you'd be with me always.* My thoughts raced with doubt and fear. *Ti-Judith. Oh, little girl. I must remember your face. I must concentrate on that.*

My hands were clammy and I felt dizzy and faint. I realized I wasn't breathing. I took the hem of my dress and lifted it up to cover the lower half of my face. I took a breath. The floor sucked at my shoes—I realized it was from blood that had drained from the corpses and not yet dried. It occurred to me that this was why the man wore rubber boots.

I turned around, and the man in his underwear appeared from the shadowy recesses of the room. He thrust a small naked male infant near my face. The child showed signs of having been dead for several days. I nearly gagged as I coughed and turned my head away.

"Is this it? He here long time!"

"No, no! A girl! Ti-Judith! She was brought here last night!"

The man flung the baby boy up onto the top shelf of the metal racks. He poked at my arm with a bloodstained finger and motioned for me to follow. I willed myself to move and then nearly fell as my shoe clung to the sticky blood on the floor.

I let go of the hem of my dress to use my hand to keep myself from falling onto the body of a young girl on the concrete in front of me. She was wearing only a torn pair of panties; on her face was the last grimace she had borne in life. As I reached up to steady myself, my hand brushed the bare belly of a woman tossed onto a concrete platform. She appeared to be at full term of her pregnancy. Her flesh was hard and cold. Between her colorless eyes was a small, blood-rimmed hole, about the size of a dime. Who would shoot a pregnant woman in the head? As I turned away I saw her gaping mouth move as if to speak. I started and began to run. I ran past the man in boots, the only other living creature in the room, and then over another body, that of a bullet-ridden boy. I was looking for Ti-Judith. I had to find her, I had to get her out of there. I tried to move quickly but the light was so dim; my eyes searched in vain through the remains of skinny children and tiny newborn babies that I discovered heaped in piles on the blood-covered concrete floor.

An eternity seemed to pass. I tried to hold my breath, and then grabbed a bunch of my hair and pressed it hard against my face. I reached for the rim of a gigantic wooden barrel to balance myself while trying to squeeze between it and a metal gurney that held the half-naked, decomposing body of what looked like a toothless old man. In front of me was a rusty metal rack of shelves that held several layers of deflated toddler-sized bodies. The sight of all the little feet hanging stiffly on top of the others tore at my heart.

Then I noticed for the first time the worms around the bodies. I gasped for air and smelled worm shit. The worms were writhing, slithering, feeding; they were shitting out what had once been mothers, fathers, sons, daughters, husbands, wives—each of them the light and hope of someone's life.

I had to turn my face. For a split second, as I held on to the edge of the barrel, my gaze fell upon a line of wide, terror-filled eyes. I was sick and tasted vomit in my mouth. *Oh, Ti-Judith, little girl. Where are you!* Was I talking, thinking, screaming? I don't know. *I will find you. I won't leave you here!* As if in answer to my vow, I heard a scraping sound and, startled, turned to find the man with the boots and underwear holding a small limp body up by its right arm for my inspection.

"Is girl," the man said as he lifted her closer. Her open eyes had sunk deep into her head, and her tiny lips curled inward. It crossed my mind that she was not stiff yet. For some reason, this felt like an accomplishment—she must have died only an hour or two ago. It was Ti-Judith. I nodded my head.

Outside, I knelt behind a rusted shell of an old car and cried and vomited. I wiped my face with my dress and rubbed my hands in the dirt. I walked slowly back and waited while the man wrote Ti-Judith's name down in an old ledger with a frayed and torn cover. The man handed me a broken pencil, and I signed my name on the line next to Ti-Judith's. I bought one of the tiny Styrofoam coffins that the man urged me to purchase, but I simply could not put Ti-Judith's body inside it. The coffin had no lining and seemed so uncomfortable for such a frail little girl. I cradled her tiny body in one arm, paid the five American dollars, grabbed the coffin under the other, and left.

Viximar and the driver had pulled up the truck near the entrance of the morgue. They were both silent as they opened the back of the truck and cleared enough space to place Ti-Judith's coffin and body. I shook my head and climbed into the front seat. I'd hold her, I told them. Viximar found a piece of plastic from a nearby pile of garbage and wrapped her in it. From their expressions, I could tell that her corpse had begun to smell. We drove to the orphanage to wash and bury her.

There was no consolation in this moment, this tiny funeral procession for a dead Haitian child. There in the truck, my teeth were clamped together so tightly that I felt a bit of tooth break off. I spat it out and tilted my head back so far I heard my neck crack. I opened my mouth and began to scream. I screamed willfully, as loud as I was able. I didn't recognize the sound as my own. It was scratchy and high-pitched and agonizing. The sound of my voice terrified me as much as the fear of being locked in the morgue. I had completely lost it. Words spilled from me, and I ripped at my hair. There was no gauge by which I could measure reality any longer. Every face, every set of eyes, every pair of little feet was now part of me forever. I screamed again and again.

Ti-Judith lay wrapped in that torn piece of plastic on the seat beside me while I buried my face in my dress. She had died in the early morning while I fought off the usual monsters in my dreams. She was taken to that horrible place all alone. We found out later that the mother of the little burned boy had tried to rouse her to give her some of the formula, but she would not wake up. She had given the guard three gourdes to take the body to the morgue behind the hospital.

"Ummmmm, hmmm, uhummm, uhmmmmmm." Inside the truck, Viximar began to hum a song he had learned from missionaries when he was a boy. He opened his mouth and began to sing

"Amazing Grace," quietly at first, then louder as the words came to him.

"Sing, Susie, sing for her," Viximar said. "Sing for Ti-Judith. In this world, she was loved."

That last phrase caught at my throat, a small comfort on the surface, but deep as a silver mine in truth. I wondered if Ti-Judith had ever known anybody who hadn't looked upon her as a burden. Ti-Judith's mother had loved her, I knew that. And I loved her. That was two. I imagined Ti-Judith in heaven, resting in the arms of Jesus. Her pain and suffering were over now. There would be no more hunger or tears where she was. Ti-Judith was indeed loved.

At the orphanage we cleaned Ti-Judith's body. We bought a used dress from a street vendor and put Ti-Judith in it. The dress was made for a little girl's party, pink with lacy trim and a white collar. It hung on Ti-Judith's tiny frame. We buried her in a small plot at the city cemetery. As the men lowered the coffin, I asked them to stop. Viximar ran to the truck and grabbed a scrap of paper, and with a pen from my purse I wrote a note.

On that note was a phrase I would write from that moment onward. I would write it repeatedly, and I would write it too often. I would write it in tribute to every child I ever knew who died. It was the phrase I wanted everyone who had ever been hungry, poor, alone, destitute, or sick to somehow know and feel and remember and hold close. Over time, the phrase would come to symbolize all that I held to be important.

The note read, "In this world, you were loved." I opened Ti-Judith's tiny coffin without a word, and slipped the note inside.

Chapter 2

Muscadine Stains

THE EVIL I CONFRONT in the slums of Haiti first visited me when I was a child, growing up in small-town rural Alabama in the mid-1960s. Most people think back to childhood as their best time. I hated mine. As a four-year-old, I used to lock the bathroom door behind me, cry, and study my reflection in the mirror. I looked old and wise. So many Haitian children have the same look of awareness and maturity—too much maturity for a child; facial expressions that children should not wear, feelings that children should never feel.

Mostly, like all little kids, I just wanted to be loved.

One day I was with my babysitter, LaDora, at a shopping mall near Lacey's Spring. Barefoot, I stubbed my big toe on a crack in the concrete floor. My toenail broke in half. LaDora frantically tried to stop the bleeding. She was so upset, I was afraid she was going to start crying. So I started crying first. It felt good. It was the first time I cried without being afraid I'd get a whipping with the belt. LaDora never carried a belt like my mama did. I decided to cry the rest of the day. Maybe LaDora would want to cry a bit with me. She was black and fat, and I figured she liked ice cream. I wished I had money so I could buy her a cone. I remember thinking it would be nice if she would adopt me. She wasn't beautiful, like Mama, but she was clean and smelled like rosewater. I was having the best kind of day pretending LaDora was my new mama.

You see, crying was never tolerated by my real mama. If any of us kids started to sniffle, she would threaten us: "Dry it up, or else I'll knock your teeth down your throat." Hers weren't idle threats. Mama often used belts and sticks. She called it "spanking," but really, it was whipping. We'd often appear at school with bruises, welts, cuts, and scrapes. After a while it took a lot to force me to tears.

My mama, Betty, was a stunningly beautiful woman. But in her secret self-loathing, she could not see her beauty. My father's mother begged Daddy to leave her, arguing bad genes. Mama came from a bloodline of classic possum-eaters. Pure hillbillies to the core. Picture the Hatfields and McCoys—only worse; that was my mother's upbringing. Jealousy, insanity, cruelty, feuding, and suicide were heavily laced throughout the Powell gene pool.

My daddy, Frank, was an engineer and brilliant. He built houses on the side. We lived in the houses briefly, then Daddy sold them, so we moved around a lot—Athens, Cotaco, Huntsville—mostly in the same area, but always a different school. When we lived in Lacey's Spring we lived on twenty-four acres. We had a catfish pond and a pig shed, and Daddy built a barn with stalls so we could board horses for extra money. I adored and worshipped Daddy. For some reason he also adored and worshipped my mama. His main concern with us kids was having us not upset her. I can't explain why my father never did anything to help us.

Mama's violence wasn't a secret in our small town. Other kids were seldom allowed to play with us. Some folks called us monsters. Mama was diagnosed as a borderline schizophrenic and had a host of other mental problems. She always took pills—she called it her "nerve medicine." When we were a bit older Mama lost all control. I believe she suffered a complete mental breakdown. Over the years she underwent six electroshock treatments and was in and out of psychiatric care.

Knowing all that doesn't make it any easier for a kid.

At age four, I considered myself very plain looking. I had a large gap between my front teeth, basic brown eyes, and blond hair that was never cut. Mama said I had walnuts in my cheeks because my face was so round. I began to keep track of the days that passed without a spanking. My sister, Tammy, and I lay awake on the tenth night—we couldn't believe we had made it that far. I climbed into Tammy's bed and scratched her back while she gave me well-thought-out advice.

"If you cry when it first starts, then it doesn't last as long," Tammy said. She was brilliant for her age. She was two years older, and her techniques, tried and tested, were listened to with reverence.

"And if they know what your favorite thing is," Tammy added, "that's the first thing they take away. You gotta act like something else is what you like best. Then when they tell you they're taking it away, you gotta cry and act sad for at least a day."

Man, I really loved her. I could have lain there scratching her back all night just to keep her giving me this kind of information. From then on, I tried to follow Tammy's advice whenever I could. I was terrified of my mother's wrath. I learned never to do anything "wrong"—meaning anything that would provoke my mama's anger. So I purposely didn't have a doll, like other girls my age, because if I got Mama upset I knew she would take the doll away. It's crazy, but I had this little pet rock instead. It almost seems silly now. I named it Sugido—*Su* for me, *gi* for a girl at church named Gina Faye whom I wanted to be friends with, and *do* for Donny Osmond, whom I had a crush on. My reasoning with the rock was: Mama won't know it's important to me, so she won't ever take it away. I didn't dare draw a face on it—it was a plain old rock. But I gave it a name known only to me.

To say we were a religious family is an understatement. Whenever the doors opened at Sommersville Church of Christ, we were there—three times a week at least. It was a tiny church of about seventy regulars, and we had all met in an old trailer until enough money was saved to build it. The new building was redbrick with white trim, no cross or steeple (icons meant idol worship), with a large baptismal tank inside behind where the preacher stood. Across the street was a cemetery where folks had been buried for a hundred years or more. Some graves had collapsed over time and left body-sized crevices in the grass. About five other kids beside the four kids in our family attended the church, and after Sunday- and Wednesday-evening meetings we'd play in the cemetery, sometimes tripping and tumbling into the sunken graves. One of my little friends, Diana, coughed all the time. Her red-freckled face was always drawn tight, and she was always grouchy. We knew she had cystic fibrosis but weren't sure what it meant. After she died she was buried in that cemetery. We never played there anymore, but we'd hang out on the church steps and watch from across the street. When it got dusky, we'd all swear we could see a glowing lantern hanging over Diana's grave.

Mama's interpretation of religion dictated everything for my family. Mama was convinced that God was very strict and didn't like bare skin, so Tammy and I could never wear shorts or short sleeves. No pants either. Ever. They were for boys. In summer, we had to swim with dresses on. My brothers swam in pants and shirts. Even in gym class we couldn't wear shorts. This was all just Mama. She was convinced you should never be able to see a woman's shape. None of our other friends at church or school were under rules this strict. According to Mama, folks were bad for just about everything they did. "You'll go to hell!" Mama shouted. It was common for adults to stand in front of our conservative church congregation and confess their sins out loud. Mama thought we kids should have to do that too. I still prayed to God, though, all the time. I knew He was looking down on us, thinking something—I just didn't know what.

At school, my mother was not known as a nice woman. She yelled at our teachers and principal. She craved control. A school bus went right by our house, but Mama said, "No, you're not taking it again today, either." She was scared we'd learn bad words on the bus. So she picked us up from school every day, but she might show up an hour or more later than promised. We hung around, playing on monkey bars, swinging on the swing set. She eventually drove up—no explanation or remorse. We assumed she spent the day sleeping. Our house was always the same as when we left it in the morning. When we got home, Mama was eager to have us start on our chores. Mine were to clean the bathrooms and vacuum the house, and then after dinner clean the kitchen with Tammy.

Before my brother Mark was old enough for school, he often spent the day over at my grandmother's. Mark, who is five years younger than I, was hyperactive, Mama said. He made her nervous, and whenever Mark cried, she hit him. Mark favored my sister, Tammy, because she rocked and held him twenty-four hours a day if she could. I loved Mark too, and called him Baby Markett when I played house with him. I made our brother Matt, four years younger than I, play the daddy, while I was the mother. Matt liked to play until I yelled at him the same way my mother yelled at my father. Then Matt would quit and play with his G.I. Joe instead. Somehow I'd find ways to pry Baby Markett away from Tammy, and over time, we became the closest, I think. I don't believe Tammy minded much. As siblings, we all looked to each other for support. Years later we would struggle to maintain this bond as the trauma of our childhoods reverberated through our adult lives.

WHEN THINGS GOT REALLY bad in our house, we stayed with my grandparents—Daddy's mama and papa. Although we moved around, it seemed they always lived half an hour down the road. They were religious—Grandpa was an elder at the church they went to—but never as strict as Mama. I had a little bedroom that Grandma called my room. It had a twin bed in it, and when Tammy and I stayed overnight we would sleep together on it and talk about picking some muscadines the next day so Grandma could make us some jars of jelly. The wild grapes grow easily in the warm, humid South.

I thought there was no cooler woman than my grandmother. Sometimes we sneaked into the old den, where Grandma often fell asleep after watching *The Price Is Right* or *Let's Make a Deal* or one of her "stories," as she called them. Most of the time she didn't wake up when we got the ice cream out of the freezer box, but whenever she did, she came in to help us. She'd cut open a cantaloupe and scrape out the seeds and scoop vanilla ice cream into the hollow. "Cantaloupe à la mode," she would say, like it was the best of French desserts. I loved that old woman to the very marrow of my bones. We sometimes talked about how Mama was too rough on me when she hit me with a stick or belt. Grandma asked me if Daddy ever spanked us like that, and I told her "not usually," only if Mama made him do it. Daddy didn't like to; I could see it in his face.

One spanking stands out vividly. Daddy's belt stayed on his pants for this one, but the greater injustice of the incident blisters to this day. On that summer afternoon my toy oven was taken away from me because, after I returned from my grandparents' house, Mama saw that I had muscadine stains on the back of my dress. She twisted my elbow over my head in her vise-grip hands to look me over and put her face right in mine. I was a "wicked, evil child," she screamed—Daddy was going to whip me when he got home. I stood in the playroom—the garage where Daddy had put down carpet—looking at my new toy oven; I couldn't play with it now for three weeks. I could feel the red rising to my face and a bruise form-ing on my arm. I wanted to scream back at her, "I would never get my dress dirty if I could help it! I love my new dress!"

But all too often kids stay silent.

Earlier that morning we had gotten up early so we could pick the muscadines for Grandma's jelly. Grandpa said he would drive me and Tammy down to the creek bed since both of us were bare-foot and refused to put on shoes. The muscadines grew thick on the banks of the old creek, even though the water had mostly dried up from the kind of hot summer people in Alabama talk about for years afterward. I was thinking to myself that this would be a fine day. Tammy was there, and I felt very fine myself to know that we'd be having muscadine jelly on Grandma's biscuits for supper.

We rode in the bed of Grandpapa's old powder-blue pickup through the back pasture where most of the hay had already gone to seed. I was looking at the ground intently as we bumped over rocks and through cow pies in hopes I'd spot a little bird's nest that had fallen from one of the grand old maple or oak trees. Sometimes when the wind gusted, the tiny sparrows' nests would dislodge and fall into the tall weeds. I raised many abandoned baby sparrows during those summers and cried every time they matured and flew away.

I didn't find any nests that day. When we reached the old creek bed that meandered like a serpent through our grandparents' land, Grandpa announced that he had forgotten to bring grocery bags for gathering the muscadines, and Tammy would have to walk back to the house to get us some. I don't think Tammy knew, but when I looked at Grandpa, I could see the evil coming. Tammy began her walk back across the pasture to the house. She argued at first that Grandpa could drive, and we could all go together back to the house. But I knew it would never happen that way, and she reluctantly left.

Grandpapa told me to lie down in the creekbed. In my head I tried to remember all my Bible verses and wished I had done my Sunday school memory lesson for the week already so I would have a new one. He unzipped his trousers and got on top of me. He was heavy and I felt his weight crushing me. In my head I thought of the words to a hymn: "I will cherish the old rugged cross, 'til my troubles at last I lay down," then another: "Rock of ages cleft for me, let me hide myself in thee. . . ." I had heard my preacher consoling the parents of a sick child one time. He had opened up his Bible and read something akin to "The Lord does not give you any trouble that you cannot handle." Those were the nicest words I had ever heard. The Lord, I concluded, must think I am the strongest little girl in the world, because I have more trouble than anyone I have ever met.

I was not there when this happened to me. I was never there. Not then, not for any of the years my grandpa did this to me. I was not there on the riverbank with the back of my new dress getting dirty from lying in muscadines. I was never there when Grandpa would pull his truck to the side of the road when he and I went to get ice cream. I wasn't there when he would come to my bedroom in the night when Tammy wasn't around and take off my pajamas. I only watched from beside me.

I remember his ugly fingernails that day on the riverbank, because they were thick and yellow. I saw his thing. He went back and forth, with his eyes rolling back into the top of his head. Detached, I observed him, and for an instant he looked at me watching him and became very angry. He had not been successful.

When Tammy came back with three grocery sacks, all she saw was her grandfather. She did not know the look he wore was that of an unsatisfied rapist. I said nothing to Tammy. Grandpa had told me that if I ever said anything to anybody, my mama would beat me real bad. Maybe kill me.

This was my life. This was my childhood.

I told no one. I was too scared. I figured out really soon that nobody was ever going to help me. Not even my kindly babysitter, LaDora. I felt totally isolated. I had no real friends. No one to talk to. I was too embarrassed and terrified to bring any of my classmates home to my house, because I didn't want them to see me get a spanking. And I wasn't allowed to go to anyone else's house unless it was someone from church. So I just kept my mouth shut.

I was raped by my grandfather from age four to eight. It's hard to remember how frequent the incidents were. I remember rooms in his house. I remember his penis. I remember his eyes narrowed to slits. I don't remember ever sitting in his lap when he didn't have his finger in my panties. He probably raped me every time I was alone with him. When you're little, you forget on purpose.

◆ ◆ ◆

I TOOK LIFE AS it came. I hoped to see goodness wherever I could. Before I was old enough for school I would spend most of my days by myself out in our garage playroom after making the beds, cleaning the bathrooms, and folding my little brothers' diapers. My mama would put me out there after lunch and I'd wait the rest of the day for my sister, Tammy, to come home from school. I adored Tammy and was so amazed to see the letters she drew on the papers she brought home from school while she sat in front of the TV watching *Popeye* and *Gilligan's Island*. I'd just sit there welling up with pride and staring at her in amazement. The girl could write a whole sentence, and she was my sister!

One day Mama gave me a MoonPie—as she often did when she needed to have time to herself. It was one of those Little Debbie cookies with marshmallow cream inside. I tried to save it for Tammy so when she came home from school she would have a big surprise. I sat there and talked to myself. I talked to the MoonPie. I thought if I made it my friend maybe I wouldn't eat it. But soon half my friend was gone, and I just talked to the remaining half.

I was never able to talk to Tammy about what Grandpa did to me. I couldn't tell her. Years later, when she was ten and I was eight, she told me Grandpapa put his hand down her panties once and she socked him right in the face. Now, *why* in the world didn't I ever do that? Whenever *it* happened, I was just so scared and couldn't even make a scream come out. I couldn't think a thought. Maybe that's why I could never talk about it—when it came to that area of my life, I was just shut tight. I could not wait to grow up and run away. When I was suffering through all this—the constant discipline from my mother and the sexual assaults from my grandfather—I wanted to die. When I was five, I sat in the play-room saying over and over to myself: *I wish I was dead. I can't take this anymore.* By the time I was eight, I would've walked in front of a bus—gladly. There was no one in my family to talk to: no one, no one, no one! It was just the way my family was—we all kept our mouths shut, even to each other.

One day my mother came to my grandparents' house unexpect-edly to pick me up. I never got a chance to ask why she decided not to let me spend the night as Grandpapa had requested. Grandma was in the hospital with something called syphilis, and Grandpa told Mama he didn't want to be alone, so she had let me go home with him. I wonder now if Mama ever questioned where Grandma's syphilis came from, but those are the questions you don't ask as a child.

That evening Grandpapa was sitting on my little bed, telling me that it was more important than ever to never tell my mean mama about the things he did to me. He had unzipped his trousers and was about to do something else when he stopped, very abruptly. The kitchen door opened and my mother's voice was calling to see if anyone was there. Grandpa tried to get his trousers zipped, and I think he must have hurt his thing on the first attempt, because he said a bad word. My mother was coming down the hall, and then she opened the door to my room. I was afraid. I think he was afraid too, because there were many words coming from his mouth but they were not whole sentences. He seemed like he needed to run. On his face was the same look I surely got whenever I knew Mama was going to whip me. I'd never seen that look on a grown-up before, and when Mama opened the bedroom door, she saw it too. This time, she yelled at him, not me. My grandpapa explained I was sick, so he was putting me to bed. The old liar. I must have been possessed at that moment, because the sound that came from me was not my own, a woeful dirge of "No, nooooooooooooooo-ooooooooo! Please no! Help me! Help me!"

Wailing, I ran into Mama's arms. I looked at her face and saw terror. I knew that she knew, but could not fathom the crime that had been committed. She picked me up, and we were both crying. I loved her very much then. We drove home, and there were questions that I could not answer, because the only words I could scream through my tears were "Help me." My mother saved my life that day, because God knew I had taken all a little girl like me could take.

Mama's grief boiled into hysterics by the time we got home. She told Daddy. He telephoned his father and ordered him to come over—*now!* We kids were all sent to our rooms.

"Why would you do that?" Daddy said over and over to Grandpa when he showed up. Daddy was crying then. Mama just kept yelling.

"Because she asked me to," Grandpa finally said. I grabbed the doorknob to go out and defend myself, but Tammy held me back.

The things that happened were not spoken of again from that day on. Only many years later, after we had all grown up, we found out that Grandpa had done the same thing to Baby Markett and many of my cousins.

Mama did not have to feel the pain of what she now knew for very long. Her mind became more ill, and she was prescribed a new medicine for that type of thing. Drugs were never a lasting solution for her. Before too long, the new medicine did not work as well, and Mama was given to fits and talking to us kids about killing herself with the pistol she kept in the drawer of her nightstand. She'd moan to us: "When I die and you're looking at me in my casket you're going to be sorry for the way you've treated me." How, after all the things she'd done to us, could she think we would even be sad? So many nights I had prayed to God that she would die. Truthfully, I longed to see her in a casket, or just to never see her anywhere again.

I knew what I needed to do. I needed to run. I needed to flee from my house and away from the abuse. I needed a job, money, and an apartment of my own to share with Mark. Tammy and Matt were savvy enough to make it on their own, I reasoned, but Baby Markett would never make it without a stronger hand.

You become very mature when sex is forced on you at age four. I saw things that no little kid should see, and I bore these feelings all by myself. One day in my childhood there was a moment of clarity: I knew that someday I would do something significant, more significant than all these people who were hurting me could ever imagine. I promised it to God—I would fix it so no child ever suffered like I had again.

Chapter 3

I'll Fly Away

BY THE TIME I WAS thirteen, my mama's beatings consistently left red marks all over my body. And although I loved him deeply, Daddy was no help. Mostly he just took it while Mama yelled at him too.

One day Mama got really angry at Daddy and began to hit him. I don't even remember what it was about. She had been crying and yelling, threatening all sorts of evil, and when Daddy grabbed her shoulders to calm her, she began flailing. Mama's fists closed like a boxer's. She coiled and uncoiled, landing haymakers on his chest and arms. Daddy stood there and took the punches, no longer holding her shoulders. His hands were clenched, but they were by his sides. "C'mon, Betty," he kept saying, "stop . . . just stop."

All us kids were there in the living room. We watched, silent from shock at first. Again and again Mama bashed him, and our dam finally broke. We howled. We pleaded. We yelled at Mama to stop. But she just kept swinging.

I'd had enough—I was afraid for my daddy; I couldn't let any-one hit him like that. In a flash I leaped on Mama's back and tried to wrestle her away from Daddy. My elbow was looped around her neck. I could feel my heart pounding against her back. Mama's hair was in my eyes. She felt sweaty and flushed.

"Stop . . . hitting . . . Daddy!!!!" I yelled.

"Get off her!" Daddy commanded, stern and abrupt. "Don't ever touch her like that again!"

We were all surprised. Mama stopped punching Daddy. I let go and slumped to the floor. There we were, all of us wide-eyed, pant-ing, crying—a family in complete chaos.

Someone whom I will always love, and may never know, soon reported us to social services. I was taken away within twenty-four hours, and for the remainder of eighth grade and until I finished tenth grade I was never again whipped.

It's amazing how life can change in an instant. I could not be-lieve my good fortune. I was out of the house—maybe not for good, but I was out. My trip to my first foster family felt like escap-ing from Alcatraz. I was finally in the home of a real family. There was no screaming, the mother seemed happy, and I never saw her cry or hit her children.

But Mama wanted me back home. Having one of her children in foster care must have been a huge embarrassment to her. After several months she began to threaten lawsuits against the state. "Those people," as she called my new family, were letting her daughter run wild!

Mama was referring to my new clothes. She had driven by school and spied on me, and she had seen me wearing blue jeans. After about a year, the judge complied and moved me to another foster home. It was a good home, too, and I stayed for almost a year before the judge caved in again to my mama's continual pressure.

This time I was sent to a state group home for disturbed and abused adolescent girls. Two policemen showed up at my school one afternoon and took me there. I didn't even get to go to my locker first. My roommate at the home was thirteen and almost full term in her pregnancy. The girls across the hall told me the girl's daddy got her pregnant. Those girls were there for drug addiction, so I didn't know if I should believe them, but such a thing was not unheard of in Alabama. I shuddered, aware that it could have been me, pregnant with my grandfather's child.

I hated the home immediately and wanted to run away. The first Sunday, we were bussed to church, and I went to the bathroom and snuck out a window. From a pay phone I called my parents and asked to come home.

Mama answered the call. She had expended so much energy the past two years trying to get me home, I figured she'd want to have me back immediately.

"I think you need to stay there for a while," Mama said after listening to my description of the place, then hung up.

Two days later, my parents came and got me. My father drove. He looked straight ahead the whole ride. I must have had a faraway look in my eyes because I was not coming home, not really. I had tasted life on the outside for two solid, glorious years, and I was not coming to their house to stay. I would bide my time, and I would leave again. Only this time it would be for good.

THAT SAME YEAR, WHEN I was fifteen, Daddy got a new job and we moved to Salt Lake City, Utah. It felt like a completely different world for an Alabama family, and for non-Mormons. Although all the houses we had lived in had been close to one another, I had still been to seven schools in ten grades, and I didn't want to switch again. Mama was never an advocate for girls' education and said I didn't have to go, so I quit.

I applied for several jobs, working first as a hostess in a Greek restaurant. The legal age was sixteen, but they offered to hire me if I accepted a lower wage, which I quickly agreed to. After several months of being chased around the restaurant by the owner's son, I quit. For three weeks I scoured the *Salt Lake Tribune* employment ads, but each time I was interviewed I was turned down because of my youth and lack of a high school diploma.

Finally I decided to take matters into my own hands—twenty-one was a good age, I decided. My next interview was at a large computer software firm. I would lie about everything—my age, where I lived, about my not having a high school diploma. Chances are they would never do a full check or call Alabama to find out about my transcripts. For the interview, I wore a knee-length dress bought at a secondhand store. My little brother Mark and I made the necessary alterations so it would fit. I wore the highest heels I could balance on and pulled my hair into a bun.

"Ever have experience as a receptionist?" the supervisor asked. She was intimidating and aloof.

"Of course, ma'am," I choked out. I was lying through my teeth.

She pointed to a PBX machine. "Know how to use one of those?"

"Yes, ma'am," I said, turning bright red.

"Okay, we'll let you know."

A few days later I had heard nothing and started making appointments for restaurant jobs again. I needed money. My parents told me I had to pay rent if I didn't go to school. I thought about going back to the Greek restaurant and begging for my old job back. I knew the owner would give it to me if I agreed to date his acne-faced, big-nosed, spoiled-rotten son. I had just decided I would go the next day and prostrate myself when the phone rang.

"Can you start Wednesday?" the software firm supervisor said.

I ran downstairs and told Mark. The job was mine. Actually mine! Mark rummaged through every inch of my closet until he found a dress that made me look like a businesswoman.

"You don't think that one makes me look fat?" I asked.

"No! I love you in that dress!" Mark said. "The only thing is you don't really have any shoes that match!"

I held up some light-brown platforms. "What about these?"

"Susie, please! *Beige* with a navy-and-white dress?" He clucked his tongue at me and shoved a ten-dollar bill that he had gotten for his eleventh birthday into my hand. "Let's go to Deseret Industries."

We went to the Mormon-operated secondhand store, where Mark found the perfect pair of navy pumps for me. I just loved my baby brother.

WEDNESDAY MORNING, I KNOCKED on the door of my new boss's office at 7:50 a.m., ten minutes early.

"Thank you so much, Mrs. Stokes," I said. "I will be the best employee you've ever had. You won't be disappointed. I promise."

"Call me Caroline," she said, and escorted me over to the reception area. "You'll be working with Brenda. The phones have gotten so busy that work has begun to pile up. The two of you can take turns answering the phones and handling the filing and mail." She turned around just as a woman came to the counter and reached over to drop a file in one of the fuller in-boxes.

"Oh, Kari, this is our new PBX operator, Susie!" Caroline motioned toward me. "She'll be working with Brenda."

There was that terrifying phrase again—the one that had kept me from sleeping since I first found out I had the job. I had gone to the library to see if I could find an operating manual. I found only enough information to scare me to death. I asked my father what a PBX machine was. They had one where he worked, but he only knew that it was a sophisticated phone system.

I extended my hand to Kari. "Nice to meet you," I said. I felt myself redden. Her face was heart-shaped and she had a pronounced overbite. She was not beautiful, but nevertheless attractive.

"Oh, welcome aboard! I love your dress!" Kari said, shaking my hand.

"Thank you! My brother made me wear it," I blurted out.

"Oh, you live with your brother?"

"Uh, well, yeah, he lives with me." I didn't want them to think I still lived with my parents.

Kari shrugged. "Do you want to come out for a drink with the girls after work?" she asked.

I was getting in deeper by the minute, and it was only ten after eight in the morning. I calculated quickly. *Does she mean a Coke, or is she talking about alcohol? If so, that means a bar. What if they ask for ID? The bartender will throw me out for sure when he finds out I'm only fifteen.*

"Uh, I can't tonight." It was true, and I stammered only a second. "I promised my brother I would take him for ice cream."

"Oh, how sweet! How old is he?"

"He just turned eleven," I said, happy to be back on the safe ground of nonfiction again.

"How come he lives with you and not your parents?" she asked, showing curious concern.

Oh, man! Shift to fiction again. "Well, they're not around. Long story, ya know?"

"Well, Caroline here never joins us girls; she's in bed every night by eight." She and Caroline laughed at her joke.

"It wouldn't hurt you to be in bed by midnight every once in a while, young lady!" Caroline said, good-heartedly. They were obviously fond of each other.

"Well, gotta get back to work!" Kari said as she strolled back in the direction from which she had come.

I smiled but didn't say anything. Just then, Brenda, the girl I was to work the phones with, came through the front door. It was 8:15 a.m. She was a couple of inches taller than I, with well-rounded hips and her hair cut in a dark, shoulder-length shag. She looked irritated.

"Sorry I'm late," Brenda said to Caroline. "I won't take my break this morning." Brenda shifted her attention to me. "May I help you?" she asked coolly.

Caroline put her hand on my shoulder. "This is Susie. I'd like you to explain the filing system and how to separate the mail. Also, she's used a PBX, but you'll have to help her memorize the extensions. And teach her which customers are routed to which customer-support rep."

Brenda shrugged her shoulders. "Fine," she said, shuffling through the mail. She sucked the back of her teeth, as I later learned was a habit of hers when she grew impatient. Caroline excused herself, and Brenda sat in front of the big black box. It had at least a hundred buttons on it. I leaned against the counter and pretended to be interested in a programming brochure that looked like Russian to me.

"It's by number," Brenda said. "Each customer has a number assigned to them." She handed me a binder. "The customers are listed alphabetically. I assume you know the alphabet?"

I wondered if she said that because I didn't look twenty-one.

"You get a document or invoice, you find the company name, look it up here in this binder, and *voilà!*" Brenda pointed to a number beside a company called Edge Tech. "There's your number! Find the file with that number and put it in." She pointed at all the in-boxes full of files. "Those you'll need to refile. *By the number! Don't forget!*" She opened a cabinet door above the countertop behind the workstation and pulled out a box about a foot deep. "I haven't had time to file these invoices. You wanna do 'em, and I'll take the morning shift on the phone?"

Oh! Thank you! Thank you, God! No PBX phone thingamajig just yet. Maybe now I wouldn't be fired until at least after lunch. "That would be great," I said. "I'll get started!" I tried to watch her every move while trying not to make any mistakes in the filing.

At 12:00 sharp Brenda called Caroline to say she was taking lunch but had not had time to show me the extension chart. Caroline asked Kari if she would sit with me while Brenda went to lunch. Kari had started working for the company as a front desk person, the same position I now had.

With Brenda gone, Kari sat down beside me at the PBX panel. The phone rang and a light lit up. Kari removed one of her gigantic hoop earrings, picked up the headset, and put it over her tiny ears. The phone continued to ring constantly for the next several minutes as I sat, petrified, and watched and memorized her every move.

"I miss this job!" Kari said. "It's much more fun to just pass 'em off to someone else and not have to deal with their problems."

"I'm just thankful I have a job," I said. "I hope I can do it." I looked at her with some reservation.

"Course you can! Here, I'll watch. You take the next one."

"No!" I blurted—too quickly. "I don't think I better."

"Why? Caroline said you know the PBX. Just pick up and say, 'Libra Programming, may I help you?' then take this list and find the extension they want to talk to and patch 'em through! It's easy!"

"Kari . . ." I couldn't look at her. "Listen, I have to have this job. Please, please don't tell anybody. I've never seen one of these

PXBs or whatever before in my life. But I can learn anything. I learn fast. Please help me. I'll pay you part of my first month's salary. I'll clean your house on the weekends. Whatever it takes . . . I—"

She held her hand up. "Listen!" She lowered her voice. "Brenda will be in Caroline's office the minute she finds out. She's a little witch. Look, I'll stay after work tonight, and when Caroline leaves I'll come up here and help you. I think I can teach you enough to handle it on your own in a week or so, but you better figure a way around Brenda. Man, you poor thing."

"I'll give you half of my first paycheck," I said. "Just please teach me everything." I paused and looked at the PBX machine with its flashing lights. I thought about why I got the job in the first place. With this I could afford my own apartment and be away from my mother. "I'll handle Brenda," I said, with renewed determination.

"Man, you're a mess, girl!" Kari laughed. "But you're sweet." She shrugged her shoulders and shook her head, then continued the lesson until Brenda returned, smelling of French fries.

I MANAGED TO TALK Brenda into letting me catch up on all the neglected filing and mail while she answered the phones. Kari took her lunch hour every day at the same time Brenda took hers so that she could man the PBX machine. Caroline gave her a strange look each time she passed and saw Kari on the phone instead of me. Each time I quickly gave Caroline our well-thought-out explanation and pretended that Kari and I had become good buddies and she was helping while I caught up on the weeks' worth of neglected filing.

I stayed after work every night until 10 p.m.—11 p.m. when Kari was willing. By the fourth night Kari made calls to me from her office. By the sixth call I managed to patch her through to a neighboring desk phone without disconnecting her. Six more times we practiced the procedure successfully. I was so proud. By 10:30 p.m. we were both tired and said good night. That was my last lesson from Kari. She drove to her apartment and I drove home. I had learned my job.

Mama and Daddy didn't seem to mind that I drove without a license. I had my learner's permit, and in their minds that seemed enough. How else was I going to get to work? Daddy was busy with his own job. Mama slept all the time.

After I'd worked for two months, except for the money I paid Kari, my car payment (sixty dollars a month for an old stick-shift Bobcat), gasoline, and the ice cream Mark and I bought for ourselves, I managed to save $130 and started looking for an apartment. It didn't take long to discover I would need a roommate. I asked Kari if she knew anyone who wanted to split expenses.

"I have a two-bedroom apartment," Kari said. "I'd let you move in with me! You don't smoke, do you? My last roommate smoked. I hated that."

"Well, I only have a hundred and thirty dollars. Is that enough?" I asked.

"My rent is three hundred a month. You'd have to pay half and utilities."

"I don't know what utilities are. How much would they be?" I asked, hoping she would say a very low number.

"Usually not more than thirty bucks."

I thought about it for a moment. I didn't want to ever have Kari mad at me if I couldn't pay my half. "Can I pay you a hundred and thirty and the rest at the end of the month when I get my paycheck?"

She said yes.

I hugged her.

That was the moment I had dreamed of my entire life. There was no fanfare, just a simple decision I made that day, sixty-three days before my sixteenth birthday. Daddy never said I couldn't. Mama walked into my bedroom while I was boxing up my clothes.

"You leaving?" she asked.

"I sure am," I said.

That was all there was to it.

MY FIRST NIGHT AT Kari's she had a date with a young basketball player named Karl. I was very lonely. I spent an hour on the phone with Mark, then went to my room and cried myself to sleep. Later that night Kari came home with him. He was a very nice, very tall black man, and I could tell he was a few years older than I, but I was sure he was quite a few years younger than Kari, who was about twenty-nine. Having been raised in Alabama in a town inundated with Ku Klux Klan members, I felt strange seeing a black man kissing a white woman.

Kari and Karl stayed in her room all night. When I got up for work he was in the bathroom taking a shower, so I decided to skip the shower and get to work early. I felt embarrassed when Kari came into work, and I tried to stay on the phone as long as possible.

"Hey, Karl wants us to go to the Utah Jazz basketball game on Thursday night and go for drinks after!" She acted as if everything was fine. I was relieved.

"Well, actually, that would be great," I said, "but I have a little confession to make—I'm not quite twenty-one yet."

"I didn't think so," Kari said. She smiled. "How old are you anyway?"

"Eighteen," I said. Another lie. But I didn't think Kari could handle it if I told her I was fifteen.

Kari laughed some more. Then she rubbed her chin with her dainty hand and looked away with a furrowed brow.

"Hey, Charlene!" Kari called to a stocky blond programmer. "Do you know anybody that we can borrow an ID from for Suz? We're going to the Jazz game on Thursday and for drinks after with Karl."

Charlene produced an old driver's license of her that could feasibly be mine if I had a bad perm and a hangover. She told me to try it out first at a liquor store near our office. I should also buy her a bottle of vodka for the favor, she said. On my lunch break, I tried it. The man glanced my way and then tossed the license back on the counter. Charlene complained about the cheap brand I chose, but we all celebrated my success by having a shot in our coffee in the office kitchen when no one was around.

I hated the taste but drank a full cup and went back to work feeling rather happy. That evening after work I picked up Mark and we went to the grocery store and bought my very first groceries. I had allocated sixteen dollars from my paycheck to buy groceries for the month. We bought three loaves of white bread, Velveeta cheese, wieners, mayonnaise, peanut butter, two plastic jugs of Dr Pepper, and eggs. Kari and I shared groceries, so I really hoped Karl would not eat all of my food.

Mark and I lay on the floor with pillows from the couch, ate grilled-cheese sandwiches, and watched an old black-and-white movie. During the commercials Mark told me about Lisa, a girl who lived two blocks over from my parents' house and who he thought was pretty.

"Well, ask her out, dummy!" I said. "I'll take you guys to a movie or something."

"She already asked me on a date," he said shyly. "Well, kind of a date, I think."

"What d'ya mean 'kind of a date'?" I asked.

He fidgeted, rolled over onto his back, and covered his face with his arm. "She wants to . . . you know . . . *'do it'*!"

I sat up and reached for the off button on the television. "No! I do not know! She wants to do *what*? How old is this girl, anyway?"

"Thirteen," he said, still not looking at anything. "I think I want to, anyway."

My jaw hung to my knees. Mark wasn't even twelve yet. I had never thought about him as anything but my baby brother. But Mark was serious. I could see he was embarrassed and felt guilty. The thing that came out of my mouth next would either destroy him or make him the happiest person in the world. He just kept waiting and watching me as I let out a deep breath. I had no idea how to answer.

"Mark, you know the Bible says you shouldn't do it before you're married," I said, trying to sound as gentle as possible. "It doesn't matter if I'd be mad or not. God would be mad."

"I think the kids at school would stop making fun of me if I do it," Mark said. "All the other boys have done it."

"Trust me," I said. "I guarantee they have not *all* done it."

"Well, Lisa said she's done it before. We found a bunch of magazines in her father's toolbox, so we were lookin' at 'em and talkin' about sex and then she kissed me and then put her hands on my . . ." His face turned a crimson color as he tried to finish the sentence. "You know, down there . . . my pants."

I wanted to go—immediately—and find this thirteen-year-old hussy and choke her. How dare she seduce my sweet little innocent brother? Instead, I put my hand on Mark's shoulder. "Look, I think about it too. I've seen those kind of magazines and I just don't think you should be looking at them. You remember when Mama found one of them in Daddy's briefcase, they almost got a divorce over it. They're nothing but trouble."

"I know," he said slowly. "But there's more." He looked at the floor, his eyes full of concern. "Susie, do you think I'm a homo? I thought maybe if I did it with Lisa, other kids wouldn't make fun of me all the time."

Mark? A homosexual? I had never even considered such a thought. Was he asking me because he really might be? All these visions suddenly filled my head, like how he knew more about women's fashion than any woman I ever knew. I grabbed him and held him close. "Of course not, silly! You're no homo!" I convinced myself that it was true that day. "Now go make us some peanut butter sandwiches!"

I DID MY JOB VERY well, and when Brenda moved on I got promoted to another department after training the new PBX operator. After my promotion I was able to spend some money on clothes.

It became a habit. On Friday and Saturday nights Kari, Charlene, and I would go to the Utah Jazz basketball game and hit the bars around Salt Lake City afterward. No one ever challenged the authenticity of my fake ID. I became accustomed to older men paying for my drinks and food. I never had a date with anyone my age. I soon learned that the sexier I dressed the more attention I got from men, and the more attention I got, the more they wanted to buy things for me. One night after drinking several margaritas at a bar called Dooley's, I told Kari how old I actually was. I had lived with her for about a year by then. She laughed so hard I thought she would hyperventilate.

That same night a tall, stocky man paid for my drink. He wore a floor-length fur coat and had a diamond-encrusted gold watch so huge I wondered if he had problems lifting his hand. His name was Paul Baker, and after the drink he invited me out to his car. Some others were going, so I figured it would be safe. Parked diagonally at the VIP parking area was the most beautiful green Rolls-Royce. It took up three parking spaces.

Paul opened the door for me. "Hop in, gorgeous!" he said, and motioned to the car. "I call her Jade."

"It's a beautiful car!" I said.

He opened the glove box, took out a gold container, and tossed it to one of the guys in the backseat. Paul reached under the seat and took out a hand mirror and what looked like a straw cut in half. The overhead lamp reflected on the mirror for a second, and I watched the guy in the backseat pour a tiny line of white powder on the mirror. He put the straw to his nose and whiffed, wiped his nose with his fingers, put more of the powder on the mirror, and handed it back to Paul.

"You want a bump, sweetie?" Paul held the mirror in front of me. I was glad I had finished my daiquiri or I would have been more nervous.

I shook my head. "Naw, I better not tonight," I said. "Thanks, though."

He shrugged and repeated the sniffing action through the straw. Everyone in the car seemed to be in a very good mood. I listened to them talk about themselves for over an hour. After they had taken one more "bump" each, we returned to the bar.

I knew what had just happened inside the Rolls-Royce was wide of the mark. But at sixteen, it's easy for lines to begin to blur. *It's his car,* I reasoned, *and an incredible car at that. Besides, I didn't do anything myself. I'll be careful. I won't get hurt—he was so nice.*

Back at the bar Paul ordered me another daiquiri. I gulped it, then two more. As the rum and lime juice swirled through my head, I couldn't begin to guess I had already begun to lose traction, and underneath my feet was the slickest grease imaginable.

Chapter 4

Behind the Doors

THE DEVIL LOVES A HUMAN ego; it's so easy to work with. He loves our insecurities too.

As I sat in first class on the American Airlines evening flight to Los Angeles from Salt Lake City, I asked the stewardess if the champagne was real. I held the glass to my lips and drank. I knew Mark would want me to remember every detail: how the leather seats felt; what the bathroom looked like in first class; were any movie stars sitting near me? These were the same things I had always wondered myself. I had flown before—but it had never been anything like this.

My photographer friend Steve Wayda sat beside me and drank a Tanqueray and tonic. He had just scribbled a list of all the things I must and mustn't do while at the Playboy mansion:

1. Always wear high heels.

I leaned over and read number one. "Dad-gum it!" I said. "I didn't have any time to change after work, and even if I did, this is the best pair of shoes I own! What's wrong with them?" I leaned over my knees and surveyed the shoes Mark and I had bought at a thrift store. The soles had peeled away from the tips slightly and the little silver buckles that fastened the cracked white leather straps were a little bit tarnished. My eyes followed Steve's to the chipped fuchsia polish on my left big toe. He continued writing:

> *2. Always have a manicure and pedicure.*
> *3. Always carry yourself like a Playmate.*

Steve shifted his chubby frame in his seat and placed both pale freckled hands on my shoulders. He was in his mid-forties and experienced in posing models. "Sit up straight," he said. "Shoulders back, chest out." He illustrated by doing so himself. He patted my stomach. "Tummy in!"

I opened my mouth to say something, but stopped.

"Number four," Steve said under his breath, and wrote:

> *4. Do not talk like a "dad-gum" hillbilly.*

"Now, sweetheart," he said as he dropped his red-bearded chin and peered at me cautiously over wire-rimmed eyeglasses, "I won't be allowed to come in with you at the mansion, so here—" He tore the page from his notepad and placed it on my tray table. "Memorize it for me like a good girl."

Steve hadn't told me that before. I could not fathom being in the Playboy mansion on my own. I had seen it on television and heard about "what goes on there." I wasn't sure why I was going to the mansion in the first place. This was Steve's big break as a photographer—he had told me so a thousand times. To have one of the models he'd discovered "make it" into an international magazine—he had begged, pleaded, sent flowers. Steve was a good friend; I didn't have many of those. We spent hours on the phone together. When *Playboy* had called and said they wanted me to come to L.A. for a "test shoot," I said I couldn't go through with it. "What if they're having sex all over the place, right there in front of me?" I wondered. But word got out, and friends started talking about the possibilities. Everyone was so excited and yammered about it every time we got together. I must admit I was just a bit curious too. *Playboy* was a huge magazine.

Founded in 1953 by Hugh Hefner, *Playboy* was considered a much classier magazine than *Penthouse or Hustler,* the other more explicit porn giants of the early 1980s. *Playboy* magazine was all about art, so they said—it was an attitude, a gentleman's magazine, a glossy holdover from the Rat Pack era of high-class drinking buddies and boys'-club nightlife attitudes. Published monthly, the magazine featured one main centerfold spread of a nude woman, plus several smaller nude features, along with various articles on sports, fashion, consumer goods, and public figures. It also had a fiction section that drew top writers like Arthur C. Clarke, Ian Fleming, and Margaret Atwood. The magazine was known to express liberal opinions on most major political issues and quickly rose to be the most popular and bestselling men's magazine in the United States. By the early 1970s, 25 percent of all American college men were buying the magazine every month. The magazine grew into Playboy Enterprises, Inc., an international company reaching every form of media. When *Playboy* first contacted me in the early 1980s, I was pretty sure I would never make it as a big-time model, but still, I wondered. The photo shoot seemed to take on a life of its own.

It all started one night at Dooley's bar after a Utah Jazz game. Kari and some of the girls from the office sipped daiquiris and talked about guys. Paul, my friend with the jade Rolls-Royce, joined us. Paul was always welcome because he never left without paying our bar tab.

"Susie, you should model," Paul said. It sounded like the easiest thing in the world.

I just laughed. Like most seventeen-year-old girls I fantasized about being a model, but I was totally flat-chested and only about five feet five inches tall. My blond hair still fell below my butt, and I spent every penny I earned on clothes and mascara, but I was an Alabama tomboy at heart, much more comfortable climbing trees than posing in front of a camera. Of course I would never voice my desire to model out loud—what if someone said "You're not pretty enough"? I wanted to be pretty enough—the beautiful one—the girl who received attention. I had never gotten that before.

"Why are you laughing?" Paul said. He looked serious. "You're gorgeous!"

"Yeah, well, you've never seen me without makeup," I said. I decided to play it safe in case he was making a move on me. I covered a run in my stocking with my hand. "Thanks for saying so, though."

"No, really," he persisted. "I know a great modeling agency here in town called Susie McCarty Talent Agency. The owner is a friend of mine. Why don't I talk to her about you?"

The image of myself wearing beautiful clothes, walking down a runway with everyone admiring me, flashed before my eyes. I reveled in the moment. Paul reached down and cradled the hand I was using to cover the run.

"I'll take you shopping and we'll get you a nice dress and some shoes," he said. I followed his eyes down to the white flesh that showed through the run on my thigh. The drop in his voice was barely perceptible. "And anything else you need, okay?"

I took my hand back and scooted my chair closer to the table. I scrunched my nose, furrowed my brow, and planted my chin on a locked fist. I could use extra cash, sure. My car had just broken down again. Paul waited for me to say yes.

"Are you serious?" I said weakly. "Do you think I could really be a model?" I so wanted to hear more good things about myself.

Within a month, Paul's friend with the modeling agency, Susie McCarty, landed me two jobs—one a swimsuit ad for a local department store and the other a fashion show at a ritzy country club in Salt Lake City. For a total of four hours' work, I got paid $125 for doing the ad and $100 more for the fashion show. I would have had to work forty-five hours at Libra Programming to make that much.

Mark gathered twenty-five copies of the department store ad and passed them out at school, making sure everyone knew the girl in the bathing suit was his sister. For a few days all the sixth-grade guys wanted to hang around him and come over to his house the next time his sister dropped by.

To celebrate, I took Mark and Paul to the Village Inn restaurant for dinner. With dinner over, the three of us rose from our booth and walked arm and arm, Paul in his floor-length fur coat and cowboy boots; me in my short strapless black dress, black patent leather high heels, and white rabbit-fur jacket I'd bought at JCPenney after six months on their layaway program; and Mark in a brown tweed suit and green turtleneck he'd found on the sale rack at Deseret Industries. All heads craned toward us as we reached the cash register, where I paid our seventeen-dollar tab. I handed the matronly cashier a twenty-dollar bill.

"Keep the change," I said for the first time in my life. I said it loudly. I wanted Mark to hear. I wanted my brother to feel this new success down deep. We grabbed toothpicks and strolled out.

So much was going so right, thanks to the modeling. Mark had a reprieve from the constant harassment at school. I had enough money to fix my car, pay all my bills for the month, and buy a membership to a gym. I worked out nearly every morning. Lunch hours were spent in a nearby field. Somewhere between an old railroad track and a herd of dairy cows I'd spread a towel in the dandelions, strip to my underwear, and tan. I'd wash the smell off with soap and paper towels in the ladies' room when I returned to work.

But modeling made it tougher for me to concentrate at Libra Programming. I fell behind. Stacks of contracts soon sat on my desk. My boss watched me from behind her glassed-in office, smoke swirling from the invisible slit between her microscopic lips.

"Susie, have a seat," she said after calling me into her office one day. She noticed I was fifteen minutes late coming back from lunch—again. I stank of coconut oil and cows.

I chewed on my bottom lip. It wouldn't happen again.

"Well, I'll let it go this time," she said. She stubbed out her cigarette in the center of a souvenir ashtray from a Las Vegas casino.

Modeling proved a tricky business. After my initial success, four months went by without any more modeling jobs. Kari's landlord raised the rent. My car broke down again; this time I'd have to buy a new one. I had been back to my parents' house a few times, and Mama's manner had softened a bit. When I told Mama about the part-time modeling work, she even said: "I always told ya you were perdy." Now, that was a change. My parents agreed to let me move back in, provided I help with rent and groceries. Kari's boyfriend decided to help her with the rent, since he was there so often, and we parted on good terms. I had tasted such a small sip of success. Now here I was back home with my parents. Work at Libra Programming was becoming frustrating. With my limited office skills, it felt as if I could never do good enough work to get promoted. At least it was a steady income.

One day a dozen yellow roses were placed on my desk by a uniformed delivery boy. The card read: "To *Playboy*'s next centerfold! Please . . . ? Love, Steve."

I just laughed when I saw the card. There was no way.

Paul had introduced me to Steve months before and we'd agreed he'd take some photos for my portfolio. Steve said he'd work for free if he could submit some to *Playboy*. He had dreamed all his life of becoming a *Playboy* photographer. I'd seen the magazine and knew what the women looked like in the foldout pictures. They were the prettiest women I'd ever seen—perfect and sexy, nothing at all like me. I was just a kid. The furthest thing from a centerfold. Besides, posing naked in a magazine was just *wrong*.

"STEVE, YOU KNOW I'D do almost anything for you." I grabbed his hand in the seat next to mine in the airplane and begged. "Please, please don't make me spend the night in the Playboy mansion by myself!"

"Susie, they don't allow outside photographers on the property without special permission," he said. He took another sip of the gin and tonic. "They put me in a hotel close to the *Playboy* studio on Sunset Boulevard." He reached up with his soft white fingers and pulled my chin toward his face. "Susie, hon, you will have the time of your life. You have to trust me on this. You'll be so spoiled by the time I see you Monday morning you won't want me around." He fluttered his red eyelashes.

I just shook my head. This was going to be awful. I started feeling like I did in eighth grade. I'd spent all my recesses and lunch breaks in a stall in the girls' bathroom with my feet up on the lid of the toilet so no one would know I was in there. Only this time there might not be a place to hide.

Why was I doing this anyway?

I DIDN'T WANT TO LAND.

From the air, Los Angeles at night looks like one mass of lights and brightness in every direction. I was a long way from Alabama. I was a long way from Utah. I was a long way from any state I had ever been in. I, Susie Scott, tenth-grade dropout, computer company phone operator, was in L.A.!

At the airport gate, a man in a black suit and tie held a large bouquet of red roses and a sign with my name in big letters. He seemed to know who I was the minute he saw me. "Miss Scott!" he said, lifting the carry-on bag from my shoulder with a smile. A long black limousine was parked at the curb. Inside was a bucket of ice with more real champagne in it. I looked at Steve, my eyes huge.

"You think it's okay to open it?" I asked.

Steve grinned and popped the cork. "Just a little—you should never drink too much when you want to make a good impression." He filled my crystal flute halfway.

It was nearly 10 p.m. when the limo began climbing the rolling, gated streets of Bel Air—movie star homes. I wondered how people ever got to live in places like these. The limo stopped in front of a massive set of wrought-iron gates: 10236 Charing Cross Road. In the moonlight the gates looked like something out of a scary fairy tale.

Steve grabbed my hand. "This is it, sweet girl!" he said.

The limo driver rolled down his window and waited expectantly in front of a huge boulder.

"Yes, may I help you?" came a voice from inside the rock.

"I'm bringing Miss Susie Scott to the mansion," said the driver to the boulder.

"Who is that with her?" it asked.

"How can it see us?" I whispered to Steve. It didn't look like anything other than a rock. No speakers. No obvious camera eye. Later I would learn there are hidden cameras all over the mansion.

"That's Mr. Wayda. I have to drop him at his hotel next," said the driver.

"Tell him to remain in the car, please."

"Will do, sir," and with that the gates began to part very slowly.

We passed through and headed up the long hedge-lined drive. I turned around and watched the gates closing . . . slowly closing . . . now closed behind me. We pulled into the circular drive and stopped in front of a giant wooden door. It looked like the front door to a medieval castle. Light emanated from leaded glass and heavily shrouded windows. In the courtyard, a white marble fountain spewed streams of water from the mouths of lions and the penises of cherubs. The streams created a mist in the warm California night air. Through the darkness I watched the front door open. Candlelight emerged from the darkness. I could just make out a great hall. Above was a bronze chandelier with dozens of long white candles. A butler in a black-and-white uniform stood ready to help the driver with my bag. I said good-bye to Steve.

For one long moment I stood outside the Playboy mansion, wondering what to do next. From deep in my memory came an image. It was early in high school, and a social worker and two policemen had come to my school to take me out of class to another foster home. No one had asked me what I wanted to do then.

What *did* I want to do?

I stood up straight, pulled my shoulders back, and followed the butler into the mansion. The limo drove away.

"Would you like to say good evening to Hef?" asked the butler.

"No!" my voice cracked. "I mean, I better not. I don't want to wake him up."

"Oh, he just got up an hour ago," said the butler.

Far above the butler and me, standing behind the heavily carved railing of a Gothic balcony, stood the most beautiful woman I'd ever seen. Her hair was platinum and fell in waves over her shoulders. With her fingers resting lightly upon the banister, she began to descend. One stair, two. She seemed to float rather than walk. Flowing layers of white chiffon swayed to reveal her legs. There was no hint of undergarments. I stood, transfixed.

From a darkened hallway behind her emerged an old man. He wore pajamas and clenched a black pipe in his teeth. The woman waited until he caught up to her, then they descended the rest of the double-balustered staircase together. The old man grinned with accomplishment as he made it down the stairs with his arm around the beautiful woman's waist.

"Welcome," said the old man. He gripped the unlit pipe in his teeth. "I trust you had a lovely trip."

"Yes, s-sir, thank you," I stammered. "I've never been in first class on a plane. . . ."

"Call me Hef," he said, "and this is Shannon." He gestured with his pipe toward the tall woman. I caught myself looking at her breasts. They were not covered well and it was hard not to look.

The woman looked down from her height and spoke. "Do you want to join us in the pool?"

"Uh, no, I better not." I felt my face turning red. "I didn't know you had a pool. I didn't bring anything to wear."

"Don't worry," Shannon said. "You don't need anything. But if you want to wear a suit we have hundreds to choose from in the bathhouse." She paused, waiting for my reaction. They were sizing me up. Shannon looked me up and down, pausing at my chest. "All . . . um . . . sizes of suits," she added. Her voice did not match the way she looked. Not sweet and angelic like her face.

Hugh Hefner and Shannon Tweed both bent to kiss my cheeks. They strolled away.

"Are you okay?" the butler asked me.

"I'm gonna faint. I'm so embarrassed. I could die."

He smiled, though not unkindly. "I'll show you your room." He sauntered across the great hall, my luggage in his hand, and climbed the staircase. At the top of the stairs we went down a long hall. He turned on the light switch in an elaborately decorated guest bedroom. "Hef's room is at the end of the hall. If you need anything at all just dial the butler's pantry, extension one."

"Wow!" I said, looking around. "This is all so beautiful!"

"Would you like something to eat or drink?" he asked. "Anything you want."

"Do you have champagne?"

"Of course!"

With that he was gone. I surveyed my new surroundings. On the nightstand were a bowl of candy and several *Playboy* magazines fanned into a half circle. On the covers were big-breasted women in various seductive poses. I was sure that would never be me. Frankly, I would be relieved to get the weekend over with, go home, and find some other way to make a lot of money.

I wrapped myself in a pink silk comforter and sat on the king-sized bed. I didn't want to leave the room.

MY CONSCIENCE (OR MY fear) got the best of me, and I hid in my room for three days. I spoke to no one except the butler, Laurent. That first night he brought me champagne and Chinese food. He wasn't interested in girls, but he was so kind. I learned later that almost all the guys who work at the mansion are either gay or pretend to be gay. We hung our heads out the window. He smoked a joint. I tried a couple of puffs. The pot loosened us both up, and we stayed up until 3 a.m. talking. He was the first gay man I had ever met who admitted he was gay. Prior to that I would have laughed or not believed it. I thought gay men were just prissy guys whom everybody made fun of.

The next morning the house was quiet. Everyone slept most of the day. I slept until the afternoon, then snuck out to look at the monkeys and peacocks kept on the grounds. Saturday passed, then most of Sunday. Laurent brought me food and magazines while I hid in my room. I had every intention of going home Monday morning. I had tried to keep everybody happy—including Steve. But this was not me. This was not the life I wanted. Not this way.

Still, there was a strong pull at the mansion. You could eat or drink anything you wanted, help yourself to free clothes, bathing suits—parts of the mansion felt like Christmas. Laurent encouraged me to head down to the pool and pick out some bathing suits and robes. Late Sunday night I snuck down, set for a clandestine shopping spree before I left.

In the bathhouse the light was low. I could make out rows of swimsuits. A movie party had just let out somewhere on the grounds, and I could see girls in various places, but no one was near me. Suddenly I heard someone say my name.

"Susie . . ."

The voice sounded welcoming, not mean or threatening. I didn't have any makeup on and was wearing an old pair of Walmart pajamas I had brought from home. I tried to hide.

"Susie," it said again. "Can I talk to you?" It sounded innocuous, even charming.

I had met Hugh Hefner only the one time, when I first arrived. Evidently he remembered my name. He held out his hand for me to follow, and I took it. His hand felt kind, safe. Without speaking, he led me to a table by the pool, where we sat.

"I want you to know there's no pressure here," he said. "We want you to have the time of your life." He was convincing. "Anything you want, you can have. You don't have to do anything at all that makes you uncomfortable or that you don't want to do. But if there's anything you'd like to try, I'd like to know so that you are safe."

He looked directly at me. "You're a beautiful young lady," he added. "The world is yours. We just want you to be happy and comfortable. Always."

I believed him. I wanted to please him. I loved what he said to me. I loved how he said it. How could I not do anything for such a generous, sweet man? I wanted him to be my father.

Hugh Hefner sat for a moment, then kissed me on the forehead. He walked away.

I STAYED AT THE mansion.

The photo shoot was scheduled for Monday morning, and I decided to do it. It wasn't nude anyway—just lingerie and swimwear. What harm could there be in that?

The session started slowly. The lingerie still had price tags on it, and it was mine just for doing the shoot. I was given a set of underwear that was worth more than I made in three months at Libra Programming. There was more, too. Free jewelry. Beautiful negligees. And oh, the attention. Makeup artists, assistants, hairstylists. Everyone's attention was so complimentary—and it was all on me. They curled my hair so it hung in chunky swirls down past my hips. They lined my lips and painted my nails. I looked in the mirror and was stunned. I had never felt prettier in my life.

Steve was behind the camera. I felt safe with Steve. He led me over to the set. It looked just like a bedroom. All around me were candles and a rich mahogany four-poster bed with flowing canopies of purple, pink, and blue. Then he took a picture to check the lighting. Then another, and another. He worked slowly, carefully, kindly. Everyone was so helpful, so generous. I felt compelled to do anything anyone asked. Somehow in that first session, the negligee fell away. Seeing the first nude Polaroid picture of myself, I was pretty sure I would look like a petrified version of those girls on the covers of *Playboy* in my room at the mansion. But I was surprised at how comfortable I looked. The enchantment had worked. The seduction was complete. I really looked like one of those girls.

Beautiful.

Really beautiful.

Me.

Tuesday morning I flew back to Salt Lake City to my job at Libra Programming. I flew back to my old car, my secondhand clothes, and renting a room from my parents.

Life at the Playboy mansion looked better than ever.

Chapter 5

Inside the Mansion

I COULD EXHALE AT LAST.

Back at home in Salt Lake City, I just wanted to lie on the couch in baggy sweatpants. The taste of champagne was still in my mouth as I tried to focus on getting back into my old life and catching up at Libra. Mark arrived home from school, fetched a Dr Pepper for himself and a diet Pepsi for me, and planted himself on the sofa.

I was already asleep.

When I woke up I went down the hall to my bedroom to start unpacking my suitcase. My bag lay open beside where Mark sat on my bed. Between his fingers he held a Polaroid picture.

"Susie!" he exclaimed and dropped the picture, horrified. The offending thing landed faceup. I saw myself naked, smiling, dangling lacy underpants from my forefinger. I had saved it as a memento from the photo shoot. I flushed crimson in front of my little brother. His mouth hung agape. I felt my eyes growing wide and panicky. "Susie," he said again, "what dee-id yee-ew do?" He filleted each word as if his tongue were a sharp knife.

"Well . . ." I choked. "Well, uh—I was going to tell you. . . ."

"Did that Steve guy tell you to do this?" Mark was close to screaming now. "I've always hated him! He's a—"

I cut him off midsentence. "Listen, will you!" I strained to whisper. "Just simmer down! And be quiet! Mama's taking a nap!"

He shook his head. "They're gonna kill you," he said.

I ran my fingers down the length of my face.

"You know that, don't you?" he reiterated.

We sat on the edge of my bed, refusing to look at each other.

"You said you were doing bathing suit pictures!"

"I know, I know, but listen, they would have killed me for that too!"

I told him about the old man who made everybody call him "Hef," and the girls who were even prettier than Mama used to be. I told him about the butlers and limos and the people who gave me beautiful clothes to wear and combed my hair and painted my nails for me. I told him about how nice Hef was to me and how he really just wanted me to be happy.

"You can have just about anything you can think of at his mansion!" I said.

The more I talked, the less disgusted Mark looked.

"It doesn't matter anyway," I said. "I'm not going to be in the magazine or anything. Those girls are way more pretty than I am. And they all have huge, you know . . ." I cupped my hands and held them several inches from my own breasts. He understood the gesture. He laughed a little, and the skeptical, judging twist of his mouth softened at last.

"You know you're pretty, Susie. Except for Mama I think you're the prettiest girl in the world."

I nudged him with my shoulder. "You wouldn't say that if you saw what I saw, but thanks. Don't be mad, okay?"

Mark hugged me and wiped his runny nose on the shoulder of my T-shirt. "Please tear that thing up and put it in the garbage disposal before she sees it!" he said. He shook his head again and mumbled a barely audible revelation. "She's gonna kill you, I just know it."

I sighed. I was home. Home in Salt Lake City. Home with Mark. Home with Mama and Daddy. Maybe someday I'd tell the story of my stay at the mansion to a table of friends at Dooley's, or Kari and the girls at the office. Maybe it would just be forgotten.

ONCE YOU'VE HAD A taste of the mansion, it's not easily forgotten.

I tried. Steve went on with his photography work, and I went on with my typing skills. On a coffee break at work I thought about Laurent the butler and Hef and all the beautiful girls I had met. I had stared at Laurent in disbelief when he told me some of the girls had sex with each other.

"Yeah, right!" I said. "That's just crazy!" I didn't want him to think I was a prude, but there was just no way! I tossed myself back into the pillows and laughed as hard as I could.

"They do! I see it all the time!" Laurent said.

"You mean they're gay?" I poked him in the chest. "Like you?" I said teasingly.

"No, just bored." Laurent shrugged. I wondered how anybody could get bored in a place like L.A.

I had never been drawn to girls or intimately excited by them. Boys, and especially men, captivated me; I'd been wrecked by now, and used by a few of them. Mostly I just couldn't fully understand the life Laurent described. It disturbed me. It seemed so foreign, far removed from anything I knew. And how? They weren't made with the right equipment. I tried reasoning the thing out in my head. Possibly it was less trouble, like when you mention that you have PMS to your boyfriend—instead of watching him grab his coat and run for the door I imagined a look of the tenderest sympathy and compassion. My woman lover would rush to get me a pillow, something chocolaty, and the remote control. Yes, that might be one benefit, but I couldn't imagine any woman trading a boy for another girl.

A FEW WEEKS LATER, right before I turned eighteen, the call came. The voice on the phone sounded excited, like I was being offered an opportunity of inconceivable proportions. It was *Playboy*. I had been accepted as a centerfold candidate. This meant not just having my picture in the magazine, but an entire spread—the best spread—focused on me. The layout would continue for six or seven pages at least. And it was a benchmark, an opening. Each year there were twelve centerfolds, one for each month, and the lucky dozen vied for Playmate of the Year, the gold-star achievement of the industry. Playmates of the Year received a $100,000 bonus plus a new Porsche, plus more base pay on all other assignments, plus more travel and tons more freebies. It was the dream of every Playmate. Steve Wayda would be my photographer for the entire centerfold layout. Hef had loved the test photos.

"You're going to be famous," Steve said later, with such excitement that I wanted him to stay that way forever.

"I can't go back to L.A.," I said. "I'll lose my job."

"Who cares?" Steve said. He waved his hands. "You're going to make a lot of money. You'll probably become a movie star! You certainly won't need your old job anymore!"

Could I really become rich and famous? Who would ever have believed that I would fly first class or stay at a mansion with butlers waiting on me?

It was hard to resist an offer like that.

Maybe Steve was right, but what if he was wrong? And what about my parents? I just wouldn't tell them—they'd never know. I could explain things to Mark and convince him it was a good thing. And God—where had He been lately? I didn't feel like praying anymore. Why should I be ashamed of my body? God made it in the first place. This would probably be my only chance to do something with my life, to be somebody. Shouldn't I have an easy life for a while? The worst that could happen is that I would have to find another job.

WE WENT TO WORK on the centerfold shot immediately. I felt swept up, swept along. I was slated to run as a centerfold in May 1983. Getting the perfect shots would take more than six months of work beforehand. *Playboy* sent out a makeup artist, a stylist, and an assistant photographer for Steve. I found out that the girls in those foldouts don't look like "that" so easily. We shot virtually every day, starting early in the morning for hair and makeup, and continuing for six or seven hours once I looked "perfect." Steve took thousands of pictures of me. I was sure I would never look that way again.

Playboy spreads are all about providing fantasy—it's about clothes coming off, about standing naked in a stream, about frolicking in a field so your dress comes up to reveal everything. Steve wanted an outdoor pose in Utah, but as the weeks passed it began to snow. I froze while everyone stood watching in parkas and gloves—the shots didn't work. An outdoor set was re-created in an

L.A. studio, and we all flew there. Poses were always about arching my back. Arch. Arch. Arch. Twist that way or this way. Make your waist look thinner. Make your legs look longer. Poses were often painful, always in high heels, sometimes leading to a collapse.

Sets were supposed to be private, but it seemed there were always a lot of guests wandering by. After a while it didn't bother me too much—when you're nude in front of strangers, you can either feel shy or turn completely uninhibited. I found the more you do something, the more comfortable you get with it—that's how habits are formed. After a while my nakedness was nothing special.

The tone on the set was always complimentary. There are a lot of gasps, a lot of Polaroids, a lot of oohs and ahs. You start feeling very quickly that this is all about you—and it is. You can ask for anything, a certain kind of wine, a certain food. I seldom ate anything throughout the day because I couldn't stand the thought of my stomach being round. At night I would eat sushi and have the makeup artist massage my shoulders. I felt loved, worshipped, adored.

A lot of girls have affairs with their photographers, and I was no exception. You ignore the insecurity. You ignore the fact that another month will come and another girl will take your place. This is your time. Your moment. Your glory. Your majesty. You.

Finally, several months after we'd begun, the perfect shots were taken and I flew back to Salt Lake City to start working at Libra again until the pictures were published. I had told Mama and Daddy I had a new love for camping. When I was in L.A. I explained I was somewhere in a tent on a mountain, just in case they tried to phone.

It was exactly 5:15 p.m. one February evening back in Salt Lake when it hit. From the blaring living room television I heard it all the way up in my bedroom. Mama heard as she lay curled up in front of the TV. Daddy heard it from the kitchen, where he was fixing supper. As if from a loudspeaker, we all heard it. It reverberated through our house. The newscaster's voice was cheerful, sincere, jolly even—nothing like this had never happened before in Utah. . . .

"We'll be back in a moment for a look at Utah's first Playboy centerfold—Miss Susie Scott. . . . Stay tuned!"

The next thing we heard was my mother's screaming.

I was clutching my heart. I could only imagine what might be shown after the commercial.

"Frank! Frrrrrr-aaaaaaa-nk! Hurry! Git in here, you're not gonna believe what she's done now!!!"

Mark was at the top of the stairs, nostrils flaring, jaw clenched, fear in his eyes as they locked with mine. "Su-zeeee!" he said as we listened to the bloodcurdling screeching coming from Mama. The commercial was clearly over now. Daddy, in shock, was by her side.

"What do I do?" I gasped. My hands shook.

"Get out now!" Mark said. "Leave before she sees you!"

It was too late.

Shoes, clothes, hangers, pillows, my blanket—all came flying toward me. I ran, sprinting for my car, grabbing pieces of clothing from the muddy lawn as Mama continued to throw them.

"Filthy tramp!" Mama screamed. "Whore! Get out!"

Daddy tried to hold her back as I tried to get the key into the ignition.

"You whore! You slut!" was all I heard as I peeled out of the driveway.

I found myself in the parking lot at Libra. I put my head in my hands and cried. As the parking lot began to darken without the sun, I sat and tried to assess the damage.

Until now, I had felt I was safely outside that magazine—that world—and if I chose to, I could look in. Now I was inside, and others could look at me anytime they wanted. By posing nude for *Playboy*, I had given every man in the world permission to use the foldout of me for his personal needs any time, any way, any place he chose. Any disgusting creep could look me up and down and fantasize that "she wants it." For a few bucks now anyone could look, forever.

What have I done? I wondered. I must be crazy. My poor father. What must he think? The hardest photo to deal with would be the one of me masturbating. Steve had instructed me to touch myself like I loved it, but I found that very difficult. I knew my parents, my brothers, my sister, would see that shot eventually. All the shots. All of me. Someone would give them a copy of the magazine. Someone would show it to them at work or school. Someone would mention the spread in an elevator, at a store, or—Lord forbid—at church. Now it had happened. I wanted to vomit. Instead, I went inside the building. Behind the cubicles I could hear the steady clicking of the computer keyboards. The night programmers—the ones the girls at the office made fun of—would be there until morning. I made it to the ladies' room and splashed cold water on my face. That night I slept in an unused, unfurnished office on the second floor. I woke up with the sun the next morning, washed my face in the ladies' room again, and tried to rub away the carpet pattern on my cheek.

I couldn't go home. *Playboy* told me I could work all the time if I lived in L.A. There would be auditions for movies, commercials, television shows. They had invited me to stay at the mansion if I needed to while I looked for an apartment. I would get paid to sign autographs when the centerfold was out. I could make a lot of money.

Steve was understanding when I phoned.

"This is your time!" he said. "Be happy! Be proud."

"I sure don't want to be around here when it comes out on the stands," I said.

"You're a centerfold!" he said. "A *Playboy* centerfold! You are Miss May 1983! Can you think of anything better?"

A lot of things came to mind.

I PACKED MY LIFE into my little red Bobcat and told my supervisor I would be back if things didn't work out. I got word to Mama and Daddy that I was moving to L.A. to be a clothes model or an actress—which I really hoped I would be. Mark begged to go with me until Mama relented.

"She'll never find California by herself, Mama!" he reasoned.

Mark's attendance at school had been sporadic at best. I promised my parents he would only come for a month to help me get set up, then I'd send him home on a plane. Mark pleaded and whined. In the end Mama caved. Daddy marked out a path on a map of United States freeways for us. My first check from *Playboy* had come in the mail only days earlier. I had never had $2,000 before.

Mark and I drove and drove. This was our dream of moving out on our own. I doubted whether I would actually ever send Mark home. We talked nonstop for hours, changing subjects like songs on the radio. We fantasized about our new apartment, cooking together. He'd keep the place clean and I'd bring home the money. He'd have to obey me since I was older, but I promised not to be mean or yell, ever. We talked about people we'd miss, things we were afraid of, things we remembered. We told each other secrets and things we hoped to forget.

Somewhere outside Vegas we saw the lights of the huge neon city. We had never seen Vegas before.

"It looks like a Christmas tree fell down," Mark stated with awe.

"Yeah," I whispered reverently. "It sure does."

We didn't talk anymore. We just tried to remember that moment as we kept driving.

Hours later we found ourselves stuck in bumper-to-bumper traffic on the Pacific Coast Highway. As the morning sun reflected off the ocean and forced us to shade our eyes, we both felt a breath of new life surge through our hearts. As if on cue, our favorite song came on the radio. I turned up the volume. Diana Ross's voice could barely be heard over our wailing: *I'm com-in' out!*

It was our new theme song. Clutching the fabric of our T-shirts, we sang for all we were worth. The horns blowing around us prompted traffic to move an inch.

"Dad-*gum*! I love California!" I squealed as the song faded. It was going to be a new chapter for me. I was going to prove I was not a whore. I was not a bad person.

IT HADN'T OCCURRED TO me then that all the things that came flying out of my closet that day and onto my parents' lawn had broken the lock on Mark's own closet, too. Soon his secrets would take on a life of their own. I made arrangements for Mark to stay with Laurent, the butler, while I stayed at the mansion.

My centerfold would be out in a matter of days and I found myself in high demand as the new flavor of the month. Everyone wanted to meet me in the flesh in anticipation of seeing me naked on the pages of *Playboy* magazine. I was at the mansion only a couple of days before the month was fully booked with autograph signings, parties, and a media tour with flights to the East Coast, the South, the North, and back to L.A. I saw little of Mark. As the tour progressed, I could barely keep track of what city I was in.

Several times I asked the radio DJ before an interview, "Where are we again?" I often traveled with other Playmates. Some of the other girls were new and green just like me. Many were seasoned and helpful. For the most part, I felt taken care of and secure.

The *Playboy* life hit full force. More tours were booked. More parties were thrown. As a Playmate, you get used to lots of attention very quickly. It's easy to get spoiled. Everywhere we went men would line up—sometimes hundreds would be waiting, anticipating our arrival. We spent hours signing our own centerfolds, T-shirts, beer mugs, baseball caps, autograph books, even cowboy boots, and on one or two occasions a hairy back or shoulder. Some of the men were kind and friendly. Some were not and called us bitches if we refused to write something vulgar. It was give and take on both sides. We knew we used our beauty to cause a ruckus. In our minds, it was absolutely necessary that all eyes were on us—always.

Television and radio interviews terrified me at first but soon became the norm. Flowers and champagne arrived with other gifts that were sweet and thoughtful, and sometimes with ones that were tempting but too expensive to take lightly. Some of those I chose to return, but not many. I loved getting gifts. I quickly learned to party with abandon. Cocaine kept me slim, I discovered, and Scotch was as chic as champagne. Together they kept me "ready to go" and mellow enough to endure the endless hours of sitting, signing, and smiling. I dated a lot then. Boyfriends were everywhere. Some lasted a night. Some lasted a week. None lasted for long. None needed to.

I made $15,000 from my centerfold shoot, bought some clothes and a watch, and invested the rest in stocks. Six months later, the stocks bottomed out and I lost everything. But when you're a regular at the mansion, it's hard to notice you're broke. I did calendars and TV commercials. I wined and dined with celebrities at the mansion. Cocaine became a more frequent friend. Once I ate and drank nothing but Scotch and vitamins for twenty-nine days. After a while, there was no place in my life that felt right or wrong anymore.

MANY OF THE PLAYMATES I met and traveled with were sweet. Some became friends. A few I learned to watch. Despite its air of easy opulence, the mansion is also a brew of ego and insecurity. There is always someone prettier than you. Even though you've been a centerfold, another girl soon comes along. Playmate life is characterized by envy, instability, and emptiness.

One in particular was so sweetly cunning I believed her when she proclaimed me "the best friend she had ever had." Veronica loved cocaine and Viviron, an over-the-counter caffeine pill. She loved her football star boyfriend, though he could be "rough" and jealous. I felt protective of her and gave well-thought-out advice. We were Playmates the same year, just months apart. We vowed to always be friends, and when the time came for Playmate of the Year to be chosen, we would root for each other.

One night the mansion's guest rooms completely filled with out-of-town Playmates in for a group photo shoot to be held the following day. Veronica and I would share a room. It just so happened that the last room available was the one I had stayed in my first night in the Playboy mansion. We giggled and laughed and drank champagne until late into the night.

"Who do you think will win Playmate of the Year?" she quizzed me. "I heard it might be you! Have you heard anything?"

"No! Did you ree-al-ly hear it might be me?" I squealed.

"Well, it's so hush-hush right now. No one will talk. I think you should go ask Hef," she said matter-of-factly. "I know he's in his room; just go talk to him. You never talk to him. I'm sure he'd like to see you."

"You think I should?"

"Yes, do it," she urged.

"Well, I'm scared. I don't know what to say. . . ."

"He's so sweet; just come right out and ask. I'll wait here."

I looked at her for confidence one last time before I closed the bedroom door behind me and made my way down the dimly lit hallway toward Hef's bedroom.

What am I doing? I must be out of my mind, I thought. But still I kept putting one foot in front of the other.

By that time, I had spent many nights in the various bedrooms of the mansion. Apartments in L.A. were expensive and I soon realized I would need a roommate. I had rented a room in the home of a man who did little but sit all night watching porn and eye-balling me, so I moved out. Reluctantly, I sent Mark back home to Utah until I could afford my own place and had more time to spend with him. I just had to know if I would win the $100,000 prize that came with becoming the next Playmate of the Year. I knew I wasn't the prettiest Playmate, but I thought I was smart, and that had to count for something. If I won, I'd buy a house, a real home. The air conditioning in my Bobcat no longer worked. It would be so nice to drive a Porsche like the one last year's Play-mate of the Year, Shannon Tweed, now drove.

I stood in front of the old man's door and knocked.

"Yes, who is it?" came the familiar voice from inside.

"It's Susie. Susie Scott. May I speak to you for just one minute?"

The door to Hugh Hefner's bedroom opened and he asked me to step inside. A visceral fear made me immediately apologize and turn to leave.

"Is something bothering you, Susie?" came his voice, enchanting as always, fatherly, secure. "Do you need to talk about something in particular?"

I ventured to look about the room.

"Would you like anything?" he asked. Warm, gentle, safe. "Something to drink, perhaps?" He turned as if on an errand and returned with a Pepsi and two glasses of ice. He set the glasses of ice down and reached into the chest pocket of his scarlet pajamas. He opened his palm. "This might help you relax, would you like one?"

"Oh, thank you, I guess so," I said, and watched him pop the tiny tablet into his mouth. I did the same.

I remember telling him it would be nice if I knew if he had plans for my career with *Playboy*.

And I remember wondering out loud if I should take my old job back.

I don't know if we discussed Playmate of the Year.

I don't know if I told him how smart I was.

When I woke up, Hugh Hefner's spongy white body was stuck to mine. His eyes were small slits, his mouth a deep cave. I thought at first it was my grandfather.

Suddenly he rolled off me.

"Grab your panties, quick!" he said. "Shannon's coming."

I felt blurry. Drugged. I had taken what he gave me freely, but I hadn't chosen unconsciousness. What had I done? I stumbled around the room. I couldn't find my robe. He had gone into his bathroom and I couldn't find my panties. I ran out of the room without them. My head hurt as I groped my way down the hall in the chill of early-morning light.

Later I found out that Veronica already knew she had been chosen Playmate of the Year and had already started planning the photo layout.

The reality of mansion life had become all too clear.

I was a whore; now it was true.

Chapter 6

Roadblock

I 'VE ALWAYS HAD A sense of orientation. When I fell, fast and hard, it wasn't that I lost interest in God. I knew I needed a savior— someone who made me feel better, at least. But in my quest for sanctuary, discernment got clouded. How easy it was to pick the first savior I saw.

Paul, my friend with the Jade limo, flew to Los Angeles and in- troduced me to Jewel, a stripper who entertained him on many business trips. I wanted to leave the Playboy mansion, and Paul thought Jewel would make a good roommate. Jewel was not com- fortable with the whole "clothes thing" and flitted around her apartment without a stitch. We sat in Jewel's tiny apartment, watching with part fascination, part disbelief, as she lifted her pet boa constrictor from a large glass box beside the refrigerator.

"This is Fuzzy," she said, and tried to wrap the creature around her bare breasts. "He's part of my act."

When the snake wouldn't cooperate, she dropped him into the box and opened the freezer.

"Want a Klondike bar?" she said. "I'm on the ice cream–only diet. It's all I have in the fridge." She ran her hands down her midriff and let them rest on her hip bones.

I closed my mouth and looked in Paul's direction. *This* was the girl he thought I should room with? Still naked, she bent over to lift a heavy bag of snake pellets. The scene grew disenchanting. Even at the mansion people wore clothes most of the time. But who was I to judge? Besides, I needed a cheap place to stay. At least the apartment was clean. I moved in.

Fortunately, I was on the road most of the time. When in L.A., I went on auditions and got parts on shows like *The Jeffersons* and *Cheers.* For some reason, I passed on an audition for a movie called *Splash.* I'd often fly Mark out to be with me on sets. He'd sit for hours while professionals applied my makeup and stuffed my bra.

One night after a poster shoot for Miller Lite and hours of standing in the salty surf holding a beer I was told not to drink, Mark told me he was gay. We sat in a sushi bar on Sunset Boulevard, drinking sake, both looking at guys.

"That guy is gorgeous," Mark said. He flipped his wrist toward a tall blond hunk. "He just winked at me."

I went to the bar and demanded a lot more alcohol. Returning, I folded my arms and looked away. "This is ridiculous," I grunted. "You're gonna kill Mama and Daddy, ya know."

"I think you already did that," Mark said sarcastically.

"How can you be gay?" I said. "You've never even had sex." I glanced to check his reaction. I cringed. He daintily lifted his sake cup to his lips and sipped.

"Remember when I was staying with Laurent, the butler at the mansion?"

How had I not noticed? And I had introduced them! I looked at my chopsticks and wondered if I could inflict a fatal wound on myself. "Please, Mark—you're not even sixteen yet." I took his hands and held them between my own. "I know you don't want to hear this"—I focused hard to make sure the booze did not slur my words—"but the Bible says *homosexuals*"—I tried to utter *homosexuals* with the same inflection as *algebra* or *leukemia*, words that make you feel uncomfortable—"uh . . . dad-gum, Mark . . . dontcha remember Sodom and Gomorrah?!"

He fluttered his eyes and said nothing.

"Well, it says it's a sin, Mark!"

His hands slipped through mine. "Hah!" he said. "Looks like we're partners in crime." A single tear slipped down the side of my nose. "I know about Steve—your photographer," Mark said. "I bet you slept with him! And what about your cocaine!"

Why should I listen to this? The little creep. I threw my napkin on the table and went to the ladies' room. In the stall I removed a small square of folded paper from my purse. I rolled a dollar bill into a cylinder and sniffed white powder up my nose. Better. I took another sniff and left the bathroom.

"I'd like to go to the bathroom too," Mark said when I returned. "I've done it before, Susie. Come on—give me a bump."

I handed him a tiny packet under the table. This day was quickly rising to the top of my list of worst days ever. I ordered another large sake.

Hmmm. Sex before marriage. Was that adultery? Maybe fornication? Was that one of the Ten Commandments? My mind raced. Man, I needed to look that up. I knew I wouldn't find anything in the Bible that said it was good.

Mark returned with a smile.

"Well, do you wanna start going to church or something?" I said.

"Yeah," Mark said, more sarcastically than before. "Let's find a church for homos, centerfolds, and cocaine addicts. Oh, yeah, and strippers—that way we can invite Jewel."

I ATE ALL OF JEWEL'S Klondike bars, and she kicked me out.

One of her ex-boyfriends, Johnny, had a room to rent. He said he'd love company, and I could stay as long as I needed. He lived in a beautiful condo with windows overlooking a bluff. From the balcony I could see surfers and sailboats. I had my own bathroom and two huge closets. It was better than the Playboy mansion.

In my new bedroom, I started to unpack boxes. Stuffed in one was a bunch of old junk—pictures of me and Mark, costume jewelry, cocktail dresses . . . and in the bottom, an old, old book. On the broken and faded white leather spine were bold, crooked letters, penned by a six-year-old—SUSIE SCOTT'S BIBLE. I held it and leafed through the pages. So many passages underlined. Notes and quotes from Alabama preachers written on most every page by my first-grade, second-grade, third-grade, fourth-grade hands. So precious, so sweet. Man, I was so different then. I must have talked to God fifty times a day.

I closed the book and went in search of dirt. I needed to clean something. Johnny said the apartment came rent-free, but surely he wasn't letting me stay out of the goodness of his charitable heart. Nothing was free. The novelty of living with a centerfold would wear off quickly if I didn't make myself useful. I had cleaned my mother's house most of my life; I could certainly clean his. After cleaning the bathrooms, mopping, and vacuuming, I walked down the hill to the grocery store and came back with dinner. When Johnny came home from work he was so happy with what I'd done.

"I just cleaned up a little for you," I said, pouring him a soda. "I made a salad and some pasta for dinner. Are you hungry?"

"You didn't have to do all this! Really."

"To be honest, I enjoyed it. It feels like a home now."

He beamed. I could tell he was very happy. "Do you watch *Cheers*?" he said, and picked up the remote control.

That became the ritual we settled into for two years. I cooked. We watched television. Home. It was wonderful.

Johnny had a lot of angry girlfriends, and I went out whenever they came by. Paul occasionally came to town, and we'd meet at a restaurant called Giuseppe's, in Beverly Hills. One night I sat at the bar waiting for him when Rod Stewart, with his famous shaggy hair, asked to buy my drink. I'd had a crush on him since I was twelve.

"No, I better not," I said. "I'm waiting for somebody." I was used to meeting celebrities at the mansion, but Rod made me shake. He shrugged and strolled away. Immediately, after convincing myself I did right by not forgetting about Paul, Julio Iglesias sat down at a table five feet from my barstool. Within moments a man from his table asked if I would join Mr. Iglesias.

"Sorry, I'm meeting someone," I said.

"Well, perhaps you could join us tomorrow for lunch at Mr. Iglesias's home?" the sun-baked Latino man urged. "Here is the number."

I paid for my drink and decided to wait for Paul outside. I was a nervous wreck. As I headed for the door, I heard Rod Stewart's scratchy voice. "'Scuse me," he said, "would you mind if I give you a call?" It was so much easier to talk to these people at the mansion. "What's your number, baby?" he asked.

After I remembered it, I told him.

I went out with both Rod and Julio. Rod was clean—no drugs

and only the occasional glass of wine. One night we walked on the beach below Johnny's apartment. Rod was quiet, sweet, and tender. A few days later he called and asked me to come to his house. It was late, but I wanted to see him again. He invited me to sit on the couch and have a drink. Then, the question I knew was coming: "Don't you think it's time we had sex?" Rod asked with one leg on the sofa, his arm draped across the back.

I probably would have gone into the bedroom that moment, but something about how he said the word *sex* turned me off. Ugh. It sounded like porn. In a split second I imagined the aftermath—the "walk of shame" to my car, carrying my high heels, with smeared makeup and disheveled hair, the drive home in the daylight wearing the same clothes.

"No," was all I said.

Rod asked me to leave. I did so quickly. I saw him about a year later at Giuseppe's with the supermodel Kelly Emberg. Funny, he remembered my name. I wondered if he would have if I'd had *sex* with him.

Julio was one of the nicest gentlemen I have ever met. He always had women around him. They adored him. Julio and I met sometimes in Las Vegas or Mexico City or his home in L.A. I always had my own room.

Julio forbade any use of drugs. Once in Vegas during his concert a friend of his offered me cocaine. I dug in, wiped my nose, and retouched my lipstick. I felt good. I was wearing seven-inch strapless heels, a spectacular bustier with black lace—tight and studded with clear diamondlike stones—and an elegant black silk skirt. A private party was set up at a Benihana restaurant, after the concert, reserved for friends of Julio. Like a queen, I floated in. From the top step of the entry, I looked for my man. Julio spotted me. I smiled. He did not. I felt as if I had a front tooth missing.

He came closer, stopped, and stared. I felt the corner of my mouth twitch. Everyone was looking at me, then him, then me. Julio kissed me full and long on the mouth. He looked at my eyes, and then, in full view of all the spectators, licked my nose. He looked at me like I was a liar, turned, and walked away. I went to my room, looked in the mirror, and cried.

LITTLE DECISIONS BRING ON consequences. One night, I decided not to go home.

Johnny and I were regulars at a restaurant called Dudley's. The owner knew we were only roommates, not dating. I had discovered that a lot of guys I dated just wanted to be able to say they had slept with a centerfold. There was no love, no care, no tenderness or attraction in it, just bragging rights. So I started saying no to requests for sex. The decision had little to do with morality; it was more a calculated plan for me to get something more—the longer I held out, the harder a guy pursued me. When I gave in, it was usually because I was a little bit interested and didn't want to hurt the guy's feelings. It rarely had anything to do with physical pleasure. It never felt emotionally fulfilling. Something wasn't right, and I just couldn't put my finger on it. It seemed like I was always just looking for the next romance, the next passion, the next excitement.

One night I was alone at Dudley's, reading a horrible script before an audition. I decided to walk home and watch television, but Dudley asked me to stay and watch the door for a while. He had an important client coming and wanted to make sure he was seated right away.

In the entryway, I saw the huge oak-and-leaded-glass door open. A breeze caught my sleeveless dress. Chilled, I tried to cover my arms with my hands. A man entered. He smiled without opening his mouth and reached for my hand. I thought he was going to shake it, so I didn't pull back. He kissed it and didn't let go.

"My name is Steven Robson. I would be honored if you'd join me at my table." He never broke his gaze.

"Oh, well . . . I can't. I'm helping Dudley."

Steven Robson did not blink. He did not look away. "Dudley is a friend of mine," he said, his voice steely. "I'm certain he won't mind." The mysterious man led me to a dark table in a private corner. As if on cue, a waiter brought us a bottle of Dom Perignon.

"Susan," Steven Robson said, "may I hold your hand?" His hands were manicured and darkly tanned. He wore a huge gold ring with the largest marquise diamond I'd ever seen a man wear. "I met you once before with Rod Stewart. Do you remember?"

Ordinarily, I would never have forgotten a man like this, but if I was with Rod, who knows? Steven wasn't handsome—just striking. His face was wide and his cheekbones unusually high, which made him look like he was smiling when he wasn't. It made me uncomfortable, as if I was obliged to smile back.

"I found out who you were that night," Steven said. "I waited until you weren't dating anyone. I must admit I had someone keep an eye on you."

I took a long sip of the fine champagne. "What else do you know about me?" I wasn't sure I wanted to know.

He squeezed my hand gently. "I know I don't want you to ever date anyone else again. I know I care deeply for you."

"But . . . you don't know me," I said. I felt like an eight-year-old. I looked up at him, hoping he had some kind of reassuring reason for wanting me so badly. No one had ever made such efforts to win my affection. I wanted to know why. I was starting to wish him victory.

"I know everything about you, Susan," he said. "Get to know me. Spend all your time with me. Give me a chance to make you love me."

"I'm not quite sure what you want," I said. "I'll date you. But you should know that I won't have sex with you. I'm not that way. . . ." Anymore, I thought.

We sat in the dark restaurant for four hours. It felt like I was negotiating with him for the rest of my life. After a while he let down his guard. He made me laugh and trust him. He looked into my eyes the entire time except for several trips to the men's room. When we left, he put me in the driver's seat of his red Ferrari, climbed in beside me, and handed me the keys.

"I've never driven a car like this," I said, stammering but excited.

"Don't worry," he said. "It's easy."

We took off like a rocket up the hill. I drove back to Johnny's apartment. Steven danced around the car to lift me from the driver's seat. When we reached the front door he kissed my hand again and then hugged me—just hugged me—for a long time.

For two weeks we saw each other every day. Every evening he kissed me good night at my door and never pushed to come in. Money was never a problem. He said he helped foreign diplomats form companies in the United States to move money out of their countries. He never told me more, saying I didn't need to know. I didn't want to. In my eyes, he was becoming fabulous.

Suddenly, at the end of two weeks, Steven Robson disappeared.

I called, I left desperate messages, I drove by his house, always with my makeup on, just in case. For three months, he was completely gone.

It was too late.

I had fallen without a backup plan. I had handed this man the potential to destroy me. Passion, I learned, could not be turned off so easily. As weeks turned into months, I reached the end of myself. One night, alone in my room, I knelt down and wailed. My heart hurt so badly. I could only hold my chest and give in to missing him.

Winter arrived, and L.A. was gloomy with rain and fog. Word came that Julio Iglesias was auditioning for a female backup singer. All Playmates who could sing were welcome to try out. Several of us showed up and sang our little hearts out, but Julio had the intelligence to hire a professional.

This prompted the *Playboy* office to spring into action. The idea was to resuscitate the old "Singing Playmates" group that died in the late seventies. A group of four Playmates with questionable stage presence and marginal talent was helped musically by modern technology. They traveled the world, bringing money to *Playboy* and smiles to large audiences of wealthy men.

Playboy needed four Playmates who fit the costumes. I was the right size. I got the job. Would I go to Acapulco? In a heartbeat. I was dying over my loss. Was Steven dead or did he just stop loving me? Which was worse? My life was without value if he didn't love me. I went from wishing he was dead to wishing I was dead. I called Steven's machine and told him where I was going to be (just in case he needed anything).

We four Playmate centerfolds arrived to see our images plastered over Acapulco billboards. Newspapers bid us a hearty welcome. We rehearsed daily from 5 to 6 p.m. Our first show was at 11 p.m., our second at 1 a.m. We were free by 2 a.m. and danced most of the night at the famous nightclubs, Baby'O and Boccaccio's. At 4 or 5 a.m. we took the testosterone-driven Latin boys we danced with to buy us pancakes. We slept until noon, drank margaritas, sunbathed, and water-skied on a private brackish lagoon.

We all went out with the young Mexican men. I needed friendship and someone to talk to. It was torment not to be comforted.

During the tour I was called back to L.A. for a three-day preapproved appearance on *Simon & Simon*. After one thirteen-hour shoot I left the set and drove by Steven's house. Through the grandly styled iron gate I could see his house ablaze in lights. I buzzed the intercom several times. No answer. The machine played "Ain't No Mountain High Enough!"

I scaled the stone wall and landed on the inside, dress around my waist and heels clutched in my hand. I straightened myself, walked to the front door, and knocked. And knocked. At last the door opened a crack, then fully.

"Susie! Uh, how are you?" I recognized a man from one of the restaurants Steven liked to take me to. "Uh, I don't think Steven's here. I'll check." He closed the door on me.

What was going on? Steven's bedroom light was on. . . . Oh, no. I pushed my face into my hands. I ran back to the wall and prepared to jump back over. Before I could escape I heard Steven's voice.

"Susan," he said. Just one word.

I felt weak but kept going. I pulled myself up the rest of the way and slid over the gate. I looked back at him through iron bars. He stood in a long ebony robe that hung open, revealing very small underwear. I had picked a bad time to come. The gate opened. Steven ran to my car and held on to the door.

"Let me just talk to you, Susie," he said.

I drove several yards with him attached to my door, then stopped. I rolled my window down. "Why? You killed me. I died."

"Please, Susie—she's just a friend."

Suspicions confirmed. I groped for dignity, slammed the door, and drove away. When I got back to my hotel in Acapulco the front desk clerk handed me an envelope stuffed with pink message slips.

"They all from Steven, except one from your brother. Steven say very urgent. He call hundred time a day."

I didn't phone him back, not yet. Not yet.

I finished my work in Mexico several weeks later and returned to L.A. Bad news. Johnny had taken part in a sour business deal and had to sell his condominium. I was broke—always broke. Soon I would be without a place to stay. I tended to lose a lot of modeling jobs because I could not fill out a bathing suit "up top." It was time for drastic steps. I took the $1,200 I made from Mexico and went to a plastic surgeon. Overnight I went from nothing to a 34C with new confidence. Hospital time soon over, I couldn't resist driving by Steven's house one last time—"for closure," I told myself. He drove up at the same time I did and parked his car directly in front of mine. Skies were gray. It was raining heavily.

"I know you still love me," he said, through my closed car window. "Come inside."

I wanted things the way they were. Oh, how I wanted things to work out. Inside, he went to his office and returned with a tiny velvet box. He got on his knee and took my hand the way he used to. My heart pounded. I could hear rain crashing on the roof.

"I want you to marry me," Steven said. It wasn't a question. He opened the box and took out a marquise diamond as big as the one he wore.

"Really? Really?" He could keep the diamond. I just wanted the man I met in Dudley's so long ago, the man who was sure he knew me and wanted me, the man who kissed my hand and hugged me—just hugged me—for a long, long time.

I took the diamond and put it on. It was proof.

"I'd love you if we lived in a shack and had to live off bread and water," I said.

It thundered outside—the sky roared and cracked in two. Steven and I ran out into the rain.

We were married on the courthouse steps in Beverly Hills.

The evening of our wedding day we changed out of our marriage clothes. Steven suggested we go to a sports bar. He sniffed several lines of cocaine, then made a Scotch on the rocks for the ten-minute drive to the bar. We arrived as the sun went down and stayed until closing at 2 a.m. Steven invited everyone who was still there home with us, including a topless dancer, to celebrate our wedding. Steven brought out a mound of cocaine for our newfound friends. I didn't take any because I was exhausted and wanted to sleep. When the sun came up everyone was still playing pool in the game room. No one noticed when I left for the day for a shoot. Three days later the topless dancer was still awake, along with Steven. She told me I was the "coolest girl she had ever met!" She told Steven he "was lucky his new wife wasn't jealous" like most girls she knew. I knew they had slept together.

When the party dwindled, Steven pulled me close. He hadn't bathed in three days and stank heavily of Scotch. The mound of cocaine was gone. Steven demanded sex, or else I could leave and take my things. I followed him to bed. He was drunk, high, elsewhere, nowhere. After forty-five minutes of foreplay, he couldn't achieve an erection. He decided I was a poor specimen of a wife and got mad. Everything was my fault. I brought him a glass of Scotch and watched him start to snore. I snuck out and went back to the *Playboy* office to tell everyone I was married.

After a couple days of sleep, Steven was kind again. I was glad. I called Mark and told him the news and asked him to come to L.A. He couldn't right away. He had officially quit school and had a job at an antique shop.

"Okay," I said. "But call me. I really want you to meet Steven. You'll just love my new husband."

AS MY HEAD HIT the metal frame of the bed, I woke up. I felt myself being pulled by my ankles. How many days had we been married? My head landed on the marble floor. I heard bad words. Curses. I tried to sit up but something held me down. It was dark. The weight lifted and I tried to crawl away. The lights snapped on, glaring, hurting. He lunged over to me and lifted me off the ground.

"Give me back the f—— wedding ring!" Steven yelled. He snatched at my left hand.

I felt as if I was in the middle of a movie and had missed the beginning. "Steven," I said, "what did I do?"

"You know what you did, you bitch!" His mouth was an inch from my face. I could feel his spit on me. "I spoil you and you ignore me like this!" He shoved me, and I fell. "Get up!" he screamed. "We're going out—now!"

"Steven . . ."

"Now! I said do it *now*!—and give me that ring!"

I pulled my wedding ring off my finger and handed it to him, trying to stay out of his reach, fumbling with my clothes. He pulled me to the driveway and pushed me into the passenger side of the Ferrari. Within minutes we were roaring down Sunset Boulevard, weaving in and out of traffic. The windows were down. I was cold and scared. I thought about trying to jump out but was afraid he would kill me if I survived the jump.

"You see this?" He held my wedding ring in front of my eyes. I nodded. "It's gone!" He flung it out the window.

"Please, Steven, please . . ." I sank down into the seat, sobbing.

He stomped on the accelerator. The Ferrari surged forward. "You are the worst wife ever!" he shouted.

The next day I woke up in the car. We hadn't gone anywhere. Steven had raced for over an hour up to Malibu and back, then drove us home. I was afraid to go in while he was still angry. Gingerly, I tried the front door. It was locked. I went around to the laundry room and got in. The door to the bedroom was locked.

What had I done?

I felt thin from cocaine, depressed. As the weeks with my new husband progressed, I worked for *Playboy* less and less. Steven loved Scotch with his cocaine. The two joined forces to make him hate me. Once, during a long binge, he began to hallucinate, yelling, screaming, jealous, crazy, hating me. Always hating me.

After that binge he announced we were moving to Aspen, Colorado. He told me to pack. It wasn't like I had a real job here anyway, he said.

I packed.

OUR MOVE TO COLORADO actually calmed things down. We moved into a gorgeous house on the Roaring Fork River. Steven seemed at peace for a while. I soon settled into a new routine. He confessed he had not really thrown my ring out the window and gave it back to me. I loved to cook and hike, but I still liked cocaine. Only when we did cocaine for long periods did he grow violent.

I never quite knew whom I married. Several times my husband locked me out. I had to go to a neighbor's in my underwear to call and beg him to let me back in. One night it was cold outside and I tried to climb the stone chimney to reach the vacant maid's quarters to gain entry from that door. I climbed high enough to see into our bedroom window. All emotion was severed as I watched him masturbating to a magazine. He paused, looked over to me clinging to the stone of the fireplace outside, then looked back at the magazine and continued. I climbed down. I no longer wanted in.

Steven disappeared time and time again while we lived in Aspen. He always left me in the care of a houseboy instructed to give me an allowance for necessities and groceries.

Once he disappeared for several weeks, then called and told me to meet him in Paris. When I arrived he was tanned and relaxed and took me to a beautiful flat he had rented on Rue de Berry. We stayed for a month while he completed a business deal, then went to Normandy and Cannes. For weeks we shopped and dined from late afternoon until early evening without quarreling once. Maybe he was sorry. I loved him enough to forgive him without his asking.

In Cannes we hit all the hotel casinos. I watched him toss the dice and order tens of thousands of dollars on house credit with just a signature. One night we sat inside an elegant casino. He hissed at me to go to the car and wait.

"We haven't eaten yet. Can I just—"

"Go," he said. "I'll be right out."

I walked to the car in the dark. He had rented a beautiful maroon Mercedes convertible. I took some cocaine from my Chanel bag, dipped my finger into it, and rubbed a bit on my gums to keep myself from getting hungry.

I saw Steven in the rearview mirror walking very fast to the car. Not bothering to open the door, he jumped into the driver's seat and threw a large brown envelope onto the floorboard.

"We're leaving tonight," he announced with strange jubilation.

"What about our clothes? All of our stuff is at the hotel!"

"We'll have 'em sent. Don't worry!" He laughed. "Look in that envelope down there."

It was stuffed with $30,000 in cash. I was so excited. Maybe I should learn to gamble too. I'd ask my husband to teach me when he was in a good mood. Steven always kept at least a million in cash in the safe at home, although I had never seen it. He had taken my credit cards long ago, saying I wouldn't need them anymore. We always used cash. He seemed to be a very successful businessman indeed.

As we drove out of the airport parking lot back in Aspen, we saw cars slowing in the distance. Traffic appeared to be stopped for at least a mile up the road. For fifteen minutes we inched our way forward. Steven became irritable.

"Honey, look!" I said. "The police are stopping everybody. Wonder what they're looking for." I craned my neck for a better view out the window. It looked just like roadblocks on television. "I'm going to get my camera! There are some SWAT guys too!" Nothing like that ever happened in Aspen.

"Stay put!" he hissed.

"It'll just take a minute. . . ."

"I mean it! Shut up!"

He stayed focused on the car ahead of us.

Then they were in front of us. Then all around us. The police were saying something into a megaphone. The SWAT men were on each side of our Jeep. My window was still rolled down.

"Peter Moxley," the megaphone echoed. "Get out of the vehicle with your hands up."

My heart raced. How exciting. I needed my camera. Who was Peter Moxley? A bank robber? A murderer? A terrorist maybe?

As if in slow motion, I saw Steven's hand go to the latch of the door. He got out and slowly lifted his hands above his head.

Chapter 7

Homeless

THE HANDCUFFS SNAPPED onto my husband's wrists with a deafening click. The guns, dogs, line of cars, and roadblock were for us. And I had wanted to snap a picture!

"Steven," I said, "Steven . . . what's happening?"

My husband, Steven Robson, or Peter Moxley, or whatever his name was, remained silent. It was his right. FBI agents whisked him away in the back of a black sedan. I was given quick, terse orders. I could not touch our car. I was not allowed to take anything except my purse. All our possessions, including our house, were now evidence—seized and locked. I was not to stay at home. But I was free to go. *Thanks.*

I felt people staring at me and longed for the sun to set. The line of cars began to move, slowly at first. Who was this woman walking by herself? Town seemed a thousand miles away. The sky grew dreary. My bones seemed to dissolve. Snow lay thick on the ground. I was officially homeless, alone, in winter, in Colorado. Steven always held all our money. I was also officially broke.

That first night, a friend let me stay in the loft of a barn he was refurbishing. My disturbed mind would not let me sleep. I felt orphaned—and haunted by dread. Steven and I had seldom stayed in the house in Aspen during the two years we'd been married. What had we been running from? And what would I do without him? What if he had to stay in jail? It was the kind of confusion only someone who loves her abuser can know. I longed to call my brother but could not bring myself to face his pity—it would hurt Mark so. I'd thought many times about letting myself die in the last few years. Maybe now I was free to do so. It would be easy to starve myself to death. I would think about it later when my head was clearer.

The next morning I woke up in survival mode. The challenge: trying to get through the rest of that day.

I snuck back to our house but the door was locked. I had learned to keep one window open in the maid's quarters for whenever Steven locked me out. I crawled inside, went to Steven's den, and opened the safe. Empty. From the kitchen I called the Pitkin County jail. I held the phone with both hands and waited for the silence to be broken with his hello.

"Steven," I whispered, "are you okay?"

A tense silence. "I told you a long time ago some people call me Peter," he said at last, "but I didn't like it, so I had my name changed." It was partly true. He had said that one night during a forty-eight-hour binge. I had decided not to mention it when he became sober. But I knew there was much more to the story.

"Why are you in jail? Steven, can you come home today?" I heard him take a deep breath and exhale.

"I'm gonna be here for a while," he said. Another puff. Another exhalation. Suddenly he became all business. "This is what I need you to do," he said, his tone urgent. "Get back into the Jeep somehow. Find an envelope—not the one from France, but another one—you'll need to take a knife, it's sealed inside the driver's-side door. Pry it open. Bring me the envelope. Understand?"

Of course I would. I loved my husband. How do you stop loving someone you know would kill you if you stopped loving him?

"Whatever you do, don't open it," Steven said as if my life depended on it. "Just bring it to me." The phone went dead.

I waited for night, dressed in dark jeans and a black jacket, and had a friend drive me a few hundred yards from Steven's Jeep. It was still parked on the side of the freeway, waiting for the impound truck.

I half ran, half walked along the interstate. I waited for a couple cars to pass. All was dark and moonless. I reached up to open the door. Locked. I waited for a couple more cars to zip by. One slowed. It was a police car. My heart beat wildly, and I contorted my body behind the rear tire, praying the patrol car would keep going. Mercifully, it did. I tried the rear latch. It clicked open. I crawled in and snaked to the front passenger seat, carefully keeping my head lower than the windows.

It took only a few hard yanks with my fingertips to pull the leather panel away from the metal. I reached in but felt nothing. Then the edge of a thin parcel caught the nail of one finger.

"Oh, God, please," I said, sinking deep into the seat as another car passed. I forced my arm far into the narrow space, pinching the tip of the package. Got it!

"What do you think it is?" my friend asked, back in his car.

"Steven told me not to open it."

The envelope lay sealed on my lap. Youth and naïveté told me to believe him "no matter what." Still, I was curious, and an invisible crack was forming in my soul. Steven was a phantom, an illusion. I saw Peter Moxley now; nothing like Steven was real in him.

"Don't worry, I won't forget you," Steven had said when I phoned him in jail. I couldn't forget him either: his record of lying and bullying, deceit and cruelty. One late night, not long before, Steven and I had sat in a café eating cheese and crusty bread. A musician was playing "Mr. Bojangles," one of my favorite songs, and I sang along with my hands clasped together in delight. Steven lunged over the table and breathed heavily in my face.

"So is he your little boyfriend?" Steven sneered.

"Steven, this always happens when you drink!" I glared my resentment into his dilated pupils. He stood up slowly, Scotch in hand, twirling the ice with his forefinger. He turned as if to leave, then flung the full glass of Scotch in my eyes. I gasped for air, eyes stinging with alcohol. My hands groped for a napkin or tablecloth—anything. The guitar playing ceased. I heard Steven laugh.

I opened the envelope and pulled out its contents.

Five passports. All false names. All faces the same—the man I married. Whoever that was.

"That alone"—my friend pointed at the passports—"is a felony, I think."

Now I knew the truth. My husband was going to skip bail and flee the country. There was no passport for me. My love transformed to rage. Steven intended to dump me. Back at the barn, I threw the passports into the fire, one by one.

THE NEXT DAY, I faced my situation. I'd need some sort of a job. Let's see—what were my skills? High school dropout? Hmmm, always looks good on a résumé. Software company receptionist?

Nothing like that in Aspen. *Playboy* centerfold? I didn't even have the cash for a bus ticket back to L.A.

The sun was out but it was bitterly cold. I began walking down the affluent streets. What I needed was a job and a place to live—all in one. I walked down Main Street past banks, boutiques, and restaurants, passing skiers in elaborate fashions and brightly colored ski togs on their way to catch the first powder of the day, goggles tucked over fox-fur hats and coiffed hair. I was jealous. I should be with them—shopping, skiing, drinking buttery hot toddies, tossing my hair, laughing. Something in me said: "I hate you." But it was directed at myself, not them.

I came to the west end of town, with its splendid Victorians painted in trios of ice cream–colored pastels. I walked to Bleeker Street. I decided to knock only on the doors of the nicest, biggest homes. Yes—I would choose the homes that I would like to live in. I knew how to clean. I could cook. I could take care of kids. I'd just start knocking, seeing who needed help. Someone was bound to take me in, sooner or later.

The first home was painted a delightful baby blue and had a grand front porch. I walked up the steps and rang the bell. Suddenly I felt flushed. A young woman came to the door, about my age.

"Can I help you?" She looked as if she had been taken away from something important.

I had not planned this event well. I felt ashamed. "I was wondering . . . well . . . if you might need a maid or a cook. . . ."

She must have thought I was a nut.

"No," was all she said. She seemed confused. Then I saw a flash of recognition cross her face. "Aren't you . . ." Then, as if to avoid humiliating me further, "Never mind. I already have plenty of help." She smiled nervously, and I backed to the edge of the porch, overthanking her until she finally closed the door.

This was not going to be a good day. I stuffed my hands deep into my pockets, seeking comfort. It started to snow. I continued from house to house—all the especially pretty ones. I knocked and asked, knocked and asked, partially relieved when no one came to a door.

Toward the end of the day I came upon a massive brick home painted the color of Pepto-Bismol. Since I felt nauseated by then, this was not altogether discomforting. The gate was ajar. I took this as a positive sign. I walked quickly up the brick path to the front door. Having now rehearsed my inquiry to perfection, I knocked firmly and stepped back to wait.

"God," I prayed, "will you help me? I need a place to live. I need a job. I promise I will work very hard. . . ."

The door opened. A pale, bundled man filled the doorway. He appeared to be only thirty or so and was cuddled in an oversized hooded robe that matched the house paint. I tried not to laugh.

"Hello, sir." I smiled sincerely. "My name is Susie Robso—Susie Scott." I caught myself. There was no Mr. Robson. "I wonder if you are in need of a maid or a cook. I will work for room and board." I offered my hand but he took a step back.

"I don't shake hands," he said pensively. "Germs, you know."

"Yes. Of course."

I glanced over his shoulder and saw a huge fire blazing in a marble fireplace deep inside a formal living room. It looked so inviting.

"I live with my mother," he said. "She's often sick. But she has me to take care of her—so thank you, no." He must have seen my disappointment, for he added thoughtfully, "I'm sorry, but my mother doesn't like others in the house."

"Germs," I said.

He gave a lonely nod, then paused. "You know, the lady across the street is always looking for help." He pointed.

"Really?" I said hopefully. "Thanks, thanks so much!"

I ran down the path and through the gate. "God, please, please, please."

It took a very long time for her to answer. Finally: "Let yourself in!" and again, "Let yourself in!" Her voice was irritated. I walked past a long marble bar into the formal dining area. "Sit down." She gestured with a gnarled hand toward the chair. "Who are you?" she asked, devoid of charm.

I told her of my need for work and a place to reside.

"When can you start?"

I nearly fell off my chair. My plan actually worked. "Um, right now."

"You're hired," she said.

She was bound to a wheelchair, she explained, and described my duties: bathing her, cooking and cleaning, errands, and more. I could stay in a room upstairs and would be on duty six days a week from the time she rose until she retired at night. If she needed to use the toilet during the night there was an intercom next to my bed. I would receive five hundred dollars monthly plus board.

I was delighted. God, thank You. *Thank You!*

That night, I moved into the attic of Miss Rue White's house on 30818 Francis Avenue. Exhausted, I slept like I hadn't slept in years.

COMPARED TO THE INSTABILITY I had just experienced, I considered my attic a little slice of heaven, though Rue was often drunk and mostly cranky.

The woman kept me on my toes. She'd call me on the intercom several times each night. *Arrange my pillow. Bring me a glass of water—now!* I rose each morning at 7 a.m. to help her out of bed and into the wheelchair.

Rue bathed twice a week, Mondays and Thursdays. On those days in particular her countenance was severe. I seemed to offend her with every word. Her face was set like marble, her jaws clenched so tightly I feared she would never open them again without a crowbar. When she did, she always shouted the same thing:

"You're fired!"

It was her weapon of choice. Neighbors told me I was her fourth live-in helper that year. I knew Rue needed me, so I didn't take the firings seriously. I needed her, so I let her fire me regularly.

I started going back to church on Sundays. Mostly, I prayed Steven would stay in jail. The story came out in the papers over time. He was wanted for a laundry list of crimes—most involving money.

One night while I soaked Rue's feet in a basin of olive oil (her remedy for corns), the phone rang. I rushed to answer it, praying it would not be Steven calling from prison again. He had been moved to a Denver prison and given more phone privileges. Sometimes he called several times a day. I feared the day he would be released.

Rue picked up the other line at the same time I did. Steven's phone calls exasperated Rue.

"Hello?" we both said at the same time.

"This is Susie's husband, let me talk to her."

"Stop calling here!" Rue shouted, and hung up. She slammed her empty highball glass down and shouted for me to come immediately. "I'm sick of that criminal calling here! I want you out of my house and—"

"I know," I said, "I'm fired." It was Monday—bath day.

"First get me another drink! I want to go to bed! After that, you're fired!"

I stood with my hands on my hips, my feet nailed to the floor, my eyes drilling a hole through her hardened face. I didn't move.

"I—said—*make—me—a—drink!*" Rue shouted. Her shout became a hiss.

I had taken all the abuse I could that day—from anybody. "Not
until you tell me I'm not fired!" I said.

Rue wiped the oil from her feet with the bath towel I had
brought. She flung the towel on the floor in front of me. I watched
her grasp the wheelchair with both hands and set the brake. She
lifted herself from her wheelchair and sauntered down the hall. She
was walking! Only when I heard the slam of her bedroom door did
I dare move. In all the months I had worked there I had not seen
her take a step without me holding her entire weight.

That night her voice on the intercom woke me several times.

I did not answer.

This place was crazy. Rue was crazy. Maybe I was crazy. I slept
in my attic home undisturbed, strangely at peace.

Chapter 8

A Single Light

DAYS WORKING FOR RUE White passed slowly. My two-named husband continued to phone from jail. Angry calls. Threatening calls. Steven/Peter had no love for me, but he would never let me go. His ego would not allow it.

One balmy evening I sat on the porch swing, having settled Rue at the table with dinner and a cocktail. I took stock of my situation. From moment one, my husband had lied, fooled around, abused me, and endangered me. How could I think the future held anything different? All delusions of a happy marriage finally slipped away. I turned my face away from the window so Rue wouldn't see me cry.

Divorce—it was the last resort, but we had arrived. I didn't know how to do it, or even where to start. I was sure I couldn't afford one. All I knew was I had to get out.

After putting Rue to bed, kissing her forehead, and placing a pitcher of water on her bed stand, I walked into town. I stopped by a pub and sipped a glass of cheap watery wine, remembering the taste of good champagne and how I had once taken it for granted. I pushed the wine aside and ordered a twelve-dollar glass of champagne. The expensive nectar equaled three and a half hours of work at my current wage. Suddenly I heard a voice.

"Buy you a drink?"

A middle-aged man towered above my right shoulder. He removed his cowboy hat and sat on the stool beside me.

His name was Charlie. He ordered a bottle of Taittinger and asked for two glasses. We toasted to nothing in particular. For a man of fifty, his frame was solid. He had thinning gray hair and folds on his face acquired by years of expression. Many people greeted him. He'd lived in Aspen twenty-five years, he explained.

With the bottle mostly gone, I felt relaxed and befriended. I apprised Charlie of my situation. He knew Rue White and her long history of bad behavior. "You live with her?" he said. "You poor thing."

When I broached the topic of my husband in jail and my need for a divorce, Charlie grew uncomfortable. He must have remembered the front-page articles printed by both local newspapers. His frown said he didn't want to be seen with me. Reaching for his hat, he laid two large bills on the bar. "Let's take a walk," he said, helping me from the barstool.

Charlie took my hand and led me past storefronts to the intersection behind the old Hotel Jerome to a two-story redbrick building. A single light shone through the blinds of the upper corner window. Charlie pointed to the window. "That's Joe Krabacher's office." He turned to me. "He's my attorney. He owes me a favor. I'll call him for you."

I stood in front of Charlie, looking at the light. Suddenly, Charlie leaned down and kissed my lips. The kiss was gentle but not short. "I'd like to date you," he said. "But I don't date married women. I'm not sure what category you fit into. Can I see you again?"

I wasn't sure what I had done to warrant Charlie's actions. While we were sitting at the pub a lot of women had said hello to him. I thought he was just being friendly toward everyone, including me.

I nodded.

SEVERAL WEEKS PASSED AND Charlie and I spent time together when I wasn't with Rue—which I was most of the time.

One Thursday—bath day—Rue was in a particularly cantankerous mood. She had been bathed and dressed in clean, pressed clothes and seated at her table.

"When's dinner!" she bellowed. "Hurry up. I can't wait all night—and pour me another drink!"

I scurried around the kitchen, juggling pots and pans and Rue's vodka decanter. Suddenly the phone rang. Rue wheeled over and picked it up. I hoped it wasn't Steven.

"Susie can't go out tonight!" Rue shouted. Then a long silence. It was Charlie. Good. His small talk charmed Rue long enough for me to get dinner on the table. Charlie must have pacified Rue, because she didn't fire me that evening as usual.

The next day Charlie called with a blissful plan. He had a client who had just bought a house to tear down. It would take several months to get permits. Charlie had arranged for me to live there rent-free in the meantime if I wanted.

The next day I quit Rue's. "Get going!" she yelled, waving me away, "and good riddance!"

The house was the sweetest little place, scantily furnished with worn, comfortable furniture. I ran back and forth, exploring every cabinet, closet, nook, and cranny. It was perfect. Right there on the living room floor I lay flat on my face and praised God. I promised Him I'd read my Bible more. And I did, at least for a while. It's funny what happens when you start to read your Bible.

"Charlie," I said into the telephone, "remember you said you didn't date married women?"

"Well, you're not really married. . . ."

"Charlie, I am 'really' married, and we are 'really' dating." I had looked up every verse in my Bible on the subject of adultery. My conclusion? That was exactly what Charlie and I were doing. And I wasn't going to do it anymore.

Charlie was silent for a moment. "You need a divorce," he said.

For some reason Charlie wasn't concerned about being seen dating me, but he had hesitated to call Joe Krabacher because he was worried Steven would have him maimed if he found out Charlie had a hand in the divorce. In the end Charlie kept his promise and made the call. He dropped me off in front of Krabacher Law Offices. I walked inside the beautiful old brick building.

I had seen Joe Krabacher before around Aspen. He frequented an upscale grocery store where I shopped for Rue. He always looked like a cold, stone statue . . . albeit a *comely* statue. He'd glare at me from under lash-hooded gray eyes. I'd glare back, just to show him I wasn't intimidated or interested.

I had seen his bio on a brochure. Valedictorian of his law school class, he had won five American Jurisprudence Awards and was a hard-driving up-and-comer in the Colorado law scene. He spoke two languages, played the piano, guitar, saxophone, and flute, and was an avid windsurfer and snowboarder. Now he offered me a seat in his office. I sat down. He remained standing. He towered around six feet ten inches, with his arms perpetually and impatiently crossed in front of his chest. His mouth was not unattractive but twisted upward at one side. I took it for a sarcastic smirk—one that had been there so long he'd grown unaware of it.

I did not like him.

I felt embarrassed and rattled. Instinct told me to excuse myself, run, preserve what was left of my dignity. My need for freedom overpowered my pride.

"How much did Charlie tell you?" I asked. I clasped my hands and stared at them. My knees shook.

"Just that you need a divorce. Not much more."

"Well, I *have* to get a divorce. . . . I'm afraid of my husband."

Joe sat down. He didn't sit behind his desk. He sat on the other side—nearer to me. "Tell me more," he said.

Somewhere inside me, a dam broke. Joe represented my only hope. Emotions flooded out, too many to manage. I spilled at least a half hour's worth. In the end, I was exhausted and began to cry.

Joe scooted his chair closer to hand me a tissue. We looked each other in the eye. Only then did he speak.

"Don't worry," he said. "It's all over now. You're okay." In that instant I reached some distant port of safety. I didn't look away. My nervousness subsided. I saw no haughtiness in him, only compassion.

The moment passed. Joe became my attorney again. "Are there any assets?" he asked.

"Nothing. Just some personal possessions."

Suddenly urgency showed in his eyes. "Susie . . ." He pressed his fingers on the sides of his temples. "Oh, my goodness. . . . What's your husband's name?" The office became very cold.

"Steven—" I began.

"Robson." Joe finished my sentence.

Joe shook his head, dumbfounded. That very morning, Steven had called, asking Joe to represent *him*. Legally, Joe could not represent both Steven and me.

"No!" I cried out. "Oh, God, no! I don't have any money. I don't have a job anymore." I buried my face in my hands. "Mr. Krabacher, you were my only chance."

Joe was silent for a moment. I could see his legal mind at work. "Let me make some calls," he said. "One way or another, you'll have representation."

"Please, Mr. Krabacher, I can clean your house for you. Or wash and iron your clothes." How could I tell him I was worth his benevolence? "I am not asking for charity. I am a hard worker." Again I crumbled, face in hands, sick of crying. I felt his hand on my shoulder. With one of his long fingers he brushed back my hair from my eyes. He leaned closer.

"Don't cry, Susie," he said. "And I'm Joe. Call me Joe. Okay?" Were Joe's eyes actually moist? He broke my heart with his tenderness.

I stopped crying and stood up. "I'm sorry I made a scene," I said. "Thank you for seeing me, Joe, really, thank you."

Struggling to regain composure, I walked to the door of his office. I had forgotten my purse. I turned back quickly only to find myself within inches of him. I released my bottom lip from between my teeth and slowly looked up. He had my purse in his hands. We both smiled. His chin nearly rested on his chest looking down at me. I felt weak and silly. I left.

THE NEXT DAY FELT warm. I walked the few blocks to Rue White's house. It was payday, and Rue would be expecting me to come for my last paycheck. An envelope had been taped to the door with my name on it and a check for $375 inside. I guessed that was right, as I did not complete a full last month. I sighed and knocked. No answer. I walked away.

Two days passed and Joe called. He wanted to talk about my case. Would I meet him at his office? I arrived midday and waited in the reception area.

When I had met him before, he had worn khaki pants and a casual shirt. This time, Joe emerged from the hallway wearing a suit.

"I had a court appearance this morning," he explained.

"Oh," I said, embarrassed. Was I blushing?

"Uh, do you mind if we talk over lunch?" he asked. "I'm hungry and it's such a nice day, we could walk."

"Oh. Okay, sure." Having deduced he was not one for small talk, I kept my answer short. I was nervous and wondered what to talk about on the way to the restaurant.

"You know, I do have some shirts that could use ironing," he said, after another comment on the weather. "That is, if you still want to do some work for me."

"Yes, of course, Joe." Was I the odd one to have offered, or was he the odd one to accept? I hoped this meant he would help me with my case.

Lunch lasted two hours at the restaurant he insisted I choose. Joe asked how I came to be with a man like Steven. His law partner had filled him in on my centerfold days. Talking more than he, I told him about Alabama, Utah, California, and the Playboy mansion, ending with Steven.

"Did you love him?" Joe asked with surprising ease.

"Yes," I said, looking away from Joe. "He didn't love me back." I didn't know why I wanted Joe to know.

After picking at our lunch, we agreed the food had a suspicious odor.

"I'm sorry about the restaurant," I said. "This place is usually good."

"Don't worry about it," he said, pushing his plate away.

"Well, I'm a really good cook!" I blurted. I had spoken before thinking but was on a roll now. "I could cook for you sometime. It's the least I can do after all you're doing for me."

The firm had declined to represent Steven. Joe had found another attorney willing to submit divorce papers on my behalf providing Joe did the paperwork. Proceedings would take only six weeks, if the convict cooperated.

Joe's head cocked to the side. "Really? You'd cook for me?" His features took on an adolescent brightness. "How 'bout tonight?" His brows arched with the question.

I was caught off guard. "Uh, actually, Charlie asked me to go to a movie tonight." I hesitated. "But we could do it next week."

Joe smiled. "Next week it is."

The next morning I picked up Joe's shirts. I ironed and hummed a tune on my little front porch. The day was breezy and the flowers in the window box swayed. I spent an inordinate amount of time on each shirt. Each needed to be *just so*. I placed them on hangers and hung them from the gingerbread lattice of the porch. I counted thirty-nine and figured he must have given me every shirt in his closet. I grinned.

I recognized one shirt—a light-blue oxford with faint gold checks. Joe had worn it once at the grocery store. I ran my fingers along the neck and inhaled. Suddenly I felt foolish. He was my attorney. Nothing more. Besides, at age thirty-five, he was a full ten years older than I. I left the porch in search of a cookbook.

The afternoon following our first lunch I had gone home and mopped all the floors, washed the curtains, and scrubbed the bathroom sink in a frantic effort to remove rust and lime buildup. I

planned to collect petunias and daisies from the flower bed and put
them in old jelly jars.

It was now Tuesday. I had three and a half more days to prepare
dinner. *He would be a friend, nothing more.* I checked myself to
make sure I'd thought the word *friend.* *Yep, he'd be a nice friend to
do things with. A friend like him should have the best meal ever!*

I made a list and budgeted $75 from my last paycheck. Joe was
certainly worth that. I hoped to have another, better job soon.

At the grocery store, I became all sleuth—part FDA inspector,
part gourmand. I examined eight perfectly scrumptious strawberries. I scrutinized six red bell peppers. I studied the most fragrant
rosemary. The butcher presented me with four different cuts of
swordfish. After deliberately sniffing each, I chose one perfectly
opaque and decidedly fresh portion. I could not afford two. What
did it matter—this meal was for Joe, not me.

At the register I watched the bill add up—$82.38—a bit more
than I should spend. Joe was worth it. I rushed home and donned
an apron. All my recipe books open on the countertop, I set to
work:

♦ The first course would be a welcoming, salutary soup. A red
  bell pepper puree with crème fraîche and chives.

♦ The second would be healthy, fun. An assortment of field
  greens arranged leaf by leaf, each garnished with edible flowers and herbs, accompanied by homemade balsamic vinaigrette.

♦ The third would be creative. Oven-roasted tomato and buf-
  falo cheese bruschetta garnished with rosemary and thyme.

♦ The fourth, transitioning. A tiny scoop of sorbet with blood
  orange to cleanse the palate.

- The fifth, the pinnacle—definite, grateful, unambiguous in friendship. Pan-seared swordfish with a vanilla beurre blanc across the top, garnished with blood orange slices for color.

- Finally, dessert—familiar but with a flair. Sliced strawberries arranged in a perfect spiral around a flawless scoop of vanilla Häagen-Dazs. Coffee. Complete.

AT 7:30 FRIDAY NIGHT Joe knocked. I was just running to my bedroom to choose another dress, deciding the one I was wearing might give the impression I liked him, as in "really liked."

I was too late. He waved through the glass panel of the door. I ran back to open it.

"Sorry, I was just . . ." My words trailed off and I stared. He wore black pants and a button-down shirt (one I had ironed) with the loveliest silver-and-black tie. His outfit said clearly he "really liked" me. I lowered my eyes shyly so he could not read them. Flowers appeared from behind his back.

My wits came back to me: "Come in, I have to check my sauce."

He followed me closely into the kitchen. I noticed his cologne and smiled with my back to him as I stirred the vanilla beurre blanc. A tiny eating area was set beside the kitchen.

"Wow," Joe said, "you did all this for me?" His gaze traveled from the single candle lit in the center of a cloth-covered folding table to the plain white plates with elegantly folded paper napkins tied with little purple ribbons. "It looks so pretty."

"Oh, I just love cooking," I said, welling with pride. I hoped I hadn't gone overboard.

"Would you like me to open the wine?" he asked.

I handed him a bottle of chilled chardonnay and a corkscrew. I could see his muscles tighten under his sleeves when he pulled the cork from the bottle.

We sat. I served the first course of soup and bread. I took a bite to check its taste and was relieved. Before his was half finished I hopped up to check the salad arrangement. At the last minute I added one more yellow edible flower for color. As he wiped his mouth I removed the soup bowl and replaced it with the bouquet of salad.

"Tell me when to stop," I said as I drizzled the vinaigrette carefully over it with a spoon.

"I don't think I'll ever ask you to stop," he answered, trying to make a joke. I felt jittery—I didn't know why. "It's so pretty," he said, referring to the salad. "How did you learn to cook?"

"Been doing it since I was little," I answered. I brought the next perfectly arranged course and pretended to finish my soup.

"How many courses did you make?" He wiped the olive oil from his lips.

"Just a few more."

"You must have been cooking all day!"

"It was nothing."

"Aren't you going to eat?"

I had been so busy I forgot to make myself a salad. There was only one serving of swordfish and I gave it to him. "Oh, I have to get the bruschetta out of the oven. So you just enjoy it. I've been nibbling all day." Not exactly true. I had starved myself so I would look nice in the tiny black dress I was wearing.

As he lifted the last bit of bread to his mouth I got to my feet to take his plate away. He took the plate from my hand and lightly set it on the table. I was startled.

"Come here for a minute," he said. With his right hand he guided me before him. He sat in his chair looking up at me for a long moment. My heart sent me an urgent warning that it would soon burst if not calmed at once. With both hands Joe pulled me down sideways to rest on his knees. He lifted his face to mine. With one taming hand under my hair, his lips became one with mine. It was as if no other event had ever happened in my life until that moment, and all memory started then.

Our lips separated only after what felt like a whole season of summer.

Dinner was finished quickly, and we moved to the only other room that had furniture (except for the bedroom) and sipped wine, kissed, and talked until my memory faded.

IT DIDN'T TAKE LONG. Maybe an hour. Maybe less. An unbecoming result tends to occur when you combine an empty stomach (mine) with low body weight (mine) and too frequent wine sippings (me). I was never completely sure when I blacked out.

I woke in my bed the next morning, my lingerie draped seductively over the lamp. *Oh, no. Susan Shamaine Scott. What did you do?* A nightgown lay on the floor. An evening dress lay beside it. I was a mess. Joe was nowhere in sight. No note. Gone. Nothing. I had ruined everything.

Strangely, I was neatly tucked under my sheet. I wore a clean T-shirt and flannel pajama bottoms. Matronly almost. I didn't even know I owned flannel pajamas. I could just barely remember an unexpected kiss that seemed so comforting. I sat up and looked around. What I saw confounded me.

Every inch of floor in the living room and my bedroom was shrouded with clothing. As I picked up nightgowns, evening dresses, lingerie, the mystery deepened. Just that moment the phone rang. It was 10 a.m.

"Hello," I answered weakly. My head hurt.

"Good morning. How are you feeling?" It was Joe. I couldn't believe he still wanted to talk to me. I casually inquired into the later events of last night's date. My precious victim said I should have no sense of embarrassment. Rather, he had quite enjoyed a lengthy fashion show of every piece of clothing I owned.

"Everything?" I asked. "I modeled every piece of clothing I owned for you?"

"Well, almost," he said. I could hear the smile in his voice. "You're quite good at modeling. You should make a career of it."

"Dad-gum!" I said. *I'm a disgusting piece of work. I should clean the devil's toenails for the remainder of my paltry life.* "Why didn't you go to bed with me?" I said it too quickly. Too boldly. In the same breath I thanked God we hadn't. For a split second, I wondered if Joe was gay.

"Because I wasn't going to ruin our evening," Joe said. He had tucked me in, kissed my forehead, and left. That was it.

I hung up, dumbfounded.

Four weeks later, Joe called and asked me why I wasn't returning his calls. Truth is, I was humiliated. Why would someone care about me after I had made a complete fool of myself?

"Just let me talk to you one more time," Joe said. "Just talk."

I agreed to meet him at his studio apartment above the grocery store.

When I arrived in the hallway the door was open. I walked in and saw through to the tiny balcony. He was doing something I hadn't seen a man do for a long time.

Joe Krabacher was on his knees.

He was visibly upset. I moved closer, eavesdropping. I heard his conversation:

"Lord, show me what to do" and "I love her."

I walked onto the balcony. Joe had been crying. He pulled himself up and sat down in a lawn chair. If I could just know that he really loved me . . . *but how can I ever take that chance again? I just can't. He'd be the death of me if he ever took that love away. No.*

"Joe, I just can't date you. I . . ." I swallowed back tears.

"No," Joe said. "I won't let you back away from me. I love you."

"I love you too, but I just . . . I don't know, I just can't date you, Joe, please underst—"

Joe looked into my eyes. His voice was strong and low. He nodded and cleared his throat as if to speak. I would remember his whisper forever:

"Then marry me."

Me, age five, in my first-grade class photo (I started school early) at Lacey's Spring Elementary School, Alabama.

(SCOTT FAMILY ARCHIVES)

Tammy and me with our grandfather, my mom's father, the late William Robert Powell (not the grandfather who raped me). I'm about twenty-three here.

(SCOTT FAMILY ARCHIVES)

Me, age four; Matt, age one; and Tammy, age five and a half; with our mom, Betty Jean Powell Scott.

(SCOTT FAMILY ARCHIVES)

PLAYMATE DATA SHEET

NAME: *Susie Scott*

BUST: 34 WAIST: 23 HIPS: 34

HEIGHT: 5'5" WEIGHT: 108

BIRTH DATE: 11-2-63 BIRTHPLACE: *San Diego*

AMBITIONS: *to be rich, famous and beautiful when I grow up*

TURN-ONS: *diamonds & furs; vintage champagne; faster horses; traveling & going home*

TURN-OFFS: *heartache*

FAVORITE MOVIES: *Gone with the Wind; Arthur; E.T. and Raiders of the Lost Ark*

FAVORITE FOODS: *flying-fish roe with raw quail eggs; peanut butter & jelly sandwiches*

FAVORITE PLACE: *Utah; wherever my heart is*

IDEAL EVENING: *cooking dinner at home, snuggling by the fire & someone else cleaning*

BIGGEST JOY: *being in love; winning; and children*

1½ yrs old

my 1st set of wheels

Third Grade

16 yrs. old

I'm gonna be a Playmate someday!

Joe and I get married, November 12, 1988. Top row, left to right: Don Trusdale (Betty Krabacher's husband), Betty Krabacher (Joe's mother), Joe, Frank Scott (my dad), Tammy, Kerry Smith (Tammy's husband at the time), Matt. Bottom row, left to right: Mark, me, Betty Scott .

John "Cheese" Branchizio (middle) with two unidentified Navy SEALs.

Mark in Cité Soleil, c. 1995

Me with hundreds of our children in a school near Jacmel, operated by Mercy and Sharing, 2002. It's recess, and I'm singing a creole song. We danced in the midday sun high in the mountains till late afternoon.

Joe and me at a friend's house, Christmas Day 2006, with three of our dogs, W. W. Steinbeck, Freud, and Mabel.

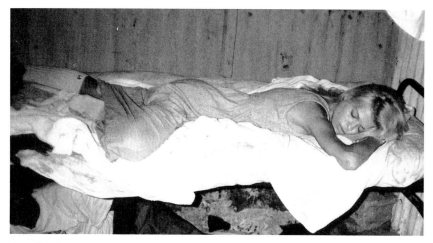

Me sleeping in a shanty in Cité Soleil, 1995. I sometimes spent the night here during construction of our school.

Me with "little Frank" the day before he passed away from irreversible complications of malnutrition. We had found him one week earlier, abandoned in the yard of the government hospital.

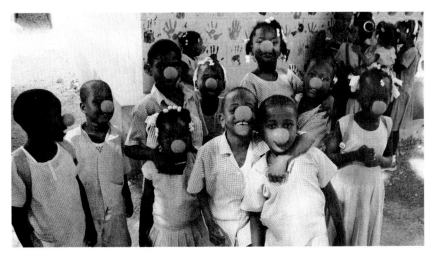

Some of our children at one of Mercy and Sharing's orphanages, emulating Patch Adams in an effort to entice him to visit (plans are currently being made).

Chapter 9

Sunrise

*I*AM NEVER COMING OUT *of this closet,* I said to myself. I could cry in here, and no one would see. The scent of my clothes, my big felt hats, my shoes—I just wanted familiar things around me. My dogs: Sheba, the big Doberman; Cosmo, the overweight Chihuahua; Strogh, the stoic American Eskimo; Flo-Dell, the sweet stray; and Mabel, W. W. Steinbeck, and Freud, the three little whatevers—all gave me sloppy kisses. I had brought in supplies: water and Snausages and fake-bacon doggie treats and the stuffed bear Cosmo believed was his life partner. I didn't want anything in this closet except us.

I would just be a recluse. *I'm an old, used-up teabag of a person anyway.* If Joe came home anytime soon he could just get used to the fact that *this is the real me!* I no longer needed him to support my failings. He should've bought extra life insurance on me while I was still physically healthy, *because I'm going to stay in this closet until I shrivel and die.* Sure—I would let the dogs go out to do their business. But they'd come back to me. I had the Snausages and Fakin' Bacon.

JOE CAME HOME FROM work at 9 p.m. and couldn't find me. I heard him calling. The dogs showed where their loyalties lay by feverishly scratching at the closet door to go visit the enemy. I let the little traitors out, and Joe followed them back to their Snausages, back to find me behind the dresses and shirts.

"Susie, what are you doing in there?"

I scrunched my knees up to my chest. That was the dumbest question I had heard in our six years of marriage. *Where has he been?* Joe, the same wonderful husband who, six months ago, told me my antique store was a failure, that I wasn't making the numbers, that I had to raise my prices or I'd be out of business, that I had used up our whole life savings, that I should quit while we still had our house, blah blah blah—*that* Joe.

Mark had moved to Aspen, and he and I played (worked?) in my little antique store. I never wanted it to be huge—just successful. It took up a thousand square feet of the historical miner's shack Joe and I had bought in downtown Aspen. Joe and I lived in the remaining five hundred square feet. But Joe was right. My store was a money pit. He said I should stay home and take care of him. That way he wouldn't have to work twice as hard making up for the money Mark and I lost.

So I tried that. Back when Joe and I were first married, that's all I did. Joe was the first normal man I had ever known—I loved being a housewife. I had the time of my life creating incredible epicurean delights for him—never fewer than four courses for dinner—and I'd spend another hour putting on makeup and mixing and matching Victoria's Secret ensembles so he wouldn't recognize the next outfit. Perfect cook. Perfect homemaker. Perfect lover. This went on, gloriously, for years. Such a wonderful wife was I!

Then last night it had happened. Joe came home in a mood so irascible that I dared not kiss him, and then . . . oh, then I asked him to sit down for dinner. He turned as red as the bloody moon of Revelations and there it came—all those words he'd pent up for years, the words that caused him to run three extra miles on his workout days and ask for a punching bag one Christmas.

He was sick of having to eat so many long, drawn-out courses for dinner. He felt forced to pretend he liked everything I made. *Just pizza would be nice every once in a while.* He was tired when he came home and just wanted to relax for once without so much of an "ordeal" every night. *And besides that, I prefer you without makeup!*

Oh, did the earth quake then. "Okay!" I snapped. "I quit. I never want you to say anything to me again."

Now, sitting knees-to-chest in my closet, I had a lot more to say to Joe. I should just get out there and discuss my feelings, talk things out. But I had been crying so long that my eyes were tired, and it was all coming out my nose, and I forgot to get more tissues before he came home. Joe and I rarely fought. It wasn't Joe's words that upset me so much. It was this: if Joe didn't want me falling all over him, what was I supposed to do?

I crawled to his side of the closet and blew my nose on his tuxedo pants. I felt a little better after that and gave W. W. Steinbeck one of Joe's dress shoes to chew on.

"Honey, c'mon. . . . Baby . . . what's the matter?" Joe said from the other side of the clothes. He hunched down, separated the clothes, and found my toe. "Aw, baby, come out and talk to me."

Nope. *You no longer exist.* I twiddled with the leg of a pair of pants.

"Honey, you're scaring me. Baby, can't we talk?"

No answer.

Joe got the hint. I heard him walk out of the bedroom and set the timer on the microwave. *He's making a TV dinner. Just like him to be so selfish and leave me in here without anything to eat.* I considered the Snausages and wondered how many calories they had. *I really am pathetic!*

I stayed in the closet until I heard Joe snoring, then snuck to the kitchen, pulled some cold chicken and a light beer from the fridge, and went to the couch. I turned on the TV and pressed the mute button. My mind continued to race.

It's my own fault I suck at running a store. But I tried so hard! I really wanted to make some money so Joe wouldn't have to work as much. I lost everything trying to prove I wasn't a miserable failure. I wanted him to think, "Wow, she's smarter than I thought!" Ugh! I'm so embarrassed. Pride comes before a fall.

On any good day, I battle low self-esteem. But this day was really taking me for a ride. I flipped through the channels while taking inventory of myself.

Is Joe even attracted to me anymore? Once I caught him with a dirty magazine in the bathroom. How ironic. I ran to old files of my pictures and pulled them out: posters, calendars, lingerie magazines, centerfolds—all featuring me. I hurled them all at Joe. "Aren't I enough for you?" *Either I'm really boring or he's seen too much of me. Joe's not a bad guy—we're just not connecting. He works too much and I . . . I . . . What am I looking for anyway? I have to say I'm not happy. In fact, even though life is going the best it's ever been for me, I'm still . . . sad.*

My eyes were on the TV. On the screen was a little boy's face. It was one of those documentaries about starving children somewhere in the world. *Mongolia, is it?* In the video, the little boy had just eaten a rat. His older brother was taking care of him and his four other siblings, and that's what they were living off: the rats in the sewers. On very cold days, when they couldn't scavenge enough trash to eat, they went down to the sewers because it was warmer. They caught rats and cooked them, and survived.

A phone number flashed at the bottom of the screen. *Yeah, right.* I was sure most of those organizations were scams—most of those children probably never saw more than a dime of every dollar sent. When a CNN headlines program replaced the little boy's face, I clicked the TV off.

But something about the boy's expression stayed with me. I knew that look. It rolled around in my head, trying to find a place to land. The child was crying and trying not to. His eyes could have been those of an eighty-year-old. I remembered that look from somewhere. The eyes said, "Life is too long"—something a child's eyes should never say. I had seen it before. *But where?*

My mind snapped back to my to-do list: *I've really got to get some sleep or I'll feel awful at my workout tomorrow. I really should run an extra mile, since I skipped today. I need some new magazines—I've read all these. I should call the salon and schedule this week's tan. I should really get my hair done, too—it's almost been three weeks—I wonder what color of blond I should be this month.*

Mongolia was far away. Children who live in sewers were far away. But my mind wouldn't turn off. *Don't worry about them, Susie—you have your own problems! They're probably all little thieves anyway. What's that little boy thinking, sleeping in a sewer like that? His parents must be worried. Why doesn't* someone *do something? There are lots of rich people—they* should do something. I'd do something if I were rich.*

There was no voice from above. No lightning. Just a moment when I couldn't escape who I was, nor the part of my life I saw reflected in the expression of that Mongolian child. I knew where I had seen that look before—that boy had the same eyes I had seen in my mirror when I was four years old.

There on my couch in Aspen, in one brief, terrifying, unyielding, everlasting moment, everything changed. Everything, everything, everything. The Mongolian sewer boy and I had the same gash—the same hurting, hungry, screaming, lifelong wound. I remembered what I had gone through as a kid, how I survived, and how I summoned the strength to get up each day. I wondered who had yelled at him most recently. I wondered where his last bruise was. I wondered what sensations his nose and tongue felt when he lifted a rat to his lips. I wondered if he would be alive tomorrow. For the first time, I glimpsed a worse place to grow up than my mother's house in Alabama.

I CAN'T SLEEP! DAMN! It's almost daylight. I may as well get up! Ugh! Okay. Make coffee, need vitamins and Paxil. I'm going to call that television station and see if they have some kind of fund set up for those sewer kids in Mongolia.

Joe was up now. He came to the kitchen and looked at me sideways, assessing my mood. I walked over and held him as close as I could. He held me back, stroking my hair.

"I'm sorry, honey," Joe said. Men forever fall victim to insecure women who demand reassurance that they're really loved. Women confirm this love by subjecting their men to test after torturous test.

"Honey, I'm sorry too," I said. "I just didn't want you to think I'm a failure. I love taking care of you, but I don't feel like anybody needs me around here."

Joe picked me up, set me on the counter, and looked right into my eyes. "Baby," he said, "I don't care if you ever get a job! I married you because of your heart. Why don't you just take some time and think about what will make you happy?"

I am an idiot. I know that. He does love me, bless his heart.

Joe showered and left for work. I peered out the kitchen window at my husband going off to start his day. "Oh Lord," I prayed, "please take care of him. If something ever happens to him I'll be ruined."

I dialed the number of CNN, the television station that aired the documentary on the children in Mongolia, and sat in my kitchen ready to take down the information from the station.

"No, ma'am, we don't have a fund set up for the children in Mongolia; we're a television station, the documentary you saw was probably purchased from an affiliate station."

I thanked the person and hung up. I flipped through the Yellow Pages and called UNICEF, the International Red Cross, CARE, World Vision—all the major international relief organizations. As I dialed, I ate an egg-white soufflé. All the organizations were unfamiliar with last night's TV show, but most had aid efforts in Mongolia. They encouraged me to send a check.

I was new at this.

"Well, can I go to Mongolia and meet your staff and help out for a couple of weeks?" I asked.

No one seemed enthusiastic about the idea.

"I am sure you guys are great"—my line became standard after a few calls—"but I don't think you realize I would be useful to you and those children." I talked fast in hopes of sparking interest on the other end. "I'll work for free, and I'm not afraid of getting sick."

Still no interest.

"I was a foster child myself! I'm not afraid of hardly anything and I don't feel uncomfortable around sick people. The thing I'm best at is taking care of people."

The response was negative with every call. Just send the check.

As a last resort, I called the Peace Corps. Sorry, no college degree, no candidate. I didn't even mention I lacked my high school diploma. Frustrated, I hung up.

I sat down in front of the window of my tiny kitchen and leafed through the newspaper. The mayor was seeking neighborly support for his Ban on Fur crusade in Aspen. The front page featured a photograph of an angry animal rights supporter spraying paint on a horrified, fur-clad blonde. Another story showed a multimillion-dollar shopping plaza coming to town—UPSCALE LIVING FOR UPSCALE LIVES, the headline read. A blurb at the bottom was a psych piece about how Americans worry more than ever these days.

I shook my head. I wondered what a plane ticket to Mongolia cost. I'd been to Russia several times when Joe worked for a telecommunications company in Moscow. Ulaanbaatar, where the children lived in the sewers, is the largest city in Mongolia— surprised I remembered that. *If I was to go there, what use could I truly be to those children?*

The dogs had all gone out to play in the yard. I called them back inside for company. They heaved through the doggie door and slid across the ceramic tiles to me.

I don't know. Let's just see what a round-trip ticket would cost. I could at least take some blankets and wool socks to those kids.

The plane ticket, it turned out, would cost a small fortune. Perturbed, I examined other means to get my good intentions satisfied. Every idea met a dead end. *I should just send a check.*

But I wanted to do something more. I wanted to see those kids, look into their eyes, hold them, hug them, tell them somehow, some way, it's going to be okay.

I was surprised to realize I hadn't looked in the mirror one time the entire morning.

At 11 a.m. I walked to my antique shop, followed by my beloved beasts. My baby brother, Mark, was behind the counter talking to a customer. Mark saw me, excused himself, and sashayed across the showroom to greet me.

"Susie, you won't believe who that is!" he squealed in a high-pitched whisper and nodded in the customer's direction. "It's Vanna White's husband!"

"Is he buying anything?" I asked.

Mark lifted the sales receipt book up to my eye level. I saw at least a dozen purchases. "I talked to Vanna myself," Mark said, flipping his wrist. "She needs me to go over to her house and take a look at their bedroom." He paused to make sure I had absorbed his words. "She wants to replace their headboard with an antique one."

"Congratulations! Consulting the stars in regards to the accoutering of the boudoir—I'm impressed!" I so loved to tease him.

He sauntered back to Mr. Vanna. I adored my brother. He was my best friend.

After Mr. Vanna left I asked Mark what the total of the sale was. He showed me. "Man, I thought it'd be three times that much!" I said.

Mark shrugged. "It was for Vanna. She is the nicest, sweetest thing. I had to give her a fifty-percent discount."

I sighed. I would have done the same thing. Mark and I both sucked at business.

I changed the subject. "So, I'm thinking about going to Mongolia." I followed him around the store as he straightened merchandise. "Joe thinks we should close the store. . . . I was thinking we could sell all this stuff and use the money to build a place for sewer children to live." I told Mark about the devastating show I had seen the night before.

Mark's eyes welled up, and I ran for a tissue. He was never one to doubt my sanity, or my invincibility. He thinks very big.

"Do you think you can go full time at your other job if we have to close?" I said.

He was certain he could. "They just love me at the other store." He flipped his wrist again.

I KNEW JOE WAS right. This failing antique store wasn't meant to be. My store was supposed to die.

As a child, I had promised God that if I survived, I would help other kids survive whatever situation they were in. That's why I wasn't happy—I had forgotten. I wasn't doing what I was meant to do. Looking at that boy on the TV screen had made me remember. Whatever it cost, whatever it took—I would go to Mongolia.

It felt like the first time I had seen the sunrise in years.

Chapter 10

Shift

N O ONE NEEDED ME.
I phoned and phoned. What was the matter? I was offering my services for free! None of the international relief organizations wanted anything except my check. But I wanted to do something. I wanted to *go*.

I decided to launch my own campaign and gather information grassroots-style. What did those sewer children really need? How could I help them get it? How about an orphanage? A big building where all those kids could sleep at night where they didn't have to eat rats? It seemed pretty simple. I called the Mongolian embassy. Property was inexpensive in Mongolia compared to the States. I could build a place for around $100,000. Hmmm, that was beyond me; maybe I'd have to start smaller—or maybe I could raise the money somehow. Surely people would want to help kids in need.

Maybe the first thing I should do is just go over there and ask peo-

ple how I could best help. I picked up the phone and called Trish, our travel agent of many years. I asked what kind of deal I could get on a plane ticket to Mongolia.

"Who the f——— wants to go to Mongolia?" Trish said, her speech trucker-style. Trish was having a bad morning. Give her something uncomplicated—Hawaii or the Bahamas. Travel agents didn't plan trips to Mongolia back then.

"Well, it's for me!" I answered. "Come on, this should be easy for you." Trish is known for her amazing ability to get people in and, more important, *out* of any country in the world. (I would literally owe Trish my life in later years.) Joe and I had learned of her existence a few years earlier on our five-year-anniversary cruise to the Mediterranean.

Joe and I had never taken fancy vacations. We splurged on this one by pawning my old wedding ring—the one Steven/Peter had given me and pretended to hurl out the car window. On the cruise, two perfumed and bejeweled men shared our dining table. They went on about their hoards of money, their countless vacations, and their undying love for each other.

"You're soooo-oooo lucky to be *doing* this cruise," one said. "It fills up ever so fast." He giggled. "But it always helps—"

"—to have Trish!" The other finished his sentence for him. They both jiggled their heads up and down, nodding vigorously, and took feverish sips from their Cosmopolitans.

"What is *Trish?*" I asked, thinking it was some sort of gay lingo.

"*Trish* is our secret." One of the men giggled and looked to his partner for his permission to reveal or his warning to hush. A nod from his partner gave him the go-ahead. "Well . . . Trish is our miracle worker, our patron goddess of the voyage, our deity of travel delight."

"Oh, *Trish* is a *person!*" I said. I'd surely been around Mark too long. I was starting to think like him; everything was innuendo.

"Do you think I could get her number for the next time we go somewhere?"

They looked at each other, not wanting to dilute the value of the requested favor.

"Well, I sup-pose," said one. "You're such a nice couple. And *he*"—looking at Joe—"is *just* gorgeous."

My husband inched away from the table.

Now when I ran my idea by Trish, she laughed and said, "Joe is never gonna let you go to Mongolia!" I knew she was on her second Bloody Mary. She and I had come to know each other well in a short time. She felt close enough to me, much to my chagrin, to thoroughly question my "schemes," as she lovingly referred to my ideas.

"Sure he is," I said. "I already told him about it."

"You're insane. Why d'ya wanna go see a bunch of kids who live in sewers and eat rats?" I heard her take a long drag from her cigarette. "You know there's no shopping over there, don't you? Besides, it's freezing in Mongolia this time of year!"

"But . . . can you get me a ticket?"

There was a long pause on the phone.

"Okay," Trish said in a singsong voice. "But you're gonna be miserable."

The ball was set in motion. In two weeks, I was going to Mongolia. After I hung up the phone from talking to Trish, I placed a classified ad to run immediately:

> *Aspen Antique Brokers is closing permanently.*
> *Clearance Sale.*
> *All must go.*

The next day the store filled with people. They fondled, inspected, and analyzed every item I had once lovingly rejoiced over as a great find. Oh, the effort I had put into that place. Once I had hauled an antique desk in a blizzard just to get it into the store on time (qualified drivers refused to deliver in a snowstorm). Mark and I sold and then hauled piece after ancient piece out the door. It could all go, for all I cared. The store was a bust.

But when I noticed one of Aspen's famous inspecting the very first purchase I'd ever made for the store, I admit I felt a twinge of regret. What was I doing, anyway—selling the store to go to Mongolia?

The item was a tall, slender hobo doll, worn and tattered, with long legs and little leather shoes. The piece hadn't sold in four years because I always hid it in a drawer if I noticed somebody ogling it. The doll had a little stitched-on grin and a plaid sweater with frayed elbow patches. I imagined it might be what Joe would look like one day when he's an old man—hopefully not as a hobo, though. Good thing I was selling my business or he might end up that way. I had found the doll for sale on a purchasing trip in London. I was lonely and slept with it each night on that trip.

I walked over and took the doll from Jill St. John's hands. "I don't think you want to buy that," I said. "It's priced too high."

"Well, how much is it; my daughter would just love to have it."

"Oh, the price would be far too much, trust me . . . please?"

She gave me an unhurried, appraising, head-to-toe look. "Fine," she said, and summoned her husband to leave.

Maybe this wasn't going to be so easy. I went through the store gathering all the things with sentimental value. After two or three trips to our little apartment attached to the store I was satisfied.

"Wow! You did great!" Mark gave me a huge hug when he returned from lunch. "Looks like you sold a lot of stuff!"

"Yeah, uh, we had a lot of customers while you were gone." I grinned meekly.

◆ ◆ ◆

JOE AND I WERE in the habit of going to church on Sundays. I had started thinking God was a good guy again. The church was cool, with a congregation of about two hundred people, mostly a younger crowd. It had a great band that played rock music. Joe and I always sat in the hand-lifting section. The pastor preached straight by the Bible. It wasn't a judgmental place; everybody seemed ready to forgive. Good thing too, because I was doing *Playboy* shoots again every once in a while for calendars and posters. What with the whole Adam and Eve thing, I didn't think God would call it a sin to be naked.

When I had married my first husband, Hef told me my days at *Playboy* were finished. I found out later that Hef knew Steven/Peter's reputation and wanted nothing to do with him. When Steven/Peter went to prison, I didn't think *Playboy* would ever take me back. But shortly after I moved out of Rue White's house, *Playboy* contacted me and asked me to do a calendar shoot. I was surprised, but pleased. Mostly, I needed the money.

My motivation for staying involved with *Playboy* was more than that, though. I was wary. I didn't want to close the doors on a prime source of income in case things didn't work out in my second marriage. By all outward appearances, Joe and I were the perfect couple. And our relationship was good, truly, in so many ways. But it was easy for insecurity to creep in. Maybe I still wanted to be in those magazines to prove a point to Joe. *See, I'm good enough to be in here, too.* Joe and I had taken a relationship class together shortly after we married. Joe's goals: to be rich and to have a pretty wife. Mine were equally superficial. He seemed quite proud that he was married to a Playmate, even if she still took off her clothes in front of other men. We had a long way to go.

That Sunday, after the preaching and closing prayer, I went around to all the women I knew to be good prayers and asked them to say a couple for me during my trip to Mongolia. This wasn't a trip I was doing for missions, or to get converts, or anything like that, but I figured I still needed God's help on my side. In the previous few days, I'd contacted a church in Mongolia that agreed to arrange transportation and a translator for me. From there I'd be on my own.

Everybody I talked to at church expressed concern and vowed to pray. Most told me how brave and wonderful I was to go to a strange and faraway land to help those poor little children.

But one member of the congregation stepped in front of me just as I was waving good-bye and leading Joe out the door. He was a manager of one of the best restaurants in town. He carried himself delicately and was eloquent in speech—cautious, not extroverted.

"I'm really disappointed," the man said, shaking his head and not my hand.

"Huh?"

"Well, it just seems so inefficient to go to the other side of the world and help a country that already receives so much aid." He was clearly not ready to let us leave. "I guarantee that since you saw that documentary every children's charity on the planet has flooded into Mongolia, which, by the way, receives hundreds of thousands of dollars from the U.S. and China and the United Nations every year! I'll bet there isn't a single child left in a sewer by the time you get there!"

I just stared, speechless. Joe stood beside me, looking curiously at him.

"They're just not that poor in Mongolia!" he insisted. The man had a shaved head, and I could see him breaking a sweat. "At least, not as poor as Haiti!"

"Tahiti?" I said. "I never knew Tahiti was so poor. I've seen pictures of the beaches, and I always thought it was such a nice place—"

"Not Tahiti!" the man said. "Haiti. Hay-tee." He stressed each syllable for my benefit.

"Oh," Joe and I said in unison.

Gary Bruyere was his name. He had been to Haiti with a group from another church and was planning to go again soon. He had such passion in his voice when he described the place. "I will never be the same," he said.

We agreed to see his travel pictures and made plans to have lunch that same afternoon. Less than an hour later, Joe and I found ourselves sitting at a table across from Gary. None of us touched our food. Gary handed me a photograph of a little baby with a head five times the normal size. "Hydrocephalic syndrome," Gary said. "It's one of the many common birth defects in Haiti."

As we picked up the photos one by one and slowly placed them back on the table, I noticed Joe wipe a tear on his sleeve. The photos grew blurry for me after a while too. It was hard to look: children standing naked with their hip bones nearly piercing through their skin; children lying in swarms of flies; children drinking from fetid puddles of greenish water.

How could I not have heard something about this level of poverty and devastation on television or in newspapers? All I'd ever remembered hearing about Haiti was that whole "boat people" thing, where everybody had tried to get to Florida or something— but that had been years earlier. I had never seen anything like Gary's pictures. I just stared in disbelief.

"Haiti's the poorest country in the Western Hemisphere," Gary said. "It's an apocalypse over there—only five hundred miles from Miami, but we hardly ever hear anything about it. If you want to travel somewhere and help someone, then go *there* and help them."

"Trish," I said into the phone Monday morning, "can you change my tickets from Mongolia to Haiti?"

"You're joking, right?" she answered.

"No, I'm not." I described the meeting with Gary. I had never seen anything so tragic. Gary had been right. That morning before calling Trish, I called my contacts in Ulaanbaatar, Mongolia. Several foreign aid groups were already helping the sewer children. Several new orphanages were planned.

"Tourists never go to Haiti," Trish said. "I mean—*never*! It's dangerous, dirty, and corrupt. You'll get robbed, or raped, or worse." She was no easy sell.

"I need to go to Haiti," I repeated.

"No, you don't," Trish said. She ranted for at least half an hour on the dangers of traveling to Haiti.

Finally I interrupted. Good intentions never amount to anything unless you actually do something about them.

"Trish, just book it," I said. I was going.

GARY AND I BECAME fast friends. He decided to accompany me to Haiti. We decided to cut costs and share a two-room hotel suite in Haiti. Gary had told me he was gay, so Joe approved of the idea, but he insisted we stay at the most secure hotel in Port-au-Prince. As it turned out, that hotel was the palatial El Rancho hotel, where Gary and his missionary friends had stayed on his other visit. He claimed Bill and Hillary Clinton had spent their honeymoon there.

I met with Gary daily for the next two weeks while Mark sold the last of the antiques at deep discounts. Gary and I pored over information we gathered from the library. We made calls to the Haitian embassy in D.C., the U.S. State Department, and the American embassy in Haiti. I watched a movie called *The Serpent and the*

Rainbow, a terrifying look into Haitian voodoo—an ancient belief system that involves zombies, demons, and a variety of disturbing practices. I ordered *Creole Made Easy* and skimmed the French-slang language that most Haitians speak. I learned that French is also spoken there, but only a few of the wealthy elite use it.

I wasn't sure what I'd do once I got to Haiti. Mostly I just wanted to see up close what the country was like. I wanted to talk to people and ask them what they needed most. It was a naïve strategy, I realize now. What could one person ever do to help such a place?

At the Aspen airport, Joe lifted me up and I wrapped my legs around him as we kissed deeply. I asked him to call me at El Rancho the minute the sale ended at the antique store to let me know how much money had come in. He mentioned there would probably not be any left after paying back the bank loan on the business.

"Yeah, but you don't know that for sure!" I said.

The airline agent at the counter tried and failed to lift our luggage. "What do you have in here," she asked, "bricks?"

"Oh no! It's candy!" I said proudly. "We're going to Haiti to help orphans." She gave a nod of approval and decided against charging us the overweight bag fee.

One more kiss for Joe. My new friend and I left through the gate.

Gary and I sparred the whole flight to Miami. He reminded me of Mark. We bought mini bottles of wine on the plane and tried talking about anything other than where we were going. The trip hadn't even begun and already we were tired and anxious. Neither of us knew what to expect.

We had done some research into Haiti's current political conditions. When we changed planes in Miami for the hop down to the island, a U.S. State Department sign urged Americans not to travel farther.

It was April 1994. Haiti was under a strict UN embargo for ousting democratically elected president Jean-Bertrand Aristide. With always short supplies now even tighter, the desperate country was in an even more frantic situation. In larger cities such as Port-au-Prince, gang members ruled the streets. Kidnapping was common. The U.S. embassy in Haiti had sent most of its staff back to the States. Just three months later a twenty-eight-nation multinational military force, led by the United States, was deployed in the country. More than twenty thousand troops descended upon Haiti, restoring public order and reinstating Aristide by force.

As the plane left the runway of Miami International Airport and headed for Haiti, neither Gary nor I spoke. We looked out the window.

"Should we say a prayer?" I asked Gary.

"Yeah," he answered, "and maybe afterwards we should switch to rum."

Chapter 11

The Invisible World

As we touched down on the landing strip that day, I knew little about Haiti. Since then I have come to know that there are more demons than humans inhabiting the little island of Hispaniola. Evil congregates on its western side, on the eroded, deforested mess known as Haiti. It's crucial to have an understanding of the word *apocalypse* in order to grasp the level of conflict that occurs here. It rages visibly and invisibly as members of its ungodly junta go to work.

Violence, anarchy, and a turbulent history make Haiti a curious study if you're an intellectual, a mysterious challenge if you're a missionary or philanthropist. Its grinding rhythm of dysfunction isn't as confusing when you begin to list Haiti's problems: the reign of rapacious dictators, a reliance on witch doctors instead of modern medicine, a legacy of slavery, and the understandable suspicion of foreigners. You might be better off to leave logic and sanity behind so as not to lose them while in Haiti.

Things could be different.

The Dominican Republic occupies the eastern two thirds of the same island—it's lush and breezy, filled with beaches and open-shirted tourists. The sharp disparity between the neighboring countries is clear. Border traffic grinds to a standstill as all Haitian dust and grime is literally washed off every vehicle entering the Dominican Republic.

Mostly, it's only island nationals who traverse the two countries. Tourism in Haiti swung for a few decades with cruise ships and buffet tables, but reports of rampant AIDS surfaced in the early 1980s and business dwindled. The door listed shut a few years later, when the Haitian government closed its promotion office in New York City. Haiti's Club Med closed, and Holiday Inn pulled its name off its Port-au-Prince hotel a few years later. Today Haiti is unknown to most of the world and forgotten by those who once visited. Lingering is a collection of television images from recent decades—riots, boat people, poverty, instability. Most visitors to Haiti today are missionaries or aid workers, sometimes a few businesspeople. Who wants to vacation in hell?

Haiti has potential. It could be the next St. Kitts or St. Lucia. By plane, it's only an hour and a half from Miami. Fly south across Cuba and the Greater Antilles, turn east at Jamaica, and you're there, a Maryland-sized isle in the heart of the Caribbean.

Haitian Shangri-Las do exist. South of Haiti's capital are the quiet, surfy beaches of Jacmel. The city's name derives from a Taino/Arawak Indian word that means "rich land." Wealthy merchants once built New Orleans–style mansions here. Residents beg outsiders to stop focusing on the madness in Port-au-Prince and realize there's still beauty and peace left in some Haitian areas.

Some outsiders even chose to invest in Haiti. For those with capital, it's a cheap, albeit risky, investment. For about $350,000 American you can snap up a five-bedroom, three-acre mountain lodge in Kenscoff, complete with tennis courts, swimming pool, and maid's quarters. A majestic landscape of peach, plum, and apple trees camouflages a security gate made of cinder blocks topped with broken bottles. Almost no Haitians own estates like these. They remain in the hands of the slightly less than 3 percent of the country's populace who control the majority of the country's wealth.

Jacmel and Kenscoff, like La Citadelle and the historic Hotel Oloffson—and a few other places—are exceptions. For the rest of the country, reports of degradation are not exaggerated. Haiti has been plagued for decades with poverty, corruption, decaying infrastructure, dictatorships, and military conflicts.

Present-day statistics come bulletlike and wounding:

About 80 percent of Haitians live in abject poverty. Haiti suffers from rampant inflation, a lack of investment, a severe trade deficit, and frequent natural disasters.

The average annual salary is $350, less than $1 a day.

For most Haitians, eating one small meal a day is considered normal. Two thirds of Haitians depend on the agriculture sector, mainly small-scale subsistence farming. The unemployment rate is more than 70 percent.

Approximately 280,000 Haitians are known to be living with HIV/AIDS. (The country has about 8 million residents. So the illness is not as widespread as once believed. Still, HIV/AIDS is a major, uncontrolled problem in the country.)

The average life expectancy in Haiti is fifty-three. In the U.S. it's seventy-seven. More than 10 percent of Haitian children will die before age four.

Some 7 percent of children in Haiti are believed to be enslaved. Some 300,000 children as young as age three consistently suffer sexual, emotional, and physical abuse.

Almost half the Haitian population is illiterate.

Some 30 percent of Haitians are either ill or underweight.

Haiti is an alleged major Caribbean transshipment point for cocaine en route to the U.S. and Europe. The country is rife with money-laundering activity, illicit financial transactions, and pervasive corruption.

THINK OF HAITI'S HISTORY as divided into four general time periods distiguished by their political climates: colonization, dictatorships, rule by tyrants, and modern oppression. This analysis is not overly negative: Haiti has been a country for the taking, and the world has grabbed.

In 1492, Christopher Columbus sailed from Spain across the Atlantic and landed on the east coast of Hispaniola on his first voyage to the New World. He met the original inhabitants of Haiti— Taino/Arawak Indians, who referred to the west side of their homeland as *Ayti*, their word for *mountains*. Columbus pronounced it *Haiti*.

Columbus wanted gold but found coffee and sugar instead, luxurious treasures for postmedieval Europe. The gateway opened, and in exchange for Haiti's commodities and labor, Columbus gave the island country Catholicism—and gave away Haiti's land. Spain instituted *Repartimiento*, a system whereby any Spanish-born person residing in the New World received a large grant of land and the right to compel labor from the native Indians. Abuse, sickness, and death followed in sweeping numbers. By 1550, only about 150 natives lived on the island of Hispaniola. Soon there were none. It is believed that none of the Haitians in Haiti today are descended from the country's original native inhabitants. Simply put, they were all destroyed.

While Spain was preoccupied controlling the right side of Hispaniola, the English, Dutch, and French began using the established Spanish trade routes to the New World. Huguenots crept around the top of the island and settled the northwest shoulder, establishing the town of Cap François (now called Cap-Haïtien) in 1670. The French also found fields ripe for coffee and sugar harvesting, but had the same problem as the Spaniards: few original inhabitants left to do the hard work.

There seemed to be a straightforward solution. Satan can offer people clear thinking when it furthers wickedness. Over the next century, France and Spain imported shiploads of black slaves from Africa. By 1791, there were 500,000 to 700,000 slaves tilling Haitian soil. Though it's a country that few people even think of today, Haiti was the world's golden star of trade in the late 1700s: the majority of the world's coffee was produced in Haiti; just under half the sugar imported by Britain and France came from Haiti; and 40 percent of French foreign trade revolved around Haiti.

The majority of Haitians today are descended from these slaves. Races mixed as the white slave owners cohabited with the slaves, creating a class division that survives today. The rich white colonialists, called *blancs*, never comprised more than 1 percent of the population. Free blacks and mulattos, called *affranchis* ("freedmen") or *gens de couleur* ("people of color") were also few in number. The remaining 87 percent, slaves, called *noirs* ("blacks") were poor, uneducated, and downtrodden. These classes seldom got along.

Slaves brought two things still found in Haiti today: an obvious resentment of their imprisonment, and a mixture of African religions that meshed and evolved into present-day voodoo.

Resentment among the slaves escalated. Some escaped and banded together, hiding in forests and mountains. They organized in simmering fury and ignited a full-scale revolt in 1791. In the end, ten thousand slaves and two thousand whites lay dead. By then the pattern for revolution was set in motion. Wars and rumors of war followed. On January 1, 1804, a final revolt led to victory, and the victors proclaimed independence. Haiti became the first free black republic in the world.

Democracy enjoyed a short celebration. A series of dictators and tyrants fought over Haiti for the next two hundred years in a struggle for control. Between 1843 and 1915, there was a succession of twenty-two heads of state: one served full term; three died of natural causes before their terms were up; one "exploded" while at his palace; one was poisoned; one was hacked to pieces by a mob; one resigned; and fourteen were deposed by revolutions.

Another course was established when the slaves revolted. On August 14, 1791, a group of *houngans* ("voodoo priests"), led by a former slave houngan named Boukman, made a pact at a place called Bois Caïman. The priests sacrificed a black pig in a voodoo ritual and drank its blood. Boukman asked Satan for his help in liberating Haiti. In exchange, the voodoo priests dedicated the country to Satan and swore to serve him. They signed no Bill of Rights. They wrote no Declaration of Independence. It would be a government of the devil, by the devil, and for the devil.

UNTIL RECENTLY, VOODOO WAS practiced mostly in secret, but voodoo is overt in Haiti today, and it's everywhere, including politics.

In 1957 François Duvalier, a medical doctor and voodoo priest, was elected president of Haiti. Duvalier was loved at first, and was paternalistically referred to as Papa Doc. He established a constitution in 1957 that prohibited Haitian presidents from running for reelection once their terms were over. In 1961 Duvalier broke his own law and ran for reelection. He won by an official vote of

1,320,748 to 0. Three years later, Duvalier declared himself President for Life.

In 1964 Duvalier established an elite military force called the President's Guard, whose sole purpose was to maintain Duvalier's power. He also established a fear-inducing rural militia called Tonton Macoutes, a Creole term that means something like "bogeymen." Duvalier became known for his corruption, for his support of industries that made money solely for the government, and for bribery and extortion.

Duvalier rose to the rank of a "voodoo sorcerer." He incorporated his friends, other sorcerers, into the ranks of governmental leadership. Few people dared trifle with a leader who was believed to have such dark forces at his command. It is estimated that during his time in office Duvalier killed thirty thousand Haitians.

When Papa Doc died, in 1971, his son, Jean-Claude Duvalier, began ruling at age nineteen by prior decree of his father. Baby Doc, as the new ruler was called, had little interest in politics but loved the money his newfound position gave him. He left much of the government's administration to his mother, Simone Duvalier, and lived the life of a playboy.

By the mid-1980s, a widespread spirit of hopelessness permeated Haiti under Baby Doc's rule. The economy worsened, malnutrition spread. In March 1983, Pope John Paul II visited and declared, "Something must change here." Haitians agreed. Within two years there were massive street demonstrations and raids on food distribution warehouses. Baby Doc tried to quell the revolts, but rioting spread. Baby Doc fled the country. Haiti was left completely ravaged.

In recent years, voodoo has seen an upswing in acceptance. On April 8, 2003, Haitian president Jean-Bertrand Aristide approved voodoo as an officially recognized religion in Haiti. Later he proclaimed voodoo the "national religion" of Haiti and a source of national pride.

IT HAS BEEN SAID that four fifths of Haitians practice or fear voodoo. Some argue this is a harmless belief system that adds intrigue to multiculturalism. But I would learn that broadmindedness does not mean we must endorse malevolence.

Many have witnessed pain, suffering, and death as a direct result of voodoo's deceptions. Voodoo encourages drunkenness, violence, lying, stealing, sexual excess, and even the rape and murder (in not altogether rare cases) of infants and young children. There is an Abandoned Infant Unit at the public hospital in Port-au-Prince that on any given day has between fifteen and thirty children who have been left to die. Many are found bent and broken in boxes, simply placed in front of the hospital gates. Some have had their anuses and vaginas ripped open thanks to voodoo practices.

This belief system goes beyond superstition. There actually seems to be some sort of spiritual force that works through it. It appears to shift the laws of nature. Using voodoo, sorcerers purportedly can transform themselves into werewolves known as *loup garou* and cause fatal accidents and illnesses. The most maleficent of sorcerers, a *bokor,* can supposedly manipulate the forces of darkness—even Satan himself—to command the dead to inflict terrifying punishment on a victim. The intended victim will become weak and thin and spit up blood and then die. It is believed that he can avert this fate by paying an obligatory fee to the bokor to break the dead spirit's hold. When asked how a loved one died, the answer from many peasants around the slums is a sad and fearful shake of the head. "Loup garou," they whisper; "the werewolf."

Haitian newspapers sometimes chronicle such practices. Mostly, it's quietly accepted. In certain quarters in Port-au-Prince, vats of human hands and heads are popular items for sale. A "long pig" is commonly understood street slang for a human sacrifice. A ritualistic dinner of a baby's arm or foot is more rare, but isn't unheard of.

In Haiti, a handicapped or deformed child is considered among voodoo practitioners a curse to be discarded. Some people label this type of selection as horse-shooting benevolence. A poor country, it's argued, is better off without the infirm; better to kill a disabled child than have her grow up a beggar. But a child breathes and dreams and feels and dies. I know. I was once a child whom some considered a curse.

Welcome to Haiti.

Come to this island.

Come to this country.

Chapter 12

No Time for Reflection

WHEN GARY AND I deplaned at the Port-au-Prince airport on my first trip to Haiti, in April 1994, we were greeted by a cacophony of dysfunction. Shoulder to shoulder, people jostled. Eyes dark. Hands outstretched. *Hey! You! Shine shoes? Sell you water? Give me dollah!* Gary and I waited two hours for our bags to be taken off the plane. Several times we were casually asked by customs agents if we had any "gifts" to be left in Haiti. Finally we got the hint and slipped them ten dollars each. Our bags appeared instantly.

A fight broke out—shoving and kicking—among men outside the airport who wanted to carry our bags. We backed away and waited, our stomachs in knots. The winners carried our two bags to a rusty taxi for one dollar each. The toothless taxi driver saw an opportunity. We asked how much it would cost to take us to the El Rancho hotel in the Petionville area of Port-au-Prince.

"Fifty dollars," he replied seriously. "Each."

"Forget it!" I said, incredulous. It wouldn't cost that much to go the same distance in Aspen. We walked away.

The driver followed, shouting: "Okay! Okay!—thirty dollars."

It still felt like a lot. I looked at Gary, who nodded. "I thought you said this place was cheap," I said as we climbed in.

In the backseat we slouched, dripping with sweat, and jerked back and forth as the cab hit potholes and swerved to avoid people and dogs. There were so many of them—both people and dogs—all very thin. Through the city we zoomed, the driver's hand planted on the horn. We accelerated past shacks slapped with bright paint and dirty stores the size of garden sheds. Graffiti was everywhere—political graffiti, gang graffiti, sexual graffiti—scrawled on buildings, doorways, fences, billboards for Prestige Beer and Barbancourt Rum.

There were no road signs or streetlights. Traffic was heavy—donkeys, kids, trucks, carts—but there were few personal vehicles, few cars. We cut in and out of traffic, gaining only a few feet with each calculated maneuver our grimacing driver made. Blockades on all the main crossroads slowed our travel. The word on the street was that Aristide, the president living in exile in the United States, was soon to return on the well-muscled backs of the United States Marines. I knew little about Haitian politics and did not care. I was concerned, however, that our driver smelled of rum even though it was still early.

Out the window I could see hundreds of sellers lining both sides of the road, sitting on upturned buckets. Women mostly, they peered from under straw hats with defiant grit as they shelled *petit pois* from long green pods and arranged their wares in brightly colored pyramids. Passersby stepped over and around them without noticing. Each seemed to be selling the same products as the vendor beside her, only in slightly different quantities and arrangements. There were bananas, small limes, oranges, and bundles of herbs, as well as packs of Comme Il Faut, a Haitian brand of cigarettes, and Chiclets gum.

Everywhere people with shiny black faces walked in and out of traffic. On many heads were balanced enormous buckets of water, charcoal, or vegetables. Everyone seemed undisturbed by the constant horns. More horns. Everywhere horns. Taxis. Trucks. Loud, backfiring, belching tailpipes.

I spoke not a word on the way to the hotel except for a comment about the smell, a mixture of diesel, exhaust, rotting garbage, and smoke. Smoke infused everything. When we had flown over Port-au-Prince I noticed a thick coverlet of smog, billions of shadowy particles floating upward from the charcoal fires—the primary heat, light, water boiler, food cooker, and all-in-one utility for most Haitians.

"Ugh," I said. "This country stinks."

I had first noticed it in the airport. Now, with the window down, it was all around me. It was the smell of sweat—putrid, sour, acrid, unwashed, old clothes, hot sun, crotches, armpit sweat. It smoldered in my throat and choked my eyes.

THE HOTEL TRISH HAD chosen for us was indeed palatial, albeit run down, as most hotels are in Haiti. We arrived in the afternoon and were whisked through the grand arched entrance by several black bellmen in red uniforms with gold braided trim. Thrilled to be back in civilization, Gary and I exhaled in unison.

Inside the lobby was an extremely short, overweight woman. She leaned over the counter on one chubby elbow, seemingly unaware of and uninterested in our arrival. There were no other guests around. We stood for several long moments at the front desk as she fanned herself. I touched her arm lightly to get her attention.

"Names . . ." she said slowly, without looking up; ". . . passport numbers . . ."

Finally we got the suite. I showered and put on clean clothes. That evening, Gary and I sat beside the hotel's kidney-shaped pool, drank sugary rum punch, and improvised a plan for the next day.

We wanted to tour Mother Teresa's home for abandoned children and inquire about specific needs in Haiti. Gary had been there once before and felt it would be a good place to start.

The heavy girl at the front desk had been replaced by the evening shift, a Haitian mulatto who spoke English and arranged transportation for us. His "friend" would pick us up at 8 a.m. the following morning and take us around. I asked two questions:

"How much?" and "Does your friend's car have air-conditioning?"

He answered, "Fifty dollars" and, with a surprised laugh, "No, no air-conditioning."

Morning came quickly. I overslept and was awakened by pounding at the door.

"Madam? *Bonjou,* madam?" came a female voice. "Your driver is here."

Gary slept on the couch. I heard him answer the door, thank her, and ask for aspirin, to which the voice replied, *"Pa gen pwoblem."*

"I hope that means 'yes,'" I called from my bed.

An hour later we arrived in front of a plainly painted building, concrete and square. Our driver announced we had arrived at Mother Teresa's home for abandoned children. I tugged at my short shorts. Gary tucked his shirt in. Surprisingly, the front gate was locked. Undaunted and not seeing anyone from whom to request entry, I started to climb over. With one leg over the gate I saw a lady in a blue-and-white nun's habit standing at the doorway of the building with a hand lifted in protest. "Wait!" she stated firmly.

"Uh, I'm sorry," I said. "I thought somebody forgot to unlock the gate."

Gary held up a bag to show the frowning nun. "We brought some candy for . . . for the children."

"No cameras," said the nun. She took a skeleton key from somewhere within her habit and unlocked the gate.

Inside, about fifty kids greeted us. Most were under age three. Some were in cribs. Some cried, gulping to regain their breath. Others lay listless, staring into space with a silence that haunted me. By third-world standards, Mother Teresa's was a well-kept orphanage, yet it was the first institution of its type I'd ever seen. We stood together, Gary and I, as the essence of despair and sorrow took shape before us. These children, although fed and cared for—this was their home. That simple fact stunned me.

I took a step forward. Dozens of little arms stretched through crib bars, reaching for us. The only response possible was to go to them. We lifted them out and held them. They clung tight against our chests and dug their fingers into our arms. To put one back into a crib elicited screams of defiance and looks of betrayal. One by one we picked up each child, hugged them, and gave little pats and kisses. We sang silly songs and danced little jigs. Setting them down often required Gary's assistance, as they held tightly to fistfuls of my clothing. After a while the nun left the nursery for other duties, and Gary and I began distributing candy piece by piece, carefully choosing softer bits for the littlest children. Sounds of sucking, chewing, and cooing filled the room, and tears began to dry.

A couple of hours passed before another blue-and-white-uniformed nun thanked us and said it was naptime and we needed to leave.

We returned to find our driver asleep in the car. Gary and I, now full of questions, asked if there were many orphanages in Haiti like this.

"Oh, yes," he said, "there are very, very many. This is a very nice one."

"Very, very many?" I asked. "Why are there so many orphans in Haiti?"

He gave a sideways glance. "Oh, you know, the mothers cannot afford doctors, so they die when they have the babies. Or kids are sick with no money for medicine, so they hope the medicine is here. Or father is out of work and cannot feed the kids, so they take them here to live."

I digested all I heard. "You said this was a very nice orphanage," I said. "Can you take me to one that isn't so nice? Where would that be?"

"That would be in Cité Soleil," the driver said. "You do not need to go there. No . . . no. The people shoot at each odder. There are many gangs. Is very, very poor."

"What would it cost for you to take us there?" I asked.

"Oh, I do not drive to Cité Soleil. Missus, even Haitians do not go to Cité Soleil. It is very dangerous. I cannot do it. I have wife and family. I am afraid of the people in Cité Soleil. You could not pay me enough to go there."

"How about another fifty bucks?" I said.

He thought a moment. "Maybe just this once."

We left the district of Delmas and drove through the center of Port-au-Prince, past the gleaming white presidential palace. Our driver proudly pointed it out and seemed disappointed we didn't want to go there instead.

Upon leaving Rue International 1, the main highway along the outskirts of the city, we passed a large water tower, and the world changed. There is no road sign announcing entry to Cité Soleil, but we were suddenly there.

The driver slowed almost to a standstill as he inched down into deep ruts. The dirt road seemed to disappear and became a vast, mud-filled ravine. The occasional pig, dog, or goat gnawed on corn husks and orange peels. A sinewy old man peed against a tin structure, widening his stance to avoid the growing pool of urine between his feet. Some naked children with dusty faces and swollen bellies ran back and forth, not too close, to get a look at me, then stumbled backward with shrieks and giggles, fingers tucked into their little mouths, and ran back to other children huddled nearby. Angry, suspicious adult faces stared at us through the vehicle's open windows.

About half a million people call Cité Soleil home. Located southwest of downtown Port-au-Prince, the district is known to be Haiti's poorest, roughest, and most dangerous area. It's a twenty-seven-square-mile sewer and garbage dump, literally. The excrement of the elite who live high above Port-au-Prince washes down via a canal. In and along that canal, people build shacks, dogs and donkeys die and bloat, and children bathe and swim. Cité Soleil, also called Du Soleil, is considered the worst slum in Haiti. Every few blocks is a different section, controlled by another gang leader; the number of gangs is said to exceed thirty-two. Random gunfire and incendiary bombs are commonplace. As I watched out the window, Aspen's snowcapped mountains and trout-laden rivers seemed a faraway mirage.

We parked and got out. Our driver insisted on waiting by the car to make sure it was not stolen while Gary and I walked down a long narrow alley into the heart of the slum. Gary knew of a school building that some foreigners had started constructing during his last journey to Haiti.

We walked perhaps a bit more than a mile and gained a following of at least a hundred children. Most wore only a T-shirt; all were curious. I realized it was unlikely they had ever seen a tall, blond woman wearing short shorts. They shouted and giggled, and came closer. They touched our hands and clothing and my long hair. They started to refer to Gary as Papa and me as Mama Blanc. (Years later, I asked them not to call me that anymore because I didn't want them to consider me their mom. I wanted them to think of me as a friend, an aunt, a sister, a mentor, but not as a mother, because I could never live up to that.) They seemed in awe of Gary's hairy arms and bald head.

When we came to the place where Gary was sure the school would be, only a concrete slab and three walls with a few glassless windows appeared.

"I wonder what happened," Gary said with disappointment. On his last trip, Gary had met a wealthy French couple who had partnered with a local Haitian woman named Maude Silverice. Maude was to oversee the project, since the couple lived in France.

"I'd like you to meet Maude, Susie," Gary said. "Maybe she can tell us why the school was never built."

As I stared at the half-built structure, I felt a strange calm descend around me. I flipped the hair off my neck, instinctively expecting relief, but the air was perfectly still. The calm was more than windlessness. It was another presence. The heat moved through my skin, and the dust floated upward, high above smoke from burning charcoal and garbage. The stench that had filled my nostrils since arriving in Haiti didn't seem to be nearly as powerful.

I took a deep breath and spoke: "I'd like to stay here for the night."

Gary laughed. "Not a chance, Susie," he said. "Come on, let's go back to the hotel. We can track down Maude from there."

I didn't move. I felt foolish passing out candy to children who needed medicine, food, water, and shelter. How could I ever know how to help the poor if I didn't spend time with the poor? I knew Gary understood this deep down, but I wouldn't ask him to join me.

"I'd like to stay here for the night," I repeated. "I'd like to visit one of the lean-tos or shanties, if someone would allow me into their home."

Gary shook his head, then thought for a moment. "Let's go talk to our driver," he said at last. "If you've absolutely got to stay here, let's go back to the hotel first. At least maybe we can find someone to translate for you."

Back at the hotel I changed into a long white sundress, modest and simple. I put a bottle of water and some toilet paper into my fanny pack and strapped it around my waist. I took off my earrings and wedding and engagement rings, and started to take off my gold cross but decided to leave it on.

I ran back downstairs to find our driver and the girl who had checked us in upon arrival in a fury of conversation. As I approached the front desk the conversation faded to hurried whispers.

"Madam!" the heavy lady exclaimed. "You are sleeping in Cité Soleil? You cannot do this! Oh, madam, it is not a good idea." The driver had one arm resting on his belly and held his hand over his mouth with the other. He had agreed to take me back to Cité Soleil and translate for me. His attitude toward me had clearly deteriorated and he was no longer the friendly, good driver he had been earlier. It became apparent he resented needing my American dollars. Who wants to risk his life for a bossy blanc?

"Thanks," I said to the woman. I turned to the driver. "Let's go."

The dilapidated, rusted blue Chrysler seemed to go slower the second time to Cité Soleil. I probed as much as I could, asking all the questions that popped into my mind. The driver answered haltingly, increasingly nervous as we drove toward the slum. The mid-afternoon air was bright, but all around me it felt dark. From the car window I stared at a long shadow cast from a dilapidated voodoo temple. Several pairs of young girls passed through the shadow, holding hands, chattering, giggling, and whispering, enjoying the single comfort of not being completely alone in hell.

I wished I had someone to hold hands with too. My tongue stuck to the roof of my mouth. As we neared Cité Soleil I looked toward the bubbling greenish brown water of the canal that separated a borough called Bellecourt from another borough controlled by a lethal gang leader named Dread Wilmer. I would search for a place to stay in either borough. That night, I would sleep in Cité Soleil.

Chapter 13

The Beginning of Disorder

EARLY EVENING WAS ALMOST upon us, and the foul stench had returned as the driver and I inched our way back into Cité Soleil. Smoke seemed to choke all the oxygen from the air. Getting out of the car, I realized I needed to go to the bathroom. The women and little girls seemed comfortable squatting while holding their ragged dresses bunched in front of them when the call of nature came, but I wasn't quite there yet.

Years later I realized with shock what the steamy bubbles were all about that bellowed up in the greenish water of the Cité Soleil canal. The sludge bubbles were caused by methane, produced when the sewer washing into the canal overheats. Flowing through this community was a literal river of shit. There is no nice way to say it.

The driver and I walked, searching for adults to talk to who would understand my desire to spend the night there. At least fifty kids trailed after us. Some seemed cherubic and shy while others were mischievous. Empowered by their peers, they made a game of running past me, grabbing my dress, and pinching me. One little boy tried to lift my dress. Stopping dead in my tracks, I put my hands firmly on my hips. The gesture alone sent him shuffling backward.

"No!" I shouted in a universal language.

As we continued to walk, several children grabbed my hand and pulled me next to a shack where an old woman lay.

"She is sick," the children said, through the driver. One little boy knelt beside her and pulled me down. "Please help her, she is cold," he said in Creole. He took my hand and pressed it down on her bare dark skin.

She had died with her eyes open. There were no adults in sight.

"She won't get well for you to see," I whispered, the driver translating. "But now she is somewhere very far from here, this place. Her body is too old for that kind of travel, so she left it behind."

I didn't know what else to do. The driver seemed unconcerned about the old woman's corpse, so we continued to walk. Slumber does not come easily in the ghettos of Haiti. Deep into the evening, I continued walking through the labyrinth of tin and cinder-block shanties, watching, and being watched.

Earlier I had noticed a group of serious-looking men following me. They peered over the rims of their sunglasses as they stood in the shadows. As darkness grew they followed less covertly. They all kept their sunglasses on in the darkness and seemed to be doing a lot of laughing. I could see their gold chains tighten around the muscles of their necks. I started to like that they were able to laugh in a place like this.

I came to an opening in the buildings where the sea came into view. Most of the children had disappeared, but a group of adults was with me now—maybe a hundred men, a few women. The group closed around me, and the light of the full moon cast long shadows that distorted their faces. No one was laughing now. We nodded, acknowledging each other. An eerie silence fell. Except for the sound of distant gunfire somewhere in another borough and the untimely crowing of a rooster, there was no sound.

"My name is Susie." I turned to search for the driver to translate. He inched his way through the crowd and stood close to me nervously. "I would like to help. That's why I came."

A frail man stepped forward. His cheekbones were so high he appeared to be smiling though he was not. His eyes were set so far apart he reminded me of a crab.

"Madam Susie—" he said, and then turned and looked respectfully back at the men, who wore suspicious faces—"they want to know why you are here. Are you with the government?"

"No," I insisted. "I'm not with any government. I want to know how to help."

The moon caught the silvery gray handle of a gun sticking out of the waistband of one man's jeans. I waited for the driver to finish translating. As he did, the man with the gun nodded.

The frail man continued as the group crowded closer. "Are you a missionary?"

"No, but I want to live as a Christian." I smiled uneasily. "It's hard."

The driver translated. The mob laughed. Then, as if permission had suddenly been given, silence was broken and questions poured forth. I breathed a sigh of relief.

The frail man introduced himself as Viximar and informed me that he loved Jesus and would help me be Christian. For more than an hour the group asked questions: Where was I from? What group was I with? Did I want to convert them? Was I looking for babies to adopt?

A woman stepped forward and placed a listless infant in my arms. "You can take my baby," she said, through the interpreter. "I cannot feed it." She lifted a bare, deflated breast. The baby was a little girl. I placed the child hesitantly back in her mother's arms. Disappointment spread like a wave through the crowd.

"How will you help us?" asked a man too far away for me to see clearly.

"I don't know," I said, shaking my head honestly. "I am here to ask you that."

"We want to leave!" shouted another.

"We need food!" came another shout, followed by at least a hundred shouts of agreement. "Yes! Yes! We need food!"

Truthfully, I knew just a little of what they actually meant. I had long since drunk the last of my bottled water. But as I stood there thirsty and hungry, I knew I could eat and drink when I got back to the hotel tomorrow. I wondered what it would be like if I couldn't.

The driver had told me earlier that on most days thousands of people stand in line before the sun comes up to wait for clean water. Often they still wait in line under the fierce afternoon sun. Water drips from a few pipes when city water is turned on. Often the water doesn't come at all.

No water had come this day. If it did not come again tomorrow the people would drink water collected in the community cistern. This water spawned mosquitoes and often made the people sick with diarrhea and vomiting. Sometimes they died. I looked down at the little girl in her mother's arms.

◆ ◆ ◆

AFTER THEIR CURIOSITY HAD been satisfied and my hopeful answers given, the crowd began to disperse. Most people disappeared back into the walls of tin. Viximar, the driver, and I continued to walk to the sea.

At the shore, we could dimly see a group assembling what appeared to be rafts. Viximar explained that this was a secret location. At this place began all the dreams of being carried to the land that flows with milk and honey.

Floating to America on rickety homemade boats is always a long shot, Viximar explained, his eyes grave. There are stories that on some beaches in Haiti, you can't walk without shoes for fear of human bone fragments piercing your feet. When the tide comes in it brings back the remnants of people who died en route to southern Florida.

"Do any make it?" I asked.

"It is said that some do."

Viximar knew about my desire to spend the night in Cité Soleil and invited me to sleep in his home with his extended family. He brought us to a cinder-block shanty with a roof made of rusty tin, wood, and cardboard.

Inside, there was one mattress and a small plastic table with four metal chairs tucked neatly around. A can of plastic flowers sat on the table. A sheet divided the room in two, separating the dining area from the sleeping area. The hut was meticulously clean though the floor was hardened dirt. Every inch of the little home was occupied by a sleeping body. I could hear random gunfire in the distance.

Viximar pulled aside a sheet and motioned for me to lie down beside a woman with a little boy in her arms. The driver had agreed to stay and was situated between several children in a corner. One by one, they woke and stared, confused at the strangers in their home. Viximar introduced us to his extended family: his wife, his five children, his grandmother, seven cousins, and a friend who had just moved from the mountains in the south. They all lived in this tiny shack. They chattered anxiously in Creole. Viximar's tone was one of reassurance. One by one, they lay back down to sleep.

I was so tired, I lay down too. That night I dreamed I was back in high school, with a final chance to graduate. I couldn't find my classes, I didn't know the right answers to any questions, so I quit. I was a failure. A failure again. In my dream I was so mad at myself. I slept fitfully the rest of the night.

When I woke the shack was empty except for a little girl. She sat beside me on the mattress, gently touching my hair. I sat up slowly and started scratching my arms, my legs, my head. Lifting my dress above my knees, I saw little red bumps covering every visible inch.

"Oh, for blood-ee Pete's sake . . ."

I touched my face and felt more itchy bumps. The little girl giggled and ran outside. I followed her to find Viximar, the driver, and Viximar's wife sitting outside the shanty on a bench against the wall. They stopped their conversation and looked at me. The driver laughed. "Oh, Madam Su-zee," Viximar said with a worried look on his face.

"I think it's fleas," I said, scratching my head. "Or maybe lice." I decided to get on with business. "Um . . . will you ask Viximar about the building the French people started but didn't finish—the one Maude Silverice was in charge of?"

Viximar said construction halted when gangs in the area started shooting one another. "The bad men stole all the blocks," he added.

It was time to return to the hotel. Viximar agreed to walk the driver and me back to the car. People continued to watch as we walked out of the slum. I didn't recognize any faces from the night before. Viximar pointed out various people I needed to watch out for.

The younger gang members, the ones Viximar said were very

dangerous, seemed to put forth a notable effort to frighten me. But in their eyes, I thought I recognized confusion, not fear or hatred. I knew I needed to better communicate to them my intentions for being there.

Viximar spoke bits of English, like "Hey you" and "Give me one dollar, please" and "I love Jesus." He never left my side, even when several young men became loud and picked up rocks. When they picked up rocks, I picked up a couple too. Mostly I worried about Viximar. I thought they were angry with him since he was with me. My picking up the rocks made the mean ones laugh very hard. I knew I could not judge these men because I did not yet know the things they feared.

BACK IN THE HOTEL lobby I was not welcome. Apparently I looked like an unsavory sort. I said I had a room and told them my name. The desk clerk looked wary. I explained I had just come from Cité Soleil. With that, the clerk motioned for the guard.

"Just call my room!" I said. "It's 202!" I didn't have ID on me or a key. I prayed Gary had not gone to breakfast. Within moments he appeared in his bathrobe, coming down the staircase. "Thank God!" I mumbled.

"Whoa!" Gary looked at me, then at the desk clerk. "Unfortunately . . . yes, um . . ." He rubbed his chin and made a show of examining me closer. "She's with me."

I shoved Gary aside and walked up the stairs.

"You stink!" Gary said when we got to the room. "I mean really bad . . . and what did you do to your face?"

"Something bit me, all over." I looked in the mirror. "Holy Moses!"

I drank all the water in the room and stayed in the shower for half an hour. I ate until my stomach hurt, murmuring new prayers of gratefulness for food.

Gary had tracked down Maude Silverice. She had a clinic and an orphanage, but worked mainly from an office at her clinic. That afternoon we went to see her to inquire about the unfinished building in Cité Soleil. We were asked to wait in an airless reception area. The heat made me itch.

"Stop that!" Gary slapped at my hand. "You're going to make it worse!"

"I can't help it. We've been sitting here an hour! Maybe she doesn't remember you."

Gary closed his eyes and slouched deeper into his metal chair. "Just be patient," he said. "This is Haiti, remember."

"Well, I'm going to see what's goin' on," I said. "This is ridiculous." I was tired and cranky and hot. I walked through an open door. There didn't appear to be any patients at this clinic. Curious, I continued up the stairs to the second level, where there were more rooms with empty hospital beds. I walked down a corridor and found a door marked "Lab." I knocked and entered without waiting. I man in a white laboratory coat was eating a large lunch.

"Oh, I'm sorry!" I said. He looked at me with a full mouth. "I'm looking for Maude Silverice."

He swallowed and stood up. "Madam Silverice is down the stairs. She is in the office." He pointed me to a door at the bottom of the stairs. I opened her door and was delighted by a blast of cool air. A heavy-hipped woman with an ample bosom and ebony skin sat eating a pastry. She wore a perfectly starched, pink, long-sleeved blouse and was flipping through a French magazine.

"Madam Silverice?" I asked, not wanting to leave the air-conditioned room.

"Who are you?" she answered. Her brow furrowed.

"I'm Susie, Susie Krabacher," I said excitedly. "I'm with Gary Bruyere." I waited in vain for a look of recognition. "You know . . . he came from Colorado and volunteered at your orphanage for a month a while ago." Still nothing. "Um, well, let me go get him." I didn't wait for an invitation. I came back with Gary in tow. Maude looked annoyed.

"Hello, Maude!" Gary opened his arms to hug her.

"Oh, Gary, I didn't recognize the name at first," she said without excitement.

Gary explained that I wanted to help with the construction project and that perhaps we could work together. Maude continued to flip through her magazine.

"I'm selling my antique store and want to use the money to do something," I said.

Maude pushed the pastry aside and gave me her full attention.

"I spent the night in Cité Soleil last night."

"You did not!" She seemed shocked.

"We went to look at the school building that you were going to build," Gary said. "What happened?"

"Oh . . . you know," Maude said, "the people in France stopped sending money. When the people in Cité Soleil stole our bricks for the third time, everybody decided it was too dangerous and gave up."

"Well, how much would it cost to finish it?" I asked.

"Twelve thousand American." Maude didn't hesitate.

I chewed on my bottom lip and figured. "The people in Cité Soleil said they needed food the most. If I can get the money to finish the building, can we make a nutrition center out of it?"

Maude smiled. "Please sit down. May I offer you some water?" She smiled again, wider this time. "It's cold."

We sat for the next hour and a half discussing details of the project. We knew we would need money to buy food each month and hire people to cook. We'd also need to hire a guard to keep the blocks from being stolen again. Everything she said sounded airtight. She described municipal politics in detail, building requirements and laws. The longer we talked, the more I became convinced of her business savvy and altruistic attitude toward her countrymen.

Maude shook our hands heartily at the end of our meeting. "Yes, yes," she said. She was all smiles as we left. "We'll get this building finished yet."

Gary and I returned to the hotel. I asked the desk clerk for an international phone line and waited. Our plan was taking shape, but how could I raise twelve thousand dollars? I wondered how much I had spent at hair salons and restaurants in the past year and wished I had it all back. Finally my call went through. Joe's voice sounded on the other end. The line crackled.

"I love you!" I shouted. "I miss you!"

I told Joe all about Cité Soleil and purposely left out the detail of spending the night there. "The hotel is really nice and safe!"

"I have some great news!" Joe said after fifteen minutes of updates about our home and the dogs. "Mark sold everything in the antique store!"

I held my breath and closed my eyes. "Was there any money left after we paid off the loan?" I asked. I crossed my legs and fingers.

The line went dead.

"Dad-gum!" I shouted.

I tried and tried to get another line. Frustrated, I went to find Gary. We sat with our feet in the pool and drank mango juice.

"I wish you were rich," I told him.

"I wish you were," he commiserated.

"Madam! Madam Krabacher!" I turned to see the desk clerk coming toward us with a huge smile, waving a sheet of paper. "Mr. Krabacher sends you a telefax. It is marked *urgent.*" I stood up as he handed me the paper.

I squinted in the sun and shaded my eyes as I read. I handed the paper to Gary and fell face-first into the pool. I broke the surface screaming and jumped out and kissed the desk clerk, who looked at Gary to see if he should be worried. "Hallelujah!" I sang over and over and danced around and then hugged Gary. "Can you believe it? *Can* you believe it?"

The paper read: *We have just over $12,000 left. Love, Joe.*

This was a sign. I knew this was a sign. The feeding center was meant to be!

That night a whole fish grilled with head and tail intact was brought to our table for dinner with a delicious sauce of fresh shallots and butter. We said a blessing for our very own miracle.

Gary flew home the next day, but I had more work to do. I knew Joe was expecting me, but I wasn't ready to come home just yet. First on my agenda: buying some more time. I threw my passport in the bushes outside the hotel and called Joe.

"Honey," I said to his office answering machine (I knew he would be at home then, so I purposely didn't call the house), "I seem to have misplaced my passport." Trying not to lie, I wiped from my head all memory of which bush it was. "I'll go to the embassy to see what I should do."

I hired a driver and went back to see Maude. Proudly, I wrote out a check for $12,000. I squealed as I handed it to her.

"Oh, Susie!" Maude squealed too, her eyes beaming. "This is just wonderful! Absolutely wonderful."

SUDDENLY I HAD A job. Overnight, I became a one-woman international relief agency in partnership with a Haitian national I barely knew named Maude Silverice.

For the next three weeks I went back and forth between Cité Soleil and the hotel. Viximar, who was not large, but was wiry and trustworthy, was hired to guard my cement blocks. Another week went by and my new passport was ready. Joe seemed quite relieved when I phoned to say I was coming home. The feeding center was close to finished and only lacked a roof. I flew home, believing the project was safe in Maude's hands.

Joe met me at the airport in Aspen. All seven of our dogs came too. Tails wagging, they licked off most of my makeup. Joe picked me up. I wrapped my legs around his waist and we kissed with our eyes closed for a very long time. He smelled so good. I hoped I did too.

"Don't ever go away for that long again!" he said.

It was strange to be back in Aspen—so much *stuff*, just *stuff* everywhere. In this city, I could have anything. I found it hard to explain to anyone what I had just been through, so I stayed quiet for many days, just remembering. Maybe I was coming down with something. I felt depressed. I didn't know I had just received the first injection of a potent and disarmingly seductive drug. I would become dependent on it, an addict to Haiti for the rest of my life. Being needed was a powerful pull for me.

One night, Mark and Joe wolfed down one of my well-thought-out dinners. Cooking gave me something to do, time to think and calculate. Nothing else I did seemed important. Mark and Joe were worried.

"When are you going back?" Joe asked. He knew I would. My eyes lit up, and I grinned at him.

"Want to go with me?" I said, looking from Joe to Mark and back to Joe.

"Honey, I just can't leave the firm right now," Joe said. I knew he wasn't lying.

"I'll go," Mark said.

I hugged him. I thought I would nearly burst.

I had called Maude at least once a week during the months I had been home. She assured me the nutrition center was finished, up and running, feeding hundreds of children a week, as well as some nursing mothers with infants. Maude gave me details of what was being served: rice and beans, dried sardines, green vegetables. With the $1,800 a month Joe had agreed to let me send if I stopped going on shopping sprees, Maude had hired seven employees, including two cooks and several others to wash the metal bowls and utensils she had purchased with the extra money we sent.

"The people of Cité Soleil are so happy, Susie!" Maude crooned into the phone one evening.

How wonderful it felt to hear that. "Well, I'm coming back to Haiti next week with my brother!" I said with excitement. "We already have our tickets!"

"Oh! You don't want to come next week," Maude said. "I am very busy next week and things are very dangerous in Haiti right now. It will be better if you visit next month, Susie."

"But I'm bringing a television crew," I said. I had called Fox News in Salt Lake City, thinking that since I was from Utah and they had shown interest when I was a centerfold, maybe they'd be interested in the Haitian project. It worked. They would send a crew and one of their newsmen with me to Haiti.

"Joe can't pay for this forever," I added. "He suggested I get other people involved. Having the TV crew there will help me raise money for the project. Maybe other people will want to help if they see it on TV!"

The line went dead. I looked at the phone in my hand. It happened often in Haiti. The phone lines were unpredictable. Still, I was uneasy. Maude didn't sound excited about seeing me. She sounded edgy. *Oh well, I know my way around Haiti. I just won't bother her while I'm there. She is, after all, a very busy woman. Besides, I can take care of myself.*

Every other time I tried to phone Maude that week, all lines were busy.

❖   ❖   ❖

MARK AND I FLEW to Haiti two days before the television crew was to arrive. I wanted to go there first and see the nutrition center and Viximar. I could not wait to show Mark Cité Soleil and the center. We found a driver and went straight to Cité Soleil from the airport.

I explained to the driver that I wanted to show my brother a place I had built to feed the poor children there. He spoke some English and seemed surprised that an American had accomplished such a thing "in that bad place." I explained I had been sending money to a Haitian women and that she was overseeing the project.

"Have you actually seen your project, Madam?" the driver asked.

A strange question, I thought.

"Many Haitians are vagabonds," he said. "They are not honest. I look forward to know if your feeding center truly exists."

So do I, I thought, suddenly very anxious to get there. We pulled up to the edge of the canal. Mark held his nose.

"It's coming from the canal," I said and pointed to the fetid green water. "You get used to it after an hour or so."

The driver stayed with his car as Mark and I walked to the center. Within minutes we were mobbed by children and young women. "Mama Blanc! Mama Blanc!" they said, or simply "Su-zee!"

But they were not smiling. It was alarm. I tried to hug my old friends, the ones whom I had come to know during my month in Haiti. They pulled their shoulders away from me.

"Ouch!" Someone hit me with a stone! I rubbed my rear end. No one was laughing. It wasn't a joke. "Mark, follow me," I said, my voice tense. "Quick!"

Still holding his nose, he followed without question. We sprinted through the small passages between shanties. Occasionally

I glanced back to see that Mark was still there. A mob followed, some jogging, hands on hips and seemingly angry. Something was very wrong.

As we drew closer to the feeding center, the smell of urine and human waste was almost unbearable. I came up to the gated iron entry, but by now the smell was so nauseating I had to take my hair and hold a thick bunch of it over my nose. Mark gagged. A guard came from behind the building. He had keys, but it wasn't Viximar.

"But, but . . ." I stammered, speaking through my hair. "Where is Viximar?"

Impervious to the intense stench, the guard opened the gate and pulled me through. Mark stepped backward and away. "Get in here!" I shouted. No time for debate—it was not safe for him outside. The gate slammed shut. The man locked it with the keys. Mark and I simultaneously reached to stabilize ourselves against the interior wall. I felt the airplane pretzels coming up in my throat.

"Oh! God!" I said. Mark pounded on the door, struggling to get out. I stood there in disbelief, my eyes burning with tears.

Spread out across the floor of the feeding center was a wall-to-wall layer of brown slime at least two hardened inches thick. It was human feces covered with maggots and a flurry of flies. They flew up around us, lighting on our flesh.

Mark and I ran outside in complete despair. The man with the keys followed. I recognized someone who spoke some English.

"Please, tell me," I said, "where is Viximar?"

"Viximar is in a deep sleep," the man answered, mournfully shaking his head.

"Is Viximar . . ." I had to concentrate to speak each word. "Is Viximar dead?"

"He is in the hospital. He has not woke up for over two months."

"But why?" I said.

"Bad men tried to steal your blocks and he fought them."

"Why," I continued, "why did the people do this to the center that gives them food?"

"We did not get food!" the man said. He was angry now. "You lie to us. You tell us you feed the children! We die, we starve, no food. You promise! I hear that from you own mouth! You say that!"

Slowly I began to piece together the truth. I had been fed a line of shit by Maude—a whole buildingful in fact. She had been using the $1,800 a month we were sending her for God knows what. More fashion magazines and pastries, no doubt. When progress halted on the feeding center, the people believed I had abandoned them, just like the French couple, and expressed their frustration by using the center for a toilet. Obviously, Maude had done nothing to stop them.

Mark wore that familiar look. "Now, Susie," he said. I ignored him. "*Susie!* Listen to me! We can figure this out. I promise. Don't do anything until we figure it out." I remembered the television crew would be there in two days.

Chapter 14

A Long, Thin Limb

IT WAS MY FIRST taste of "being had," Haitian-style: you send money to someone you trust, you assume it's being used for good, and you end up with a roomful of shit.

It felt easy to hate. Or to be mad. Or to despair. I had promised to assist the people of Cité Soleil and help supply food for their children. Maude Silverice had led me to believe the project was up and running. As I talked with the people outside the feces-filled building, more of the story came out. The center had actually opened. People had been fed there for one week. Then it closed inexplicably. Children were still starving, so the people's disappointment turned to hatred for me. In their eyes I was just another lying blanc talking out of both sides of her mouth. Naturally, their minds turned to revenge.

I could see their point. When you're in pain it's hard to think clearly. But it was tougher to forgive when I remembered poor Viximar, with his happy and sad face, now in a coma in the hospital. I told myself that not all the people beat him up. Every group's got its bad apples. But still, my anger began to mount. I felt the pressure between my tightening jaws. I needed to get out of there. Quick.

Mark hurried me back to the taxi, where I told the driver to take us to the El Rancho. It was the only hotel I knew well. Mark held my hand and pulled me from the car when we arrived. He walked me to a quiet, comfortable corner in the large, empty lobby.

"Sit!" He motioned to a chair. "Stay!" he barked, pointing an index finger within an inch of my nose. He walked away, turning to look back over his shoulder, a warning against me vacating my chair. Within moments Mark returned with a glass of cool white wine, an effort to pacify me. He placed a little bowl of peanuts in front of me and left again, taking my purse with him.

By the time Mark checked us into the hotel, he and Ghislaine, the heavy desk clerk I had met on my first trip, were chattering as if they were long-lost friends now reunited. I could tell Mark was hatching a plan of his own and had begun to recruit Ghislaine with his effervescent charm.

I wasn't so sure. I felt sapped of forward momentum. Sitting in the lobby chair Mark had placed me in, I thought about more pleasant times in Aspen. In my mind, I allowed myself to go back there. I could leave Haiti for good, I thought, fly home to Aspen tomorrow if I wanted, avoid the humiliation of seeing my failure on TV—me and a crap-filled feeding center. As I tilted the wineglass to my lips I felt the last drop slide down the inside of the glass and into my mouth. *It would be so easy just to leave.* I stood up. Suddenly Mark was in front of me. He smiled and shook his head. He took me by the hand up to our room.

"Okay, now this is what we're gonna do," Mark said. "Ghislaine is getting off work in half an hour. She's coming up to the room with a bottle of good white wine for you. You leave the rest to me." He patted me on the top of my head. His voice was part teasing, part condescending.

"Can't we just get out of here?" I said.

Mark pretended he didn't hear. "Buckets, Clorox bleach, shovels, mops, brooms, Pine-Sol, paint." In a nonchalant, singsong fashion he ticked off each item needed.

"Seriously, Mark," I said. "I think I'm finished with this place."

He rolled his eyes. "Susie, for crying out loud! Get a grip! I can get some of the guys in Cité Soleil to help. It's only one big room!" With his left hand on his hip he sauntered away, then turned back toward me, playing with the corner of his sparse little mustache with his right hand. "You just rest and drink some nice wine and take a little nappy-poo."

I looked at him. The evening light was slanting off the Caribbean ocean through the hotel blinds in a way I had never noticed. Mark looked older, wiser. He wasn't just my kid brother anymore. I wasn't sure who he was, or what he was into, but I loved him. That much I knew for sure.

Mark wagged a finger at me. "And for heaven's sake, Susie, have a little more of that faith you're always talking about!"

FAITH CAN COME IN small degrees, sometimes from nearby hands we'd never expect to be stronger than ours. While I sat on the bed and wallowed in my misery and got drunk, Mark and Ghislaine rallied and made plans. Ghislaine loved food, hence her thunderous physique, and Mark ordered from room service to her heart's desire. Ghislaine was able to track down all the cleaning supplies needed, but would not go to Cité Soleil with Mark to help.

"Too dangerous!" she said. "I want to live!"

"He's notch goin' ta Cité Soleil without me neither!" I shouted from my bed, woozy with wine.

Mark shook his head at me. "Susie thinks I'm a wimp because I'm gay," he said. "Hmph! I can take care of myself."

"I cansh still hear youse," I slurred from under the covers. "Little bro, ain't no way yer goin' anywheres without me."

Mark must have said some more things, because I heard noises after that. I awoke the next morning feeling like I should shave my tongue. Stumbling to the bathroom, I sloshed my face and swallowed from the faucet for several minutes. My eyes were puffy and red in the mirror. A memo was taped to the lower corner. "Dear guests, we would like to remind you not to drink the water from the faucet. Clean drinking water is provided in the cooler adjacent to your door." The memo was repeated in three languages. *Oh, great.* Diarrhea was sure to follow within twenty-four hours. How I loved Haiti.

I rubbed my hands over my face. Mark had unpacked my suitcase and laid out my toothbrush, hairbrush, and Bible. He had scrawled a note in his familiar handwriting:

> *You're gonna need these. Sorry, no aspirin. Ghislaine*
> *found me a driver who speaks some English. We've gone to*
> *Cité Soleil without you. Ha! Ha!*
> > *—Love, Mark.*
> *P.S. I took $100 from your purse to pay for supplies.*

It was nearly noon. I brushed my teeth, showered, brushed my hair, then read my Bible. Reading it had become more common for me then, and my little brother knew me well. The Bible had been left open. Mark had underlined a passage in burgundy with one of my lip pencils:

I put my trust in Thee.
In God, I have put my trust;
I shall not be afraid.
                    —Psalms 56

"God?" I prayed. "Do you really want me here? It sure doesn't seem like it."

Traffic was atrocious, and the midday sun beat down through the passenger window of the old taxi while the driver complained about going to Cité Soleil and how he would need to wash his car afterward. When we pulled up alongside the canal I got out to walk the rest of the way in. Heat and stench hit me in the face. Expecting to be pelted by a stone, pinched, or yelled at, I was wary and turned around frequently to check for angry faces. None was there. Everyone I saw seemed content, except for the women and children who winced while carrying heavy, water-filled plastic buckets on their heads, as is the custom. Children recognized me and ran up, squabbling over who would hold my hands.

As I drew closer to the feeding center, I recognized some of the young men as the ones who carried guns or machetes and wore dark sunglasses at night. They were laughing. Some wore brightly colored Handi Wipes tied like scarves over their dreadlocks or bald heads. The sticky scent of marijuana was thick in the air, mingled with the smell of Pine-Sol. Inside, Mark was occupied with a mop, his own head covered with a pink-and-white striped Handi Wipe. He sang loudly above the din:

Holy, holy, holy! Lord God Almighty!
All Thy works shall praise Thy name, in earth, and sky, and sea;
Holy, holy, holy; merciful and mighty!
God in three Persons, blessed Trinity!

Mark loved to sing old hymns. His favorites were that one, "Amazing Grace," and "How Great Thou Art." I stood amazed at the intense concentration of employment. The place was a flurry of engagement—everyone was cleaning.

And everyone was stoned.

I tapped Mark on the shoulder. Bent and determined over his mop, he looked up with glassy eyes.

"Heyyyyyyy." He stopped singing and giggled. He smiled his beautiful silly smile and started to fall over, stabilizing himself atop his mop.

"Gol-ly!" I said. "How in the world did you manage?"

"Not too bad, huh?" Mark said. He gleamed with pride, his pupils oversized.

I looked at the room that had only the day before been filled with feces. It was nearly gleaming.

"You are a genius," I said. "But how . . ."

A gang member sauntered up, muscles shiny with sweat, a yellow-and-white Handi Wipe tied loosely over his dreadlocks. He put his huge hand on Mark's shoulder and smiled goofily at me.

"This is my friend, Dread." Mark announced his ghoulish friend's identity. I knew the name. Dread Wilmer. He was one of the most feared gang leaders in Cité Soleil.

"Hi, uh, I'm Susie, Mark's sister."

"*Nou se zanmi!*" Dread said in Creole—"We are friends"—and pounded his fist twice over his heart. I did the same and raised my own fist to meet his as was traditional and evidence of friendship in the Haitian ghetto. One by one other gang members walked over. Mark introduced them: Tupac, Billy, Amaral, Ti-Dread . . . they were all tattooed and muscled. Some wore guns and knives. They were all grinning, all stoned.

I smiled nervously. "Uh, thanks so much. Does anybody need anything?" I asked.

Mark spoke for the group. "Um, yeah. Cookies. And maybe some potato chips. A lot of 'em. And maybe you could find some pretzels somewhere. And how about some peanuts?"

The munchies had set in. I raised a wary eyebrow.

"Oh yeah," Mark said, his eyes bloodshot, "and how about some more Handi Wipes. We're just about out."

The driver took me to Eagle Market on Delmas Road. I bought cans of soda, crispy fried plantains, potato chips, locally baked cookies and sweets, and all different colors of Handi Wipes. Back at the center, I munched right along with our new friends, the "Handi Wipe Gang."

The next day Mark and his gang brushed moss-colored paint on the interior walls of the newly cleaned building. I hired a truck and drove to Delmas to buy benches, long wooden tables, and tin utensils and bowls. The driver knew a place to get charcoal and crude grills and cooking stoves. Last, we secured some bulk foods—grains, rice, beans, and dried milk—with cash I had brought from home.

I hadn't expected the attention a food-filled truck would get as we drove back into Cité Soleil. I climbed atop the truck bed to keep people from stealing everything. So many children jumped up with me, the truck's tailgate nearly dragged on the ground. Hungry faces followed the truck to the center. The crowd slowly dissipated when the truck driver explained the center would open "officially" tomorrow.

We secured guards and left. Back at the El Rancho, Mark and I sat in silence on the balcony of our room until dusk turned to darkness.

"So, you never told me how you got everybody to help you clean," I said at last.

"Well . . ." He grinned sheepishly. "As soon as I got there I recognized a familiar smell. So I bought some, uh"—he cleared his throat—"*fine herb* from a guy. We smoked a couple and I bought a bunch more. He had some friends, and they all came over. They all wanted to practice their English and we all got to laughing."

"But how did you ever convince them to help you clean a room filled with crap?"

"Oh," he said, and smiled. "It wasn't too hard. Once we were all laughing, I stood on top of the building and announced to everyone, 'I am the grand most exalted potentate of all the shit I survey!' They all howled until their sides ached. And then I said, 'And you can be too!'" Mark lit a cigarette and blew three perfect smoke rings before exhaling in a coughing fit.

"You're crazy," I said, amazed.

"Insanity runs in the family." Mark looked at me goofily from the corner of his eye. His expression grew solemn for a moment. "So I hired them all with the spleef they had just sold me." He nodded.

I just shook my head. Mark had done all this for me, I knew that, even though I would have chosen different means. Mark never sought glory for himself. He was always comfortable in the background, whether running an antique store in Aspen or helping me with my newfound calling in Haiti. Truly, I knew little of what he felt inside. I had sensed for some time that his life back home was shaky. Mark told me once that he was convinced he would not live to be an old man. He certainly never had ambitions to be a hero. His biggest hope was that he wouldn't die bald. He was always worried about losing his hair.

We went for dinner. Mark raised his glass and touched it to my own. "To us," he toasted. "The lesser of the least." He pursed his voluminous Alabama lips around a tiny portion of the rim and daintily tilted it into his mouth. I wasn't quite sure what he meant, but I toasted anyway. We looked at each other over the flickering fire of the candle that burned between us in the center of the table, and I felt a strange sadness. Something looked finished in his careful, sweet eyes. I suppressed a shudder and winked at him.

FOX TELEVISION NEWS CAME as promised, and the feeding center was opened, just in time. Word began to spread back in the States about the small project Joe and I had begun. I had grandiosely named what we were doing the Foundation for Worldwide Mercy and Sharing. I imagined us branching out one day into other countries. It was such a long title, people back in the states complained they couldn't fit it all on one line of a check.

There was one loophole I still needed to close: the inevitable encounter with Maude. Before I flew home I steeled myself and went to her office.

"You!" was all I could say when I saw her. I felt like one of the Three Stooges, the one who always slapped his own face and improvised sounds that slid from total frustration into hysterical nonsense.

"Why? How? What?" I tried to talk to Maude again, but it was still an accusation, not a query. In my platform sneakers, I towered above her.

Maude laughed out loud. I willed my arms to remain at my sides so as not to throttle her. Mark was waiting in the lobby of Maude's office, but when he heard laughing he came in and stood beside me.

"What did you do with all the money I sent?" I said, feeling my nostrils flare and my heart quicken. "I want to know why you lied to me—now!"

"Susie, Susie, Susie," Maude said. I watched her lipstick and teeth moving. "Let's go find somewhere to sit and talk." She spoke in a hushed tone, as a mother might reprove a child. She turned to my brother. "Mark, don't you think we should all sit and talk? Your sister is too stubborn. Is she always so serious? Hmm?" As if she could count on Mark as an ally. The nerve!

"Do you have a conscience, Ms. Silverice?" I interrupted.

She patted me on the shoulder. "Su-*æe*! We could not work in Cité Soleil. It became too complicated. I did not tell you because I wanted you to sleep well at night. We used the money instead to start building a maternity ward onto my hospital. It's a very good thing you have done with your money. We will save thousands of little babies. Come with me and I will show you. With the money you sent we have bought all the bricks and have already started to build."

Maybe it was my mistake. I still had lots to learn. Perhaps I misunderstood something, or messages got lost in translation. I didn't want to be bigheaded, swooping in like some tourist with money to throw around and changing everything as if it all depended on me. I valued empathy. I wanted to work alongside the people who called this country home. After all, Haiti didn't belong to me. It was going to be here with its troubles long after I was dead.

I will not trouble you with all the specifics of our conversation that day, or the one we had the following day, or the ones we had for more than a year after that. Suffice to say, Maude won me over—again. She could speak so convincingly—you wanted to believe her. You wanted to forgive, you wanted to have faith. You wanted to trust that the incident with the shit-filled room was all just a cultural miscommunication, as she kept repeating, over and over. Building a new maternity ward was surely a worthy cause, wasn't it? And nobody would ever lie about doing something that selfless, would they?

I looked Maude in the eye when we shook hands and said all was made right.

I had confidence when I agreed to partner with her again to help construct the new hospital facility that Joe and I would now fund.

I had all assurances when I talked my husband into contributing $50,000 of our life savings, and when I raised another $40,000 through Aspen philanthropic organizations, and sent Maude checks totaling $90,000.

I felt secure when I made several trips to Haiti over the next few months to check up on the project, even though I seldom witnessed any work being done—there were always such good excuses for the delays.

And I was in—hook, line, sinker, and bloody mouth—up to the very point I discovered that no hospital was being built, no hospital would ever get built, and that Maude had taken the $90,000 plus who knows how much else and built herself an extravagant house in the mountains.

It was a shocking lesson in deceit. But this was our season of figuring out how things are done in Haiti. Not that we've completely figured things out, even today. The one bright spot was that the feeding center in Cité Soleil (soon dubbed the Mercy Nutrition Center) stayed up and running—under our management, not Maude's.

When we first started in Haiti, it took more common sense than we had, many attempts at making friends with people who had done it before, and an abundance of plain trial and error.

It felt like we were out on a long, thin limb most of the time.

Chapter 15

Mark's Horror

THE APOSTLE PETER DESCRIBES Satan as a roaring lion, prowling around looking for someone to devour.

Satan found my little brother.

Mark and I celebrated with abandon when we reached Miami International Airport Hotel. The Fox News filming went wonderfully, and children in Cité Soleil were eating and happy. Our flight for Aspen did not leave until the following day.

Mark and I went to the restaurant on the top floor, where we could watch the planes take off and land. We ate stone crabs with creamy honey mustard sauce and drank champagne. We laughed and were very silly and very relieved. He was wonderful. He told me I was the only person he knew who could actually still look good in a room full of shit.

After dinner we went to the bar, where Mark ordered a Pink Rum. I reminded him of our room number, kissed him good night on the cheek, and went to our room. After a bath and putting on shorts and a T-shirt, I called Joe and told him we were back in the States.

"Hallelujah!" Joe shouted into the phone. I told him the high-lights of the trip and about the children and the filming. "How did Mark do?" he asked.

"He was a hero. You won't believe how amazing he was." I beamed, twirling the phone cord between my fingers. "I'll let him tell you the whole story when we get home."

I crawled under the covers and glanced at the clock. 11:20 p.m. Mark should be back any second. I woke to the phone ringing. 12:40 a.m. The room was pitch black. I felt for the phone. "Hello?" I cleared my throat.

"Mrs. Krabacher?"

"Yes."

"Mrs. Krabacher, this is hotel security. Could you come down to the front desk?"

I reached for the light switch. Mark was not in his bed. Sud-denly overcome with panic, I ran barefoot to the elevator and banged the down button over and over. *Where is Mark? God, let everything be fine.*

When I reached the front desk, a security officer stood with a city police officer. "Mrs. Krabacher?" the policeman asked.

"Yes." I was shaking.

"Your brother was smoking in the bar," said the policeman. "Hotel security asked him to put the cigarette out three times. Your brother became belligerent—first to them, then to me. I'm gonna have to take him in."

"Are you serious?" I asked, incredulous. "He probably just had too much to drink. My little brother is gay—he doesn't know how to be belligerent!"

The policeman walked me outside to the squad car, where Mark sat in the backseat. Mark looked terrified. "Can I talk to him?" I pleaded. I could hear him crying. "Please don't take him. He's sorry. I'll do anything."

The policeman was a big man, not as tall as Joe, but thickset and stern-looking. *"Anything?"* he said, putting too much emphasis on the word. "Well, maybe we can work something out." His tone suddenly became less businesslike. "You'll have to fill out some paperwork, though. Come with me to the security office inside the airport."

"Thank you so much," I said. I got Mark's attention by tapping on the sealed back window before leaving with the policeman. "Don't worry," I shouted through the squad car window. "I'll be right back to get you!" I smiled bravely and gave Mark a thumbs-up to show all was going to be okay.

The airport was mostly empty. A few forlorn passengers slept in chairs and on the floor, using backpacks or wadded-up coats for pillows. I chattered uninterrupted, as I do when relieved or nervous, from the squad car at curbside to the office where we were to fill out papers. The policeman kept quiet and walked a few strides ahead of me, hurriedly, glancing from side to side.

"My brother's a good guy. . . . I'm sorry to put you through all this. . . . You must hate the night shift. . . ." On and on I blabbered. *Where in the world is this office?* I thought as we walked down the terminal. We entered a dimly lit hallway off one of the main corridors.

The policeman opened a door at the end of a hallway and snapped the light on. "If you'll just step in here," he said. It was very small for an office. There were two metal chairs and a table inside. I didn't see any paper or anything to write with. He pulled his chair close in front of me. "Are you cold? You're shaking."

The questions felt strange. The room felt strange. I became very warm and fought the urge to cry. I felt scared and very sober and wide awake.

"No," I said. "I'm fine, thank you. Where are the papers I need to sign?"

"Don't you worry about your brother," the policeman said. But it wasn't kind. His mouth had a dangerous smirk. "Your brother resisted arrest, but there's no need for him to go to jail." Suddenly I felt one of the policeman's huge hands on the inside of my thigh.

"Papers," I said, moving his hand off me. "I'm here to sign papers."

"Yeah," he said. "We can do that later." He put his hands back on me, both hands this time, more strongly, more forceful, and began to slide them up my legs. His fingers were callused and rough. My mind raced. The office was too far from a main corridor. It wouldn't do any good to scream. It was too late at night. We were too alone. I was in a very bad situation.

"I have a room in the hotel upstairs," I said, thinking fast, anything to buy some time. I tried to smile while looking into his devil eyes. I put my hands on his hands and took them off me. "I don't want to do it like this." I laughed seductively and touched the side of his face softly. I could see his mouth watering.

He shook his head. "You little slut," he said. Impatient and angry, his hands fell hard on my knees again. His thumbs dug into my flesh, trying to force my legs apart.

"I'd like us to have wonderful memories of the first time." I kept up the act and closed my eyes. He thought I was fantasizing. I was praying. I reached into my pocket and placed my room key in his palm. "Let me go get into something that will drive you crazy," I said with the dirtiest grin I could muster. "Wait five minutes and come up to room 317." I stood up and reached to unlock the door to the tiny room.

His hand grabbed my arm. "Five minutes," he said, and pushed the door open.

I walked, increasing my gait until I turned a corner in the terminal, then broke into a run. Tears streamed down my face. I couldn't think or plan. Where could I go for help? No one was in the airport. Who would believe me? I ran to the elevator. It opened on the first pound of my fist. Inside my room I bolted the door, set the security chain, and crouched between the two beds.

"Joe, he's coming to my room," I hissed into the phone, "Joe—what do I do?!"

"Call the police!" Joe shouted. "Susie! Hang up and call the police!"

"He *is* the police, Joe!" I could hear the key in the lock. The door burst open and caught with a thud on the swing-bolt. He could break that if he pushed hard enough. I was completely silent.

"You!" the policeman shouted. Suddenly he thought better of the noise and lowered his tone. "You filthy bitch," he said through the door. "Listen to me, and listen good—I'm taking your goddamn brother to jail."

I cowered on the floor. My teeth chattered and I shook all over.

Mercifully for me, I heard the policeman's steps walking away. Joe talked me down until I was settled enough to make plans for the morning: I was to call an attorney he knew in Miami, and he'd direct us in the specifics of filing a formal complaint. There was little else we could do in the moment except be shaken up.

The next morning I called Trish, my travel agent friend, who lives in Miami. She picked me up for the ride over to the Dade County jail.

"You okay, baby?" she said, and gave me a hug. "You need a Bloody Mary, sister. You look like hell."

"Yeah, well, I've been awake all night."

Trish shook her head. "I hope you're writin' all this stuff down. You oughta write a book."

"Let's go get little bro."

Mark would not talk. I hugged him and cried and then he cried. "What's this on your jacket?" I asked. He cried harder. Splattered on the front of his jacket was an opaque yellowish-white substance. I looked at the jacket more closely and then at him. I never knew the full details of what happened that night in the Miami jail. All I know is that I got away. He didn't.

BACK IN ASPEN MARK worked at various boutiques over the next few months. Often he brought young men to our house after work. I knew that one of his friends—one of the sweetest men he brought over—had AIDS. I didn't know exactly what Mark was doing with him, if they were friends or lovers, but he seldom gave me complete answers anyway.

"Mark, do you have sex with other boys?" I asked him one day.

He turned red. "Nooooooo, Susie. We just hold each other. That kind of sex grosses me out." I nodded.

Mark moved back to Salt Lake City, where it was less expensive. He fell in love and moved in with a man. I was happy he seemed happy. But when he told me they fought violently and often, I grew very worried. Mark was also drinking more and more. After his third DUI he had the choice of going to jail or rehab. He chose rehab and lived at the Salvation Army center in Salt Lake City for a year. While he was in rehab his lover found another. They broke up, and Mark moved back home with Mama and Daddy.

"How's everybody doing?" I asked Mama one day on the phone.

"Not very good," she said, her voice unsteady. "We've been up all night long."

"What's wrong?"

"Well, we had to take Mark to the emergency room. He had an overdose with that cocaine mess." She started crying.

"You've got to be kidding! What happened, Mama? Is he okay?"

"He's been putting it in a needle and putting it in his arm. And last night I was sitting here on the couch watching TV and his arm just busted open." She blew her nose. "Me and your daddy had no idea he was doing any drugs."

"Oh, Mama." I just could not believe it. "I'm going to get on a plane and come right away."

I knew cocaine was a hard habit to break. The last time I succumbed I was sure I would not live to see morning. After putting more than two grams up my bloody nose I stayed up for two days and nights. I lay in bed all the third day hallucinating, exhausted, trying to sleep, so wired I could actually see my heart beat inside my chest. At one point my left arm and fingers became numb. "I'm having a stroke," I thought. "Oh, my God!" I was terrified and too embarrassed to call for help. I couldn't let anyone see me like that. But God was watching and I was so ashamed. How could I have done this to myself? I lay there waiting to die. But, thank God, I didn't. That was the last time I ever did drugs.

The next day, bringing Mark home from the hospital, my mother and I sat in the backseat holding him. He felt frail, much lighter than normal. We hugged him and kissed him and he smiled faintly and sadly.

"Mark . . . sugar . . . honey . . ." Mama said slowly, smoothing his hair away from his face. "What's it gonna take for you to stop this, sweetheart?"

He looked up at me first, then at her with the saddest eyes. "Don't worry, Mama," he said. "Just please don't worry."

Mark regained strength after his overdose and came to visit me in Aspen. By then his skin had a sallow hue and the whites of his eyes were a faded yellow. My worry and concern translated into anger.

"Mark," I said one day, "have you taken an AIDS test, ever?"

"No, Susie!" he snapped. "I practice safe sex."

"You said you weren't having sex!" I was yelling by now. "You said you just held each other—that that kind of thing grossed you out!"

"It's none of your business, Susie!"

"You lied to me!" I stomped out of the room and slammed the door.

After that my brother wasn't as secretive with me about his life. He fell in love with another man and admitted they had anal sex constantly. Mark quit his job and fell to the mercy of his lover's whims. He confided his increasing sadness. On Mark's twenty-sixth birthday his lover announced he had AIDS and had known all along. I begged Mark to take a test. He pleaded with me to give him money to move to San Francisco. I got mad. "Take the test, Mark! We have to know!"

"What does it even matter?" Mark said, his eyes empty.

He wept when his lover left him for someone younger. After that, things began to slide quickly. Mark became more and more promiscuous. Dangerously so. He wrote bad checks to hire male strippers to perform for him. I found syringes and empty boxes of Preparation H in the garbage can. I watched his gorgeous face lose all its youth. One day, overcome with anger and desperation, I screamed, "Stop this self-destruction! Mark, I love you, I understand that—"

The word cut him short. "You could never begin to *understand* me!" he shouted.

Now I was furious. "You little fag! You think it won't matter if you get sick. You think Joe and I will take care of you if you get AIDS."

Mark slapped me so hard I stumbled backward. Holding my face with one hand I ran into the kitchen and fumbled through the drawers with the other. Finding only a metal spatula, I clung to it, daring him to come near me again. He came toward me crying and begging. "Oh God, Susie, let me hold you. I'm sorry. I'm sorry."

"Why won't you stop, Mark?" I sank to the kitchen floor sobbing, shaking, needing him to be strong. But there was no strength left in him. "What will it take? What will it take, Mark?"

"My tombstone," he said, then turned and walked out of the house. His eyes no longer reflected the spirit that once lived in him.

That March, Mark tested positive for HIV.

MORNING, AUGUST 23, 1996. Mark starched and ironed his button-down shirt and put a sharp crease in his favorite gray suit pants. Mama and Daddy had flown to Alabama to visit relatives and left Mark to watch the house. Today they would arrive back in Salt Lake City, and Mark had agreed to pick them up at the airport. Mama and Daddy would arrive at 12:15 p.m. Mark would meet them at the baggage claim area at 12:30.

On that same August 23, I rose at 5:30 a.m., read from Psalms, then prayed for everyone on my prayer list, including Mark and all of our orphaned children in Haiti.

> *My life is consumed by anguish*
> *And my years by groaning;*
> *My strength fails because of my affliction,*
> *And my bones grow weak.*
> *—Psalm 31*

I prayed particularly for strength that morning because I had not slept well. I had had a nightmare about Mark. Somewhere in the darkness, demons had visited me, taunting me with images of a coffin, a cherrywood casket, to be exact, with my brother's body inside. No one knew about Mark's condition except Joe and me.

At 8:00 a.m. I made my version of an Egg McMuffin (using Egg Beaters and turkey sausage) for my sweet Joe to eat on his way to work. I washed my face, dressed, and drove to the gym. The wife of a partner of Joe's at work was having a birthday party at one of Aspen's finest eateries. I sweated on the treadmill an extra half hour so I could eat a good brunch with a glass or two of champagne. By the end of our three-hour lunch the birthday girl was sloshed, spilling an entire hundred-dollar bottle of Taittinger Rosé on the carpet. I watched the red-colored champagne seep into the soft, lush patterns in the carpet. I had drunk quite enough and was glad to ask for a ride home.

At 1:15 p.m. Mark had not shown up yet to pick up my parents, and so they called Mark's place of work, a little furniture store in downtown Salt Lake City. Mark had not been there all day, they complained and added that he'd be lucky if he still had a job if he decided to bless them with his presence later on. Daddy and Mama sat for another hour in the airport's baggage claim, waiting and fuming. My father relented and paid a cabdriver forty dollars to get home.

They arrived at the house at 3 p.m. Mark's restored '64 Thunderbird was still in the driveway. The front door was locked.

"Betty, give me the key," Daddy said when no one came to the door, "Mark's not here." The vein that always worried Mama pulsed in his forehead. "What in dad-blame Hades!"

The house was all but empty. Where the television once sat was only a vase of faded silk flowers. The VCR, the vintage stereo my father bought when they were first married—all gone. Some knickknacks were on the carpet, arranged as if in a sad effort to make the house seem less empty. Mama was shocked. Daddy was heartbroken. In the short time they were away, Mark had sold whatever was valuable for drugs.

But that wasn't all they would face.

Meanwhile, one of the girls dropped me on Main Street in front of the little Victorian "miner's shack" where Joe and I lived. I walked around back because I kept the front door locked and never carried a key. I walked through the mudroom, still tipsy, humming "Somewhere Over the Rainbow" and searching for my silly mutts. They did not come as usual to lick me and jump up and down. "All right, be that way," I mumbled, then saw Joe in the kitchen with all six dogs huddled around him. "Humph!" I said. "No wonder. Come here and kiss Mama, you little heathens!" But the dogs stayed ever so close to Joe. "Babycakes!" I said to him, flirting. "What're you doing home from work so early, anyway?" I reached to hug him. Joe did not let go when I pulled away. "Can we go out tonight? I didn't go to the market."

Joe was breathing hard and still held my arms. His face was dark and taut. He said nothing.

"Well," I babbled on, "I don't mind cooking, honey-bunny. I can go to the market now if you don't want—"

"Susie . . ." One word. My name. Joe held me slightly away from his face and very firmly. Then it hit. "Mark died."

I pulled away from him and went to the fridge. "Mark who?" I asked, my head in the refrigerator. "Do you want some juice or a soda?"

I turned around and closed the refrigerator door. Joe's eyes were wild. I had never seen that look before. "Mark who?" I repeated. Joe looked so strange. I went over and put my hand on his shoulder. "Mark *who*, honey?"

Joe fell to his knees and looked up, reaching for me. I backed away.

"Mark *who?* JOE!" I backed farther away. In a flash I went through all the last names of people we knew named Mark. My eyes grew wider and wider, my lips tightened, I felt my nostrils flaring and my veins pulsing. My breathing took on a vicious animal sound. I stared, not blinking, daring him to answer the question.

"Our Mark," Joe said, then broke down completely. He wailed, still reaching for me, begging me to come to him. My head fell back as I went down. "Mark shot himself, baby," Joe said, "he shot himself," groping to hold on to me.

I wanted to hear Joe say he was sorry. Why would he lie like that? Why would he say such a thing when it's not true?

I screamed. I clawed at my ears, those evil messengers to my head. It was as if I could hear all the demons who had ever cursed and ravaged my life. They wrapped themselves around me, a hellish shroud of horror. *Don't touch me! Don't touch my soul!* I crawled up the counter, my nails breaking against the hard wood. I pulled out drawers, dishes, glasses, knives—anything—needing to hear crashing and breaking so the sound of my heart tearing, gripping, being gripped, burning, spilling, would drown out the world and its screams; maybe then I would know if I was dead or still living. My throat tightened. Choking, I ran outside still clutching, hurling, throwing, a sound coming from inside me like a wounded dog. All that lived inside me descended, crashed, poured out, bled.

Daddy had found him. Mark lay frozen on the laundry room floor where he had just ironed his clothes. In the oven was a cake he had just baked. A note rested on the kitchen table. Mark's mouth was open and a black jelly oozed out, his eyes fixed upward. One side of his face was scarlet and blue where it rested on the carpet. Blood was all over the floor. Daddy ran and lifted him, but he was cold by then, his lips dove gray, and his eyes did not blink.

Months later I sat in church still very numb. I could feel my hands, wet and sticky. Was it tears again, or warm blood? No, no, it was the demons again, and the tears and the haunting. Every day I still saw my father when I closed my eyes. I saw him kneeling inside the laundry room, kneeling beside a bucket of pink soapy water, kneeling with a crimson-stained dishrag, scrubbing and weeping. My daddy. I had flown to Salt Lake City that same day Mark shot himself. I had to tell my father after looking at his withered hands in the bloody water that Mark had AIDS and he had better put gloves on. The blood never went away from that carpet, nor that house. Mama and Daddy had to move. Mark was gone, and though I asked God to raise him from the dead like he had done with Jesus, that miracle was not for me.

The gun Mark used was the same one Mama used to threaten us all with when we were children. I don't hold that against her— that it was still in the house. I never have. I knew Mark well enough, even through all his lying, to know he would seek a gun any way possible. On Mark's last night, while my parents were still out of town, he paid a male stripper to come over to the house and perform for him. That was the last act of affection he sought, though what false affection it was.

Mark was my best friend. When he committed suicide he took a part of my life without my permission. I can hardly speak his name today without weeping.

Chapter 16

Scooting Chairs

I DIDN'T BURY MY BROTHER in the ground because I couldn't picture Mama having to walk through the snow in the bitter Utah winters. She would always be sad, but at least she wouldn't have to be cold, too. Joe and I bought a cherrywood casket, like the one in my dream, and a drawer in an above-ground mausoleum. One of the hardest things I've ever done was look at price tags on coffins. There was no way to reconcile it in my mind: who could possibly appraise the worth of a coffin for someone you adored?

For months afterward, I was surely the sorriest person I had ever known. I existed, zombielike, doing the work Joe, Mark, and I had started. Things went from bad to worse in Haiti, too. In the mid-1990s, corruption and violence ramped up, provoked by political tension. It was common to see bodies strewn on the streets, pierced with bullets or hacked by machetes. No one who lived or traveled there was sure what would become of them. I didn't care now. I was pretty sure I'd die young too. Death had visited my own house and created a strange confidence. On the streets of Cité Soleil, and among the gang members I worked with, I was often confronted with sawed-off shotguns, revolvers, and automatic weapons such as M-16s and AK-47s. My familiar line became: "If you're gonna try and scare me, at least cock the dad-gum thing." And if they didn't, I'd just shove the gun aside and get on with business.

Joe came to Haiti with me several times in those early years. It always proved a huge emotional shock to him. He'd immerse himself in the day-to-day details, particularly of the handicapped children. Sometimes I'd see him in a quiet corner, his head in his hands, weeping. Whenever we came home, he'd be depressed for weeks, his body in Aspen, his soul far away. Once, he confessed that after a trip to Haiti it was hard for him to do simple things like go to the fridge whenever he wanted, or take a drink out of a water faucet. He began to find his niche more in the foundation's daily management from the American side. Soon he was averaging four hours a day working on foundation business, in addition to putting in a full day at the firm. Haiti felt more and more like a partnership for us. I knew Joe was in for the long haul.

When we were first married, we had decided to wait at least five years before trying to have children. After the five-year mark, the years continued to tick by without conception. A doctor's visit confirmed that medically it wasn't going to be easy for me to get pregnant. As I spent more time in Haiti, Joe and I began to think that maybe it was all for the best. Even if we could conceive our own child, with the life we led, having a child just wouldn't work. We decided to abandon the plan.

The Mercy Center soon began to be used as a schoolhouse as well as a feeding center. After children's little bellies were filled they began to ask to learn. The women of the slum community led the charge. In many ways, they hold a lot of power in Cité Soleil. Often, the fiercest gang members fear the women will cast spells on them or put curses on their families. So the women formed a coalition and asked us for books and teachers. I was thrilled.

We built walls inside the center and created classrooms. We continued serving meals to the poor children while they were taught in Creole. We hired teachers and bought books and uniforms, as is the custom in schools there. Shoes were included, since few had a full set of clothes, much less shoes.

Viximar recovered from his beating. I paid his hospital fee and the rent on his shack and asked if he was still able to work for Mercy and Sharing. I suggested a peaceful job such as director of the new school. When he questioned my ever-present sorrow, I told him about Mark. I said I didn't understand suicide and I couldn't even try to explain.

Over that next year I often spent a month at a time in Haiti. Joe was okay without me, and I felt comfortable there, fighting my battle with grief. In some ways I felt less alone in Haiti. We all were fighting some sort of battle in this place. I spent many hours on my knees, alone in my room, praying for understanding, even asking God for a miracle.

When I was little, my favorite memory verse was John 11:35 because it was short and I could not read well. The verse says simply, "Jesus wept." Christ was crying because two friends of his, Mary and Martha of Bethany, had a brother who died. Even as a child I could relate to their sadness. Now the story meant even more. Miraculously, Jesus brings the brother, Lazarus, back to life. Oh, how I wanted that. I could imagine Mark sitting up in the cherrywood casket and scaring everyone to death—except me, because I had been expecting it. Then we'd have champagne and he'd apologize for shooting himself, and I'd make him promise never to do it again. We'd clang our glasses together and toast. But when my brother stayed dead, I wasn't angry with God. In this season of intense sorrow, I found myself clinging to God more than ever.

THE PROJECT IN CITÉ Soleil soon proved less time-intensive. Our brave staff, including Viximar and eight teachers, kept vigil and did fine as leaders, and the people in the area were mostly content because Mercy and Sharing was feeding and now educating their children.

About 200 children ate at the center daily, as well as some nursing mothers, and about 125 kids came to school at the center. For the most part we were left in peace. But one day in the mid-1990s two warring gangs battled, with our little center in the middle. It was a serious fight with guns and knives and all the horror imaginable. In the end, twelve children were killed in the crossfire.

I was in Aspen when I heard what had happened and fell to my knees when I got word of the senseless, brutal tragedy. I was seldom afraid, but somehow this felt different. It was hard for any of us to articulate. A few of the children who were killed had come to our center, but not all, as there are thousands of children in Cité Soleil. In our grief, we decided to close the school and feeding program temporarily until we could ensure the safety of our staff and the children. Perhaps Cité Soleil was too unsafe after all, as we had always been told. The mothers in the area blamed the gang members and so did I. We continued to pay our staff because they were not at fault.

I flew to Haiti and sat with Viximar and his wife and five children one night before going to my room at the Visa Lodge Hotel. I had taken to staying there because the price was half the El Rancho's, and the El Rancho broke my heart with the bittersweet memories of Mark and me, mixed with the memories of children who were now gone.

"Is there another place we could try to help?" I asked. "I'm learning how to raise money and get labor and food donated. I think I can do more."

He sighed and shook his head and tried his English. "Well, Madam Susie, der is the 'ospital." With Viximar I often needed a translator.

"Hospital?" I repeated, to make sure I understood. "Okay, we can go *demen*," I said, practicing my Creole.

"*Wi*. Madam Susie, tomorrow!" he said, in half English and half Creole.

With Viximar's help, I began going regularly to the pediatric section of the public hospital in Port-au-Prince. It was a bleak, lonely place. When the wind blew and the temperature reached above 100 degrees, the smell oozing from the city morgue nearby was ominous.

The hospital was a maze of rooms and corridors. You never knew what you'd encounter. One dusty morning I brought several bags of powdered baby food and formula to the pediatric ward plus bottled water and diapers. I found one toddler, probably two or three years old, tied by both wrists to the rails of a two-by-three-foot iron crib. There was no adult in sight. The child's head was huge, perhaps four times as big as its body. I couldn't tell its gender. The head had grown so heavy with fluid that it had begun to flatten into a thick pancake. As the child rested against the hard surface of the plastic-covered slats of the crib, I calculated that the head alone weighed thirty or forty pounds. I watched the child for several minutes before our eyes met and I found the courage to caress its hideous head. Its eyes popped out from under their lids—pressure was causing them to bulge painfully. The child convulsed at my touch, then calmed as if hypnotized by something unseen. I rubbed its crusty, concave belly and stroked its tied arms. As we stared at each other I fell in love. The child, like most others in the ward, was lying in a pool of yellow diarrhea. I untied the knotted rags that bound its little hands to the rail. Viximar helped me lift the child so I could wipe away the mess from under its body. After removing a stiff cloth from around the child's groin, I discovered it was a girl. I kissed her forehead and she drifted into a deep sleep.

The little girl's face appeared in my mind all that day. She was the most frightening human being I had ever seen. For nearly a decade of my life I lived among the most beautiful women on the planet. What would it be like for that little girl to have that sort of outward beauty for just one day? I realized that I was more aware of the dark side of outward beauty now, and somehow, oddly, I felt less sorry for the little girl. If she could survive, maybe she would learn to develop beauty from within. She might recover from her sickness. I had a lifetime of being brainwashed into thinking that beauty and wealth were the keys to being loved and accepted. True, I brought much of it on myself, but I was not sure I would ever completely recover from what troubled me.

At that time I became consumed by the writings of Samuel Rutherford, an old Scottish Pastor. He spoke of God's love:

"Had I known what He was keeping for me / I should never have been so faint-hearted."

Somehow, Samuel Rutherford believed that God's love was always good, no matter what the circumstances. That unconditional, extravagant love reminded him to have courage. I was intrigued by this old man who had lived so many hundreds of years ago. His wife and two children had died, but for some reason he didn't blame or leave God. It was said that he used all his pain to be a great comforter of suffering people. He would get up at 3 a.m. daily to read and study, then spend the rest of his hours visiting the sick, praying for people, comforting them, helping them any way he could. That's what I wanted to be like.

I BEGAN TO GO to the hospital almost daily, sometimes with Viximar, sometimes alone. One evening when the heat had subsided I asked Nolette, a front desk clerk at the hotel, if I could pay her to come with me to the hospital. I had rented a car and wasn't sure I could find my way at night. I hadn't visited since the day before and wanted to bring more formula. I dared not leave large amounts because some of the bundles I left had been stolen.

Nolette was cheery and quick. At the hospital, she was very natural with the kids. I watched her as I changed the diaper of a young boy whose body was twisted and stiff with cerebral palsy. She helped me give him some water by lifting him gently so he could swallow and not choke. We kissed him good night and went on to the next child.

Suddenly we heard an unnerving sound coming from another area of the hospital. Strange sounds were common, but this was something I couldn't place. It was a long, tortured moan mixed with screaming and laughter, almost mischievous. Night had fallen and the light inside the various wards was dim. It frightened me. Nolette and I decided to investigate anyway. As we walked toward the sound I could feel eyes that had long ago adjusted to the darkness now watching me. We reached a room without a door. As my eyes adjusted I could make out a metal cage inside. A little boy with tightly cropped hair jumped up and down in the cage, swinging back and forth and gripping the bars with his hands. He was naked and his smile was full of white teeth that could be seen clearly even in the murky light. He flipped backward, laughing convulsively, clearly happy to see someone. He made me want to be happy with him. But his eerie, crazy laughter prompted another child in the room to scream. I could not see the other boy until I walked farther inside. He was older, maybe twelve or thirteen, gaunt and frail, with feet turned inward, facing each other. His lips pursed together and were cracked from thirst. *"Mwen grongou,"* he whispered to me, *I'm hungry.* I could see now that the room was filled with children, many quiet, many emaciated, all filthy.

"God," I said to Nolette. "What is this place?" She ran to get my flashlight and came back with food and water.

"Abandone," she said. "It's where sick children come when they have nobody."

We walked through the room, greeting each child, trying to touch and speak softly to each. As I shined the flashlight into a metal crib, I realized one child wasn't moving. The crib held two toddlers; one appeared to be a year or so old. He was crawling on top of the other, sticking fingers in its mouth and collapsing on top of the little bluish-black body. The body had stiffened. It was a corpse. I lifted the child that was alive and put it into the antiquated cage/crib of the naked laughing boy.

I counted seventeen children in the abandoned-children's ward. We learned later there had been maids employed to take care of the children, but they had not been paid for many months and had stopped coming. Only one maid still came, sporadically, in hopes of getting a dollar now and then. Nolette mixed water with the dry baby food and we started to feed the ones who had strength to swallow. They were all severely dehydrated and hungry. They all had soiled their bedding. Many had festering bedsores.

I picked up one child who was awake and quiet. As I lifted her there was a slight resistance. She screamed and arched her back fiercely. I caught her head in my hand to pull her to me and comfort her. My hand sank into the back of her head and ooze ran between my fingers. I gasped and looked at the metal crib. A patch of flesh and hair stuck to the metal bars. The child had been lying so long without being picked up that her sores had healed onto the metal frame. Nolette winced and I swallowed back tears so the child would not see me cry.

I decided right then that Mercy and Sharing would start a new project. If no one was looking after the abandoned-children's ward, we would. Over the next few days I visited frequently, asking all the questions I could. I hired Nolette to go to the hospital every afternoon when she got off work at the hotel to care for the children. I learned that the hospital's head nurse, a loud, bossy woman named Madam Scarasse, was in charge of everything, including the ward. It was soon clear that the doctors, nurses, and maids all feared her. Even the hospital administrator was reverent in her presence. She had important connections and was believed to be a powerful voodoo mamba. Madam Scarasse agreed to let Mercy and Sharing sponsor the ward at the hospital. We could pay for food, water, and medical care for any of the abandoned children we wanted. Any special care or surgery required would also be the responsibility of Mercy and Sharing.

Although Madam Scarasse agreed to our being there, she made it known she wasn't happy about it. I didn't like her either. But in Haiti you learn to live with imperfect work conditions. At first I tried to get along. I named the little naked boy, the one who laughed so crazily, Henri Scarasse, after Madam Scarasse. I was pretty sure she would not hurt a child named in her honor. She didn't. Of all the children, she seemed to pay some attention to him.

Others watched us closely too. Word got out that a relief organization was spilling money into the hospital, and many others hatched unseen plans. Several children in the ward died during the first month after we had discovered them. Nolette and I asked for permission to take their bodies from the morgue and bury them in the city cemetery with a little note in each coffin. The morgue keepers realized they could charge us more to find the bodies if they were hidden at the bottom of stacks of other dead children. When they told us they could not find them, it would always cost more to continue looking, so we'd give them a few extra dollars. Finally, I told them I didn't need their help, I was on to them. If I had to go look for one of my children's bodies in the morgue, I'd do it myself.

Madam Scarasse's disappointment with us increased, but for an altogether different reason: too many children were living. With the water and food and attention they now received, they were louder and more robust. This was inconvenient. One day she cornered me, looking annoyed.

"This is a hospital, not an orphanage!" she said. "I demand that you no longer feed the children. You must leave now."

"Oh, Madam Scarasse," I said, "this is wonderful!" I had had it with her. "So *you* will take care of the children in your hospital now. God bless you! This is the most wonderful news!"

Her eyes slithered from my own to one side. Mine never left the top of her nose, right between her eyes. We understood each other's sort: formidable, at the very least, a challenge to be reckoned with. I was not finished, however, and was not going to let her off the hook.

"Madam Scarasse," I continued, "I heard that the maids have not been paid in a very long time." I paused for effect. "But I know that money has been provided by the hospital administration to you, and it came from the Haitian Ministry of Health. What happened to all the money, do you suppose?"

Madam Scarasse's face was pinched, and she looked like an angry rodent. She got so close to me that I could smell her lunch and her armpits. "Get out!" she shouted. "Who are you? Nothing!

You are nothing!" She slapped the Children's Tylenol out of Nolette's hand and stomped out of the room.

I watched the bun knotted tightly on the back of her head and
her massive, arrogant buttocks till they were out of view. I turned
to Nolette. "She's pretty classy, don't you think?"

Nolette didn't smile. I could see she was worried. The feud,
Haitian-style, had begun. Perhaps I overstepped my boundaries. I
had pushed a powerful woman very far, but I didn't care. I had decided that no more of those kids would die if they didn't have to. It
was that simple. "Bring it on," I whispered as Madam Scarasse left,
and lowered my chin in determination.

Two weeks later we were still there. The abandoned-children's
ward of the pediatric unit was thriving with twenty-seven children,
much to the chagrin of Madam Scarasse. She issued a summons for
me to appear before her.

"These children cannot stay here! Do you hear me?"

I had studied municipal codes in the meantime. Haitian Social
Affairs was responsible for placing children in the abandoned ward.
It was the government's mandate to place these children into or-
phanages. I reminded Madam Scarasse of that.

"Why are you yelling at me?" I asked. "I'm only trying to make
them comfortable, clean, and fed while they're here."

Madam Scarasse's tone shifted to one of calm business. "You,
Madam Susie, have two weeks to get them out. All twenty-seven.
All out of here."

"They are your children," I said. "This is your hospital. I'm just
trying to make sure they don't starve and die from bedsores and
neglect!"

Madam Scarasse's calm was short-lived. Her nostrils widened to
the point of deformity and she stood up from behind her yellow,
cracked vinyl-top desk. I wondered if she'd put a voodoo curse on

me. "You can take care of them," she said, seething, "or I"—she coughed slightly—"will take care of them for you."

I understood what she meant. She was a woman of guile and means. She would dispose of the children, permanently, without a second thought.

"JOE, HONEY! HEY, BABY!" I forgot for several minutes why I was calling. The lines had been down for several days and we had not spoken for a week.

"Baby!" Joe shouted into the phone.

A wave of girlish passion overcame me. Oh, I missed his mouth, his hands, his eyes, his hair—oh, man, his comfort. I had purposely not thought about the things I missed because it led to other things that led to, well, the things I could not yet think about. I listened to every syllable of every word and enjoyed even the pauses when I could hear his breathing. In Aspen, I'd get close to his face at night when he was asleep and breathe in his breath when he exhaled. I pretended to do that now, with my eyes closed while he spoke to me on the phone.

"So, baby, what about you and the kids?" he said, and I opened my eyes.

"Well, honey, uh . . ." I decided for a direct approach. "Is there any way we could buy a house in Haiti for about twenty-seven children?" I fidgeted and sucked my bottom lip.

Joe was quiet for a moment. I waited. "Well, we're tight on money right now," he said. "But let's try. Maybe we can get a loan."

I was dizzy with happiness. "I love you, I love you!" We hung up and I prayed to God to get us a house—quick—and I thanked Him for Joe.

Nolette had relatives who knew people who knew people with property for sale. We found a newly constructed house in the Delmas area. The price was listed at $80,000 "American," but when they saw my white face the price jumped to a nonnegotiable $100,000. It was the only suitable place I had seen. It had many rooms that could comfortably house twenty-seven kids. After multiple layers of fees and taxes, Mercy House became ours. Nolette agreed to leave her hotel job and work full-time at Mercy House for a 10 percent salary increase. We hired several others, all with children of their own, to be house mothers for my new family of children.

One bright afternoon we moved all the children from the Abandoned Care Ward to their new house, carload by carload. Finally we were all home. Nolette began to sing a made-up song, "Hallelujah, Hallelujah." She sang it over and over. The children shouted and laughed along with her. The ones that were able to grabbed her hands and danced. They ate a hearty dinner of dried meat and carrots and rice with bean sauce. The babies sucked their bottles and gazed like little lambs at their new mothers' faces and cuddled hard against the soft cushions in the padded cribs before drifting into sleep.

After we moved all the children out, I sweet-talked Madam Scarasse into letting us still come by the hospital to take care of kids. She must have been moved by a Hand greater than mine, because she relented. Today Mercy and Sharing still sponsors and supports a room at the public hospital in Port-au-Prince, which averages eighteen to twenty-four newly orphaned or abandoned infants. Children are frequently abandoned at the unit, or are moved from the unit, so the number of children at any one time varies. These children are made as healthy as possible and eventually moved to our orphanages, where their care continues.

There was a lot we didn't know about running an orphanage at

first. Nolette and I thought we had planned for everything: cook-
ware, bottles, utensils, beds, cribs, sheets, towels, diapers, soaps, lo-
tions, potions, medicines, and toys. Neither of us had children of
our own. We hired a trained nurse because so many of the children
required medical care.

I had been in Haiti almost a month. It was time to return to
Aspen. I missed Joe and I needed to raise money to pay the salaries
and the other expenses that had now become regular.

The first call I got from Nolette was hysterical. "Oh, Madam
Susie . . . the children, they pee-pee and ca-ca everywhere." She
started to cry. "They are like animals!"

This was something we hadn't thought of. "Okay, listen to me,"
I said. "I have to stay in the U.S. to raise money, Nolette. You've got
to get them potty-trained. That's got to be the first thing."

When I returned to Haiti, after having had marginal success raising money, I walked through the solid iron security gate and heard
the kind of noise children make only when they are content. An old
nurse waved to me from the second floor, holding a child in one
arm and a flyswatter in the other hand. Madam Jeanette was cooking something in the kitchen. The aroma reminded me of an Alabama breakfast. Nolette came from the dining area, having set the
two long wooden tables with a red-and-white checkered tablecloth.
She gave me the customary cheek kisses, which I returned. Her face
was moist with sweat and she fanned herself with a dish towel.

"It looks amazing, ladies!" I said very loudly over the din of children's noise. I was about to add "fabulous job" when a thunderous
sound broke above our heads. Loud and constant, it grew closer and
louder, like a massive piece of equipment moving across the upstairs
part of the house. I panicked. "The children!" I yelled, and ran
through the kitchen and up the stairs, Nolette on my heels.

When we reached the top of the stairs it was all I could do to keep from bursting out laughing. Samuel (we found out he was about fourteen) was standing in poofy pantaloons, wobbling back and forth behind a herd of children, all sitting on plastic potty chairs. His thin, crooked legs bowed outward as he stood holding a water gun and smiling mischievously at us.

"They are all in line," Samuel said. "They all scoot forward to see you."

More than a dozen toddlers were scooting toward me, faces full of concentration and determination. They scraped and screeched across the floor. Four mothers stood, one in each corner of the room, trying not to laugh. The children held tightly to their potty chairs with both hands, their little brows arched in excitement, some with tongues pressed against their chins, and others giggling wildly.

"What's going—" I started to say.

"Oh, Madam Susie! *Bonjou!*" the head mother shouted over the noise. "I am sorry, but they heard you come in! They got excited and wanted to see you."

Nolette explained they had decided to use peer pressure to make the potty training go more quickly. She made a strict rule that once the children got up in the morning and sat down on their potties, no one could get up until everyone had done number one and number two. The children didn't get up because not all were finished yet.

"That's a great idea!" I said. Then I went around kissing every forehead and getting sloppy wet kisses from all the kids.

"Has anyone not finished yet?" I asked. Four or five shook their heads. "Okay, let us know when you do, so we can all go have breakfast." I turned and grinned at Nolette and the head mother. The children scooted their potties back.

Our orphanage work had officially begun.

Chapter 17

Debacle

SOME VALUE PHILANTHROPY.
Some don't.

Word spread in the area surrounding our new orphanage: The crazy blanc woman would take all the "cursed" children. What did she do with them? Rumors abounded. But some saw what we were doing as hopeful.

One morning before dawn, while I was staying at the orphanage, I was wakened by a woman's wail, her voice mingling with the moans and shouts of other men and women. The sounds of human agony intensified as the mob reached the gates of my children's home. The house mothers came out of their rooms with furrowed brows, clutching their nightgowns and trying to understand the commotion.

Then we heard the heavy clanging of metal on metal. The front gates to the compound were being battered. I rushed down the stairs and through the entryway. Outside, the tall metal security gate was under siege as our elderly guard tried to fight a bevy of hands and arms over the top of the gate.

"No! Madam! No!" the guard shouted, as I loosened the chain. I wanted to talk to the crowd and see if someone had been injured.

A young woman fought to run away, kicking and cursing at a young man struggling to hold her. Another young man, who may have been her partner or husband, sobbed and spoke into her ear, trying to comfort her with trembling fingers. A very old woman held a bundle of towels. She spoke to the crying woman and glared at the crowd, silencing most, then thrust the bundle through the gate. The young woman broke free from the grip of her aggressor and ran, wailing, never looking back.

The bundle held a newborn child. It made tiny crying gasps. Our old nurse pulled the towel back. The baby had an extreme cleft lip and palate, taking up most of its face.

Slowly I pieced together what had happened. Witch doctors and voodoo priests often use the power of fear to extract money from the poor in order to lift a "curse," such as a deformed child. A cleft palate is always tough for a priest or witch doctor to "cure," so the girl was probably being pressured to dispose of her baby. The mother wouldn't throw the child in the canal, the oft-recommended method, but brought it to our orphanage instead, a hard enough decision. Opinions were divided in the crowd as to what she should have done.

Our old nurse was unruffled by "curses" and set about taking care of the child. I had slept fitfully the night before and returned to my bed to sleep until the sun rose. We now had forty-seven children and a flurry of daily crises, so situations like this were not unusual. When I woke again and asked about the child, everything appeared normal. I asked if the baby was a boy or a girl and got the singular answer *Wi*—Creole for *yes*. I wasn't sure I heard correctly, but I needed to rush off to some type of government meeting, so I did not question the response further.

When I returned I asked again about the baby's gender, wanting to give the child a name. Our nurse's hand slowly went to her mouth and then to her head of tightly braided cornrows. She looked up at me as if her entire future rested on the accuracy of her answer. At this point I was thinking, Either I have got to get a full-time interpreter because my Creole is really awful, or this woman may be short of a full deck. The nurse slowly pulled back the little sticky tape on one side of the baby's diaper. My mouth fell open.

The poor little baby had everything—or both. This poor child had an entire suite of deformities: the appearance of both sexes, as well as a cleft lip and palate. We decided to call her Pat.

After testing, we later found out the birth defect has a name, cloacal exstrophy, or ambiguous genitalia. We fell, inch by inch, in love with her. She had a deep effect on us all, the child who gave "special" a new meaning. Pat was eventually adopted. Her new family called her Patricia. It is a little girl's name, because her chromosomes indicated she was female. Today Patricia is so pretty and loves all things girlish. Her success as a person makes her an angel and a hero in our eyes.

Most of the children in our home came to us with wrecked little bodies. Some had extra fingers or cleft palates. Others were stiff and paralyzed by cerebral palsy or spinal injuries. So many were mentally retarded, it broke my heart. Often the children had been abandoned at the government hospital or their mothers had died in childbirth. Rarely did anyone claim an imperfect child.

Joe, thinking of our liability, urged me to go to the embassy and find out what we needed to do to become a licensed orphanage. The process began. One day I was heading to an office called

IBESR (Institut du Bien Être Social et de Recherches)—a branch of the Haitian Social Affairs Ministry—to apply for an orphanage license. For anyone running an orphanage in Haiti, IBESR is an extremely powerful agency. They are responsible for accrediting all adoption agencies and orphanages in the country. They also provide or deny all authorization to adopt. As I was preparing to leave, Samuel squirted me with his water pistol and Henri Scarasse (the little boy named after Madam Scarasse) crawled on his knees, chasing me, as I went to each room to say good-bye and get hugs and kisses and my hair pulled.

I have learned that government agencies in Haiti relish inflexible policies. The ladies behind the counter at the IBESR building sat fanning themselves.

"*Bonswa*," I said, "I'd like to apply for an orphanage license."

They stared blankly at me, as if I had asked if there was indeed life on Mars, and if so, what religion did Martians practice.

"You cannot come in without an appointment," said one worker.

"Certainly," I said. "May I make an appointment?"

"No," said another. She wore bright orange lipstick and chipped nail polish. "You must call for an appointment."

I took a deep breath and let the air out, slowly looking at my shoes. "Do you think I could just make the appointment now," I asked politely, "while I'm here?"

"Nooooo, Madam," came the reply. "We have protocol."

I decided to cave early. "Okay, may I have a card with the correct number to call to make an appointment?" The fingers with the chipped nails grabbed a pencil and wrote several numbers all beginning with the same prefix and ending with a different single digit.

Later, when I tried to phone, none of the numbers worked. I went back the next day and was given an appointment for the following month.

Joe and I sold shares we owned in an Aspen restaurant, and I sent letters to everyone at church and in my address book politely asking for money. I sent pictures of the children with the requests, and friends and neighbors gave. I felt relieved. Joe applied for charitable status so those who gave money would receive a tax deduction for their gift.

The *Aspen Times* did a story in their weekend edition about the children at our Mercy House in Haiti. That story led to another in *The Denver Post*, which led to another story that would change just about everything.

I WENT BACK AND FORTH between Aspen and Haiti. A full year passed before I got my license to run an orphanage in Haiti. I continued to work at the government hospital and got a one-sided contract that allowed me to use a large room behind the pediatric unit to take care of all the abandoned children. Madam Scarasse allowed me to hire eight women (chosen by the hospital) to take care of the children abandoned or orphaned at the hospital.

Mercy and Sharing provided food, diapers, mattresses, bedding, milk, formula, water, and a stove and refrigerator. We built cabinets with locks so supplies would not be stolen and sold. We cleaned and painted and installed ceiling fans.

But, as I said, not everyone appreciates philanthropy.

One day I dropped in unexpectedly and noticed that several of the smallest babies I had brought clothes for the day before were missing.

"Where are the three children that were here yesterday?" I asked my staff.

"*Morte*," came the sullen reply.

"Dead!" I shouted. "They weren't sick. They were healthy newborns!"

The women continued shuffling around the room, busying themselves. "Show me the death certificates!" I demanded.

"Oh, the certificates are not prepared yet," said one.

I marched furiously down the dusty alley behind the hospital to the morgue.

"Where are the bodies of the three infants who were delivered this morning from the abandoned-baby ward?" I asked. "I want to see them."

The men stank of death and had brown and red stains on their ragged clothing.

"No babies," said one. "None here for at least three days." He showed me the register. I believed him. The morgue workers made money from me only if they could produce the babies' bodies. I'd purchase three coffins from them, which they knew.

Distressed, I walked slowly back to the abandoned-baby ward. When the staff saw me enter the door they scurried away. I called everyone to stand before me.

"Where are those babies?" I asked, restraining my voice to appear calm.

None of them looked up. No one said a word.

I went to Madam Scarasse's air-conditioned office. I looked through the glass window that separated her domain from the pediatric unit and noticed in the far corner a pile of clothes I had brought the day before for the three babies. I recognized the clothes instantly: they were given to me by a girlfriend in Aspen whose child had outgrown them. I was livid. For a moment I wondered if it would be more sensible to calm myself, pray about this, then talk to Madam Scarasse tomorrow. Fervor got the best of me and I flung open her door. She sipped a bottle of water I was sure came from my children's refrigerator. I wanted to grab it from her manicured fingers and pour it on her head.

"Madam Scarasse," I said, "I want to know where the three newborn babies from the abandoned-baby ward are."

"Susie. Poor Madam Susie," she purred. "Didn't your staff tell you? They are dead."

"They are not in the morgue." I was seething and my throat burned.

Madam Scarasse stood up behind her desk with an arrogant, lazy effort. I looked at her bracelets and rings and knew her monthly salary could not support the clinking chains. She was a scoundrel, and a scoundrel with the power to make children disappear.

"*Bonswa*, Madam Krabacher," she said, her voice flat. It was a command to leave.

What could I do? I left without knowing what happened to those children, but I was determined to find out. I began to watch and observe more closely. When I was not in Haiti, Nolette would go to the ward to deliver supplies and food. We were not allowed to dispense medicine to the children, yet when the children were very, very sick we would beg one of the hospital's staff doctors to examine the children and administer medicine that we paid for. I started to see a pattern.

All children in the ward were tested for long-term problems such as heart defects or AIDS. The children whose tests revealed serious diseases never seemed to disappear. It was healthy children whose faces were missing.

Slowly I got the picture: healthy children are one of Haiti's greatest exports. There are many good and reputable orphanages in Haiti. But there are also many that are not. These orphanages spring up like mushrooms overnight, aiming to collect high fees from selling healthy babies, especially those with light skin and good features.

International adoptions are seldom easy. There are many people who spend enormous amounts of time navigating the legal procedures necessary for an adoption process. Legitimate adoption agencies set up safeguards to ensure the children's well-being—many protective measures are in place so children can't be "sold." Still, it happens. The average cost for a child on the Haitian black market is $20,000 (or more). And where do orphanages who smuggle children get them? A good place to start, of course, is the "free" government hospital. Who wouldn't pay for a nice, healthy, adoptable infant? Everyone gets a cut. Everyone, including the hospital, cooks the books and makes a little money on the side.

I was staying at the Visa Lodge when I figured it all out. My room at the orphanage had become a room for children contagious with TB. I sat at the bar and ordered a bottle of Chilean white wine. A scholarly-looking man with a grayish-brown beard and eyes that looked like they had seen many years of hard drinking and hangovers smiled at me and lifted his glass of whiskey. He cleared his throat. "I'm here taking photographs for a Canadian newspaper," he said. "I understand you run an orphanage." He slid a business card toward me on the bar. "I'd love to do a humanitarian story while I'm here."

I was hesitant, unsure of his motives.

"Maybe I could just follow you around for a day and take some pictures of the children," he said. "It might cause people to want to help them."

I knew that could be true.

We met in the lobby the next morning and went to the orphanage. The children were eating oatmeal with milk for breakfast. The ones who could not feed themselves were being fed by the house mothers.

The man's name was Laurence Fiende. He was a freelance photographer, well known in Europe. He seemed strongly affected by the sight of so many children with defects and handicaps. Watching them, knowing their progress, I was so proud of them. Henri Scarasse was learning to walk. His knees were deeply callused from his years of using them to get around. We had bought leg braces for the children whom our doctor said would benefit from them. They all hated the braces. (Henri often hid his from the staff.) But the supports were helping many of the children. Henri showed off by taking a few steps without falling. Laurence smiled sincerely. Henri giggled, and I laughed with him.

Laurence photographed Samuel sitting with his water pistol in his lap beside the old guard in front of the house. He photographed the children who couldn't walk or sit up lying outside on mats in the shade of an old knotted and twisted tree. The tree reminded me of my children—a beautiful tree.

Next we toured the hospital and abandoned-baby ward. I was still angry with the staff there, but that was not Laurence's business, so I did not show my anger. One employee, named Yvette, took my hand and looked at me apologetically. She cupped her hand over my ear and whispered, "Jerry, he dead."

"Why? I just saw him yesterday!" I had washed the little boy and changed his diaper. Jerry was retarded and emaciated when he was abandoned in front of the hospital. He appeared to be about five years old and could not walk or stand. He was still very thin and small for his age but he had gained his appetite back and seemed to be improving.

I went to the morgue, Laurence following close behind. Jerry's body lay in the hallway of the morgue. Laurence held his hand over his nose, his eyes red and moist and the wrinkles in his forehead visibly deeper.

I bent down to look at the little body. Just the day before, I had held Jerry. He wore the same diaper I had put on him, but his clothes were gone. I noticed dried blood on his abdomen and pulled the diaper back an inch. It looked like an incision. It had not been there the day before when I diapered him. My mind raced, trying to explain the blood. Sometime later I would learn that Jerry had been killed so his organs could be harvested and sold on the black market. But I had no understanding of this then, no fury yet, only confusion and sadness.

The metal doors opened, and the man I knew with the rubber fishing boots appeared. I asked many questions, but he seemed not to understand. He spoke to me loudly in Creole, waving his hands, clearly aggravated by my insistence. I asked if Jerry's body could be prepared for me for burial, told the man I would return with clothes for the boy, and paid him. Laurence and I watched as the man lifted Jerry by one arm and dragged his sagging body away like a rag doll. That image will be forever in my mind. I turned and met the flash of Laurence's camera. I wondered if he could feel it, the evil that lived inside this place, or perhaps he was shielded from it behind his camera lens. But I am no stranger to it. *I know you're here, Devil.*

Laurence followed me for two more days before returning to his home in France. We lost another baby, Jimmy, the following day, and again went to the morgue. Nolette and I buried the two children in the Port-au-Prince cemetery that week. I wrote notes for each coffin. As I knelt to pray and place the notes in their tiny hands, my knees were pierced by a sharp object. I looked closer. It was a bone. With my hands, I dug into the dirt that had been removed to dig the graves. There were many bones and fragments of rotting clothing. The cemetery workers had dug up someone else to resell the grave! I stood and walked to the grave diggers, leaning on their shovels. I had paid seventy-five dollars for the cemetery plots.

"How much will it cost to leave the bodies in the grave and not resell the space?" I asked.

For another seventy-five dollars I was guaranteed that the bodies would not be moved. I paid.

I HAD MADE MADAM Scarasse angry.

Another little baby, a boy, was brought to the ward. His mother had died giving birth. He was a month premature and mourned his mother and would not eat. I carried him for hours inside my shirt against my bare skin so he could hear my heart and be comforted by the sound. I was in love, head over heels.

Madam Scarasse observed all this. She and her nurses made jokes and cursed. But the baby grew strong and healthy. I named him David, after the soulful, musical king in the Bible.

All too quickly, I needed to return to Aspen. Nolette drove me to the airport. In Miami, I called Nolette to ask how the children were, missing my little King David already.

"Madam Susie," she said, "I am frightened that Madam Scarasse is going to do something terrible. When I got back to the hospital after taking you to the airport I found a piece of white tape wrapped around David's wrist. On the tape was written 'Madam Scarasse.'"

I was frightened now too. And angry. "Nolette," I said, "tell her that if she touches that baby"—I closed my eyes and thought of all the ways Madam Scarasse could be punished—"I'll make sure she regrets it."

My boldness made Nolette more angry than frightened. The braveness of a mother lion grew in her. She cut the tape from David's tiny wrist and threw it in the head nurse's face. But that night Nolette received a phone call at her home. On the other end was a woman's voice, and steely. All it said was: "Do you like the little boy, David?"

Then the line went dead.

Early in the morning Nolette raced to the hospital. She stopped to kiss Martin, a little boy with a very big head who had been in the abandoned-baby ward for many months. Martin always smiled and was learning his ABCs in English. But this morning he did not smile. He rocked in his little plastic chair and pointed with one hand, nervously rubbing his large head with the other. Nolette tried to pacify him with some water in a bottle. Martin pushed it away, crying. He pointed at the trash bin and rocked violently now in his chair. Nolette walked to the bin. Lying on top of the pile of trash was an open box of rat poison. Martin stopped crying and pointed to David's crib, in the opposite corner of the room. She looked at Martin and down through the rows of sleeping children. Her heart pounded in her chest as she walked toward David's crib. He lay on his back, milky pink foam spilled from his lips, his bottle half empty beside him.

David was dead.

As Nolette walked out of the ward that day, she saw Madam Scarasse. She was standing behind the glass door of our little abandoned-baby ward, arms crossed over her thick chest. She was smiling.

In Aspen I sat in a chair, hands folded in my lap, and watched the snow fall. Crying only hurt, and I hurt too much already. I wondered what it would have been like to have David and to raise the boy. He would not have died if he had lived with me. Tears now fell with the quiet snow.

MONTHS PASSED. LAURENCE CALLED to say a German magazine called *Stern* wanted to publish the photos he had taken while following me in Haiti. It was a reputable magazine, he assured me, and they wanted to interview me as well. I agreed.

The pictures Laurence had taken pulled no punches. They were almost unbearable to look at. But they brought attention to the plight of abandoned children in Haiti. The *Stern* article was published, and the German people began to offer donations to help the children, which I gladly and gratefully accepted.

We were able to buy a truck and hire another nurse as well as buy a generator so we could have electricity during most of the day. It was a treat to be able to run the refrigerator all the time, and the children loved having their drinks cold. I enjoyed the electric fan the most.

The *Stern* article turned into a blessing for Mercy and Sharing's children. But lurking in the shadows was the type of trouble that often follows a time of great blessing.

On my next trip to Haiti I noticed a European-looking man watching me furtively. If I went to the hotel restaurant he appeared at a nearby table. If I went to the bar he showed up on a nearby stool. After several of these annoying coincidences the man came to where I stood by the front desk trying to place a call. He leaned casually, his legs crossed and his elbow on the counter, within hearing range. He was too close.

"Do you need to use the phone?" I asked, not hiding my agitation.

"No," he said, and did not leave.

He smoothed his thinning hair and rested his chin in his palm as if to make himself more comfortable. I hung up the phone and abandoned the call. He followed me.

"Is there something you want?" I turned back to him.

"No, I just want to watch you," he smirked.

I put my hands on my hips and looked at him incredulously. I didn't know whether to scream or deck him.

He spoke first: "Aren't you the lady with the orphanage?"

"Look—who are you and what do you want?" I demanded.

"I'm a journalist," was all he said. No business card. No name.

"Whatever," I said, and left him. "I'm late for an appointment." And I was.

He followed.

In the hotel's restaurant, a Haitian businessman named Allain Thibodeaux waited for me. I was meeting with him to see if he could help me start another school and an adoption program. Mercy and Sharing was growing and I needed help on the ground in Haiti.

The nameless journalist sat down one table away. As I spoke in low tones about the children and adoptions and schools, I caught a glimpse of the man straining forward with something in his hand. I did not turn around. I leaned closer to Mr. Thibodeaux and whispered: "The man sitting at the table to the left of us . . . what's he holding in his hand?"

"Looks as if it's a microphone," Allain said.

That was the final straw. I stood up, indignant, and strode to the journalist. "What do you think you're doing?" I said. He smiled cunningly and sat back in his chair without answering.

I couldn't get a word out of him.

Two days passed and I did not see the man again. I went to the orphanage to deliver medicine our nurse had asked for. Nolette followed me up the stairs chattering excitedly. The children were lying on mats in the long, wide hall, where the breeze and the fans blew the flies away.

"What did you say?" I was paying attention to her now. "What friends?"

"Two blanc men with cameras," Nolette said, now looking at me nervously. "Your friends! They said they were your friends."

I stared at her in confusion. "Nolette, start over. What men with cameras? I don't know what you're talking about."

The story came out. Earlier, two men told our guard and Nolette that they were friends of mine and I had asked them to photograph the children. It was a complete lie. I knew nothing good would come of it.

In less than a week pictures of my children lying frightened, twisted, and crying on the floor were published in a rival magazine of *Stern*'s. The men had pulled the children from their mats and made them cry, then snapped photos. The captions underneath implied that we had neglected the children. It did not mention that the children were handicapped and in many cases near death when we found them abandoned. They did not photograph any healthy children at the orphanage. They photographed our medicine cabinets and zoomed in on expiration dates and said I had withheld medicine from the children and it had not been used before it expired. They did not mention that this particular batch of medicine had been donated once it had already expired, and was still good anyway.

Why don't you just quit? You can't save the world. Don't you think you've done enough? I listened to some of my friends who watched me grow depressed. I returned to Aspen and stared at the carpet for several days. I began calling a certain old chair "the sad chair" because that's where I sat when I was sad and all of the dogs could fit in it with me. We were sad together and I was not alone.

In the end, the credibility of our organization was vindicated. *Stern* magazine did another story on us and validated their first article. A team from Zolcer TV, a station in Germany, saw the *Stern* article and wanted to do a documentary. They did, filmed in Aspen and Haiti, and documented the same conditions as the *Stern* articles and the same level of care. Their documentary ultimately proved the *Stern* articles were accurate, but not before damage had been done and donations from Germany dropped off.

Some value philanthropy.

Some don't.

Chapter 18

A Day Without Anvils

To do any serious work in Haiti requires endurance. Weeks stretch into months, and months stretch into what feels like timelessness. The same problems creep up again and again, from different sources, taunting, acidic, threatening to destroy us.

For all I knew it was just another average day at the abandoned-baby ward, but then Madam Scarasse cornered me, fury in her face.

"I have decided you must all leave," Madam Scarasse said. "This is not an orphanage. There are too many children here. You must get out, now!"

I looked around the ward. Again, the only children I could see were handicapped and terminally ill. No healthy children were in sight—they always disappeared. Some practices—however horrible, however protested—you learn to accept so you can continue doing the good you're able to do. I knew Madam Scarasse wanted all the sick kids out so she could clear more space for her healthy-children trade. If we didn't get them out, she would dispose of them her way, as she had done with others. But we were currently at full capacity at the orphanage.

"We'll leave," I told her. "But you must give me time. I need two months—at least."

Her eyebrows lowered. "You can have time, but we cannot wait two whole months." She stormed away.

I had to fight off discouragement with a club. Expanding the orphanage was no easy task. Due to cultural beliefs, it had proved difficult to find employees who wanted to care for sick children, even when jobs were so scarce in Haiti. Sick children were believed to be possessed by the devil, or cursed. I respect other cultures. But this cultural belief raises a problem. It is completely unacceptable for me to allow anyone to treat my children like pieces of furniture simply because they're born different.

Once I threw a holiday party at the orphanage. I hired women in the area to prepare the Haitian food I knew my employees and kids liked very much, and proudly scooped mounds of peas, rice, bread, and seasoned chicken onto plates myself. But most of the employees would not touch the food. I had served it on the same plates the children used. Several got up from the table and left without touching the meal. The children and I had an extra-nice feast that day ourselves.

Good help was always hard to find, particularly since I wasn't around all the time to oversee daily operations. Since most of our children were either terminally ill or handicapped, we needed round-the-clock nurses, or "house mothers," in the orphanage. We needed constant help to feed and clean the children, administer medicines, and plan their days. The children blossomed under loving care. At our orphanage they began to smile and laugh more.

Nearly all adored being hugged. But not all our employees fully understood what we were trying to do. I fired nearly all the staff positions at least once before finding women who would not hit the children or yell at them. Even then, turnover was almost constant.

At times the orphanage was unbearably crowded. After Madam Scarasse threw down her ultimatum, Joe and I searched for a bigger place for the children to live. They were growing, and now we needed somewhere to put those left behind in the abandoned ward. I lived in constant fear of what Madam Scarasse would do in her wrath.

It was hard to talk to Joe about money all the time. We needed so many things—and Joe heard about most of the requests. We always had plenty of clothes—everyone gave us used clothes. But finding medicines at a reasonable cost was much harder. Government red tape made it hard for medical donations to come into the country. Embargoes made food expensive, and we had hundreds of hungry mouths because of the feeding center. We needed vehicles to take the orphanage children to school and therapy appointments and to purchase supplies.

Problems compounded. Disease flourishes in Haiti, and I was not immune. After one particularly rainy season I contracted dengue fever, probably from the bite of an infected mosquito. For two weeks my fever raged past 104, my head felt like it was in a vise, I had nausea and severe vomiting, and my body hurt straight through my bones. Recovery stretched into months. I felt tired all the time. Maybe even depressed.

I'd often return from Haiti with undiagnosed illnesses—severe fevers, viselike headaches, nausea, puking, lack of energy—just a general feeling of sickness that could last for weeks. Once I was positive I had a tapeworm. I named him Wally, just to keep my spirits up, and was so relieved, strangely enough, when a coworker contracted the same symptoms. I knew then it was only a virus.

Keeping clean in Haiti was always hard. From my constant contact with sick children and germ-infested places, I contracted lice, scabies, and mange, an unsightly and painful rash caused by burrowing mites. What helped me continue the work were a few key staff members, such as Viximar and Joe, and prayer.

More attacks came. One by one, month after month, the sky rained down a thousand anvils on us, season after season. About the time Madam Scarasse told us we needed to vacate the ward, the director of IBESR was replaced by the most dreadful woman I have ever known. Oh, how I wished she were even as kind as Madam Scarasse. I was summoned from Aspen to her office.

"Your orphanage license will not be renewed," was the first announcement out of the new director's mouth. Her massive frame hulked behind a metal desk. I stood in front of her like a schoolgirl in trouble with the principal. The new director did not offer me a seat. From her chin grew four long hairs. On her desk was a nameplate carved from wood and painted in puerile brightness. It read Sherlie A. Mire.

"What? Why?" I withered, searching for some place to land.

"Madam *Susie*," said Madam Mire, "I have heard you are very difficult." She used my first name condescendingly, as Madam Scarasse had grown accustomed to doing. I watched her inhale, simmering with pleasure at my fresh need. I had felt unwell for several days and had another fever and the shakes. Surrounded by the aura of my new tormentor, I could taste bile on the top of my tongue. I knew I would throw up soon.

"Could I have some water?" I said, feeling a chill. "I don't feel very well."

"It is all gone," said the director.

I sucked in my lower lip and studied her crankiness. I decided to press on with business. "Why can't I have my license renewed?" I said it bleakly, looking around for a wastepaper basket. I was going to hurl any minute.

"Because you have two sorts of children in one house." On her desk was a bottle of water. She unscrewed the cap and gulped several large swallows. "You have normal children and handicapped. They cannot be together in one house! It is not allowed!" Her fist banged her desk as she said the last word, awakening my every raw nerve.

Madam Mire lifted herself from the chair and turned her back. Her oversized buttocks clenched together, held in place by an unforgiving stretch of spandex. Still with her back to me, she spoke: "You must separate them immediately or we will have to remove the normal ones from your care!"

I was too weak to brawl. "But we only have one house."

"Buy another." She held the orphanage license in one hand, toying with the phone cord in her other. "I will not give you a new license until you do."

Perhaps it was my fever talking, but I decided to play diplomatically. We were women of mutual interest, weren't we? I placed my hand on top of her wrist; my fingers brushed the license. My voice grew stronger, but softened slightly.

"Madam Mire, I know you care about the children as much as I do," I said. "Maybe we could talk over lunch."

Madam Mire glared at me. She huffed. "You can take me to dinner at Chez Gerard restaurant," she said. "Take me tomorrow night."

When the elite rich want to eat out, Chez Gerard is where they go. That was fine; I needed Madam Mire to be reasonable. I needed that license now, and I needed time to raise money and find more space for the children.

Madam Mire was an hour and forty-five minutes late. She appeared with two hefty bodyguards and four other men she introduced as "cousins." I moved myself from the small table for two I had reserved, and arranged another table for eight. The cousins and bodyguards ordered cocktails immediately. As an afterthought, they ordered a bottle of champagne. Then another. Orders began to fly: appetizers, soup course, cocktails, salads, cocktails, entrées, cocktails, coffees, desserts, cocktails, more desserts. . . .

About halfway through the feast, Madam Mire announced that if I wanted to talk to her for the rest of the evening I must speak only French. I explained I spoke little French and was embarrassed by my poor command of Creole. She laughed loudly, shouted something down to the opposite end of the table in French, and everybody laughed raucously. Madam Mire spoke French anyway, and made one of the cousins translate for her. She said only one thing more: that she did not wish to discuss any business-related matters, and then sunk her face into a large plate of *tassot* (fried beef chunks). I could not get another word out of her for the rest of the evening. Her silence was small comfort. The dinner finally over, she stomped away from the table, her entourage following like a fox's tail. The waiter presented me with the bill, a bemused smile on his face. Still sick, I had eaten only soup. In Haitian value, the dinner cost about two years' wages. So much for diplomacy.

Two months passed. Madam Scarasse scowled and shuffled, but in the end agreed to extend our deadline. Her eyes brightened when I mentioned we were working hard to raise money. That magic word *money*—even the mention of its proximity could sometimes open doors.

Every moment I spent in Aspen, I worked on fund-raising. I sent out letters by the truckload. Cold-calling newspapers and radio stations came next, to see if they would talk about our work in Haiti. Most journalists were skeptical at first. They wanted to know about my background and what my interest was in Haiti. The mention of *Playboy* proved another door opener. I was reluctant to talk about it, but found my phone calls with media sources ended quickly without it. The centerfold days offered a unique hook: Why would a woman who once experienced so much opulence now spend all her time in a land of squalor? Over and over I honed my skill of diverting the attention and message back to the plight of the Haitian children, saying, "And it's so close to the United States—how can we ignore their need for help!"

Meanwhile, Joe and I located an orphanage compound in Haiti built several years earlier with funds from USAID (United States Agency for International Development). The compound now sat empty for lack of money to operate it. With money we raised and more of our own, we bought the site. The compound was in bad repair but spacious—five buildings in all—with wonderful potential.

I had never seen Madam Scarasse happier than the day we moved out. We weren't out of her hair completely; we were still allowed to come by and look after the really sick children. But in her eyes, our time with her would be limited. We moved all the children from our existing facility and separated the healthy children from the handicapped and sick children, just as Madam Mire had requested so eloquently. We started a school and small clinic in two of the extra compound buildings. Madam Mire scowled as she issued a new license to us. Maybe the expensive dinner had softened her after all. We were not leaving our calling, and I began to feel stronger and happy again. We turned the old orphanage into a hospital, since the one I had tried to build with Maude Silverice turned to disaster, and I knew firsthand the need for financially accessible medical care in the country.

For a short time, all felt right with the world. But in this season of raining anvils, the sky had only cleared for a spell.

THOUGH BY NOW I had been in Haiti for years, my naïveté lingered. My belief in basing decisions on trust was a habit not easily shaken. Time and time again it proved a mistake that tripled and spawned and devoured the trust.

Allain Thibodeaux, the businessman I had interviewed earlier for information on how to run things in Haiti, was made Haitian director of Mercy and Sharing. He was a good man who knew how to get things done and proved it to me several times. Had I investigated further I would have heard that among locals he had a reputation of a *vagabond*. I had heard the word in passing but dismissed it as harmless murmuring. A vagabond? He certainly didn't seem like a railway tramp. He was well dressed, polished, and polite. How I wish I'd known that *vagabond* is the Haitian term for *con man*.

It took a while for Allain Thibodeaux to show his true colors. Meanwhile, the woman who sold us the property for the orphanage compound, Poupon Pacaud, felt very bad and even wept from embarrassment when the title to the land turned out to be questionable. She could not bear to see us suffer or become discouraged, she said, so she offered to help run our orphanages and the schools to help us out. She had a foundation of her own and had ongoing support from USAID, which lent her credibility. She drove one of the nicest vehicles I had seen in Haiti and bragged that USAID paid all expenses for her relief agency, including the cost of her lovely SUV.

Astonished and impressed, I asked what I could do to get financial support from USAID as well. Mercy and Sharing now cared for more than a thousand children in our schools and orphanages, and our budget was low for the number of children. Money was always a concern. Haiti was becoming increasingly violent, and I ran into difficulty raising money in the States. Americans often asked me why we should help a country that didn't help itself.

"It's a more complex situation," became my standard reply, hopefully sounding polite yet firm. "Besides, the children are innocent." I had been an innocent child once and knew I didn't deserve the severe punishment I received. Now, as an adult, I deeply felt the Haitian children's plight.

Poupon kindly offered to help navigate the months it would take for us to obtain Non-Governmental Organization (NGO) status—for a small fee, of course. The new status would allow Mercy and Sharing to apply for USAID funding and to ship food and supplies into Haiti tax-free in most cases. I was nothing but happy.

Poupon dug in, and we began to pay her a part-time salary. She told me confidentially she would soon close her own offices and would be interested in working for Mercy and Sharing permanently. Her husband, Rodney, was also in need of a job. On her recommendation, we hired them both. The husband was crass and, as I realized a few months after hiring him, violent. One day Poupon showed up at the compound with a black eye. "Oh, I bumped into a door frame," she said, but I dug for the truth in this case, and she admitted Rodney hit her. Because she presented herself professionally, and because the children in her care seemed healthy and happy, I allowed her to continue as project director, though I fired her husband.

More months passed and our file for NGO status grew thicker with project descriptions and financial and background information. Letters from Washington, D.C., and our local Colorado government were required. Joe prepared all the legal documentation on the American side, and I delivered the originals to Poupon for her to submit and register with the appropriate ministries in Haiti. One of the final requirements, Poupon said, was a copy of our license from IBESR. I went with Poupon to visit the dreaded Madam Mire.

Madam Mire was never overly positive regarding anything to do with Mercy and Sharing, but, strangely, Poupon and Madam Mire chattered amicably in French—I understood little of the conversation, but it sounded almost as if they were long-lost friends. I sat uncomfortably, willing myself to be polite and patient. Half an hour passed. All was friendly chatter. The clock ticked.

I heard Poupon ask Madam Mire something—*what was it,* something about licensing? Or ownership? I tried to make sense of the forms on Madam Mire's desk. I heard Poupon repeat the question to Madam Mire.

Madam Mire stretched her arms out, her palms turned up, and she tilted her head to the side. *"Pas mon défaut,"* she said. I understood that, I had heard it many times before. *(It's not my fault.)* But something was seriously wrong. I could see it on Poupon's face. My patience vanished and my agitation and concern rose.

"Poupon, what's the matter?" I whispered tersely. "What's going on—tell me."

Poupon ignored my questions. Madam Mire said nothing, but ticked through files in her desk drawer. She found what she was looking for, pulled out a large file, and laid it on the desk.

"Thibodeaux—" Madam Mire said. *"Il est votre président."* She looked at me, and I looked into her eyes, revealing all my vulnerability, something I regret to this day.

What did she say?! "Poupon—" My voice was well above a whisper now. "Poupon, I need to know what's going on. Thibodeaux is our *what?*"

Madam Mire smiled and pushed the open file toward Poupon. I turned over page after page of typed documents. Again and again on line after line I saw my name and Allain Thibodeaux's name. I could make out enough French to grasp what had happened. I felt as though my insides were being held together only by the pressure of my clenched fists.

Mercy and Sharing did not exist anymore.

In its place was a new foundation called Maison d'Anges ("House of Angels"). Allain Thibodeaux was president of this new foundation, and I, apparently, had signed the agreement, line after line, making myself vice president.

"I am so sorry, madams Pacaud and Suz-zee," said Madam Mire. Her voice was rough and masculine, her smell sour from needing a bath. "We have no organization by that name anymore. There are no decisions for you to make here." I wanted to rip her apart. Instead I got up and walked out in total disbelief. I sat on the curb outside the gates and calculated the damage.

Allain Thibodeaux, our Haitian director, had assumed it was too difficult to run a Haitian company unless he was completely in charge. So, to "streamline" the process, he had forged my signature and signed our foundation over to him. My orphanage license was now in his name. All our assets were in his name. I found a phone downtown and called Allain. When I confronted him, the reason became clear.

"Susie," he said, his voice like margarine. "You are so simple. Maude Silverice makes tens of thousands of American dollars each year from adoption fees. Why shouldn't we?"

"Because I'm never going to be like Maude Silverice," I said. "I never would have agreed—you know that."

"Susie . . . ," he said. His voice trailed off. He had no answer. He didn't need one. Mercy and Sharing, in the sight of Haitian law, was now completely his. I hung up. Adoptions were a small part of our foundation, but we never charged for them—particularly under-the-table adoptions, as Allain was suggesting. If good and loving people wanted to adopt a child, I didn't want to discourage them or lessen our children's chances of getting chosen. We were getting by on the money we raised. I wouldn't sell my children.

Poupon emerged eventually from the gate onto the street. We drove in silence until we entered the gates to the orphanage compound. What we saw was another surprise: total chaos. Employees bickered hysterically. One house mother clutched another by the apron, not letting her flee as she seemed to be trying to do. Many ran toward our SUV, shouting and gesticulating wildly.

"Stop!" I shouted above the din. "I can't understand you. What's the matter?"

They pointed at one another and to the top of the ten-foot concrete wall surrounding the compound. I kept hearing "Thibodeaux" over and over. They separated into teams on each side of me, yelling again at the wall and at each other.

I listened, incredulous, as they explained they had just foiled a hideous plot happening right under my nose. Thibodeaux had hatched a plan with three house mothers: they had agreed to secretly hand healthy infants over the wall to him and an accomplice while one on the inside distracted our guard.

The three accused mothers stood against a wall in the compound. All cried and begged. More of the story came out. The women had also stolen from me, taking food and milk from our children. They all looked as if they had gained several pounds in the past months. None looked starving. They knew they were caught. One snatched a glass bottle from the curb and smashed it against the concrete wall. She held the jagged edge to her throat, threatening to kill herself. "You understand?!" she seethed, as if her blood would somehow be on my hands.

"Wait a minute," I said, and held up my hand. Breathing hard, she paused. I strolled to the SUV and retrieved a disposable camera from my purse. I walked back slowly, camera clasped in my hand. If she was going to kill herself, I would document it so nobody could say I did it. I was certainly not going to stop the wretch. I aimed the camera at her, my finger poised on the button. "Go ahead, I'm ready."

She dropped the glass and ran through the gate.

Thibodeaux, we learned, had promised several of our children to foreigners for adoption and had already taken a "down payment." But I would not go down without a fight. I phoned him again and demanded to meet. He came to the compound, and I met him outside the gate.

"You're fired," I said.

"Susie," he said, "you cannot fire me. I am the president."

"No matter what the paperwork says, I still pay your salary," I said. "You're fired."

His tone shifted as he realized control was not completely his after all. Was that actually a tear in his eye? His head slumped. He looked as sad as a basset hound. "All I want is for someone to love me no matter what I do to them," he said.

I looked him in the eyes. "It won't be me, and it won't be my kids."

For a moment he seemed perplexed. Then he turned on me. "What a Haitian man cannot control he will destroy!" he growled. The hound was now a wolf.

I met his scowl with a daggered look of my own. "Is that a threat, Mr. Thibodeaux?" I said.

He said nothing and left.

◆ ◆ ◆

I HAD TAKEN TO writing out my prayers, every so often, in my journal. That day I wrote:

> *God, I am not strong anymore, only desperate. I am completely crushed. I cannot continue to rise. Every time You place me face-to-face with the impossible I break myself in half to do it. Now I just need to mend.*
>
> *Couldn't I have a break? Please help me. Unleash Your angels to come for me, or give me some weapon to fight the tremendous forces of evil that torment these children.*
>
> *I will praise You. I will praise anyway. I promise.*
>
> *I am afraid now.*
>
> *Is this the cross You gave me, Father? I cannot comprehend it. Surely I would have chosen another path for myself.*
>
> *I will die from this. I am sure of it.*
>
> *I am not afraid to die. I just dread the dying.*
>
> *Over and over again—how can You let me walk through those piles and piles of innocent bodies? Every time I choose the color of lace for my children's tiny coffins—O God, it hurts. God! How can these children, God, be taken in their dawn of life to this dungeon of a morgue with its barrels of heads and limbs swimming in worms?*
>
> *Answer me, God, please—I am in desperate need.*

I NEEDED A BREAK. Whenever I became severely stressed, depression usually followed. Then my immune system would weaken and I would catch colds from the children.

I decided to go to the ocean. I was always able to draw solace from the waves and the smells of the sea. I thought of going to Jacmel, but it was a four-hour drive from Port-au-Prince and I was too shaky to drive the winding mountain roads to get there. I would go to Williamson instead. It was only an hour's drive, and the water was often calm and took on all the cheering colors of light and sun.

It was cooler in Williamson because of the gentle breeze that came from the sea and danced across the mountains and back down again over the rocky beach. It had been a long time since I had felt movement in the air, and it soothed me. I could see a great boat with torn sails hanging from its mast that jutted into the sky and seemed to pierce the center of the sun far from the shore. The boat sailed deeply from a heavy load of coal, and the men who perched with their feet hanging over the wooden edges looked as if they were also comforted by the breeze. I took a bottle of wine from my cooler and a fresh baguette and a couple of skinny chicken legs I purchased for a few gourdes from a little vendor woman alongside the road.

I sat on the rocks and drank the cool wine from a plastic cup. Someone in a small fishing boat, not far off, drew in the line. I watched, hopeful he'd be rewarded with a fish. This was a part of Haiti I had forgotten about. I promised myself I would make an effort to come to the ocean more often. The quiet water sipping the edge of the rocks reminded me I was very small. I liked knowing that at this moment I was not in control. I knew that God saw all this. I was not alone. Maybe his angels were already in action. "Don't forget about us," I said, gazing up into the purple and pink sky. "Okay, Father?"

My new strategy became simple: If Mercy and Sharing didn't exist anymore, I'd just create it again. I applied to the IBSER for a new orphanage license. Madam Mire was not happy about my plan. She complained and complained that I made phone calls to everyone about her.

In fact, I did.

I knew she was in cahoots with Allain Thibodeaux, but I didn't exactly know how. I contacted everybody powerful I knew, asking for whatever help they could give. Maybe someone could drop the info at a D.C. cocktail party, and it would trickle back to Haiti and connect with an official in President Aristide's office—Madam Mire's ultimate superior.

Or maybe I could talk to the president myself.

The Palacio Presidencial de Haiti, or Presidential Palace, in Port-au-Prince, is a Romanesque stronghold with white spires on top and four large colonnades in front. Phone calls were made; appointments proved a challenge to obtain. At last I received a confirmed slot to meet with Aristide's chief of staff, Jean-Claude DeGrange. I carefully chose a conservative dress and flat shoes, and drove to the palace. The day was hotter than usual, and I stood for half an hour in the sun at the gate, explaining the reason for my meeting. IDs were checked, intercoms buzzed back and forth, and finally I was ushered inside to DeGrange's office foyer, where another hour slowly ticked by. At last DeGrange emerged, a richly dressed national who wore glasses and too much cologne.

"Sit, please," he said. His voice was soothing, his manners impeccable. We sat. He took my hand in his. "Tell me your situation."

I told him all about the foundation's history, the struggle we were having at that moment with our license, and the frustration we were experiencing by not being able to get anywhere with the IBESR. DeGrange put his hand on my knee. I stood up. "Just come to the orphanage," I said. "See the children for yourself."

"No, no, I would not be able to do that," he said and looked away. The silence lasted too long. He cleared his throat at last. "The president is not available this day, but would you like to meet the first lady?"

I said I would. DeGrange disappeared for a moment, then returned and beckoned me to follow. As we entered Mildred Aristide's office, I saw her on her knees by the desk. Papers were scattered across the floor, as if there had just been an argument and someone had pushed the desk's contents on the floor. The office was not overly important looking. It had white walls and high ceilings. She stood, greeted me, and motioned for me to sit beside her on a modest green couch. The first lady was not unattractive. Her hair was carefully coiffed, her skin flawless; she wore a jacket with conservative sleeves and a prim skirt.

I explained my story again. I told her all about my tormenters: Madam Scarasse, Madam Mire, and the evilly talented Mr. Allain Thibodeaux. I explained the lengthy and expensive process I had undertaken to make right my orphanage's paperwork, and my inability so far to obtain a new license with the IBESR. I asked for her help, or her husband's help, to get our license. She asked careful questions in perfect English. Her voice was sweet, kind, and interested. At the end she took my hand in hers and began to cry. "Thank you," she said. "Thank you for what you are doing with our children in Haiti. I will do all I can."

The meeting lasted twenty minutes. I thanked her and stood up.

"I'll pray for you," was the last thing she said.

Although I found a sympathetic ear in Mildred Aristide, nothing with our license situation changed. I later heard that Mrs. Aristide called the IBESR and spoke to Madam Mire, requesting that I be given a permit to continue to operate my projects in Haiti. The answer was still no. Madam Mire must have been one powerful woman indeed.

I had heard that U.S. congressman John Conyers Jr., a Michigan Democrat, was a true and strong advocate for the poor in Haiti. I had written him on occasion and had attended a few fundraisers and events at which he spoke. I decided to write John Conyers again.

In a lengthy letter, I explained that six months had passed since I had spoken with Mrs. Aristide, and I had worked with four legal firms, but still no license. I had also gone to Eude Craan, minister of social affairs, and called Joe Baptiste, president of NOAH (the National Organization for the Advancement of Haitians). Mr. Baptiste went to President Aristide on my behalf, then worked with DeGrange again—all of them confirmed that I properly qualified as someone who deserved my permit to operate orphanages in Haiti. Even with all that pull, everyone concluded they could not help me further, and I should simply be patient and wait to hear from Madam Mire, who needed to issue this permit to me directly.

In my letter I told how Mr. Thibodeaux had communicated to me that he would put "his" permit back in my name in exchange for a "severance" check for $75,000 US. I decided this was unacceptable. I also documented exchanges between Mr. Thibodeaux and Madam Mire in which they planned to open an "orphanage" of their own, really a holding ground for healthy children to be adopted under the table. To top it off, Madam Mire told me I needed to give her my house in Delmas (which was closed temporarily for repairs) so she and Allain could run their "orphanage" in it, and that the only way I could ever have a new license was to give her the house for free.

I signed my letter: "Sincerely, Susan Krabacher, president, Mercy and Sharing." That was still the truth, license or not.

I didn't write the letter gleefully. I wrote it out of frustration and desperation. I didn't know where else I could turn. It was

2002. I had worked in Haiti since 1994 and had more than 1,700 children in our schools and orphanages. Mercy and Sharing employed more than one hundred Haitians, and supplied free water to an additional three thousand Haitians in poor areas. That couldn't all stop overnight.

To this day, I am not sure exactly what Congressman Conyers did. All I know is that Madam Mire grudgingly gave me a one-year license. And I didn't sign over my house in Delmas to this woman, nor to Allain Thibodeaux.

For the time being, Mercy and Sharing was legally back in business.

But the sky was still dark.

Perhaps Poupon was afraid. Perhaps she was just evil. She and her husband, Rodney, sued Joe and me in Haitian court, alleging that Rodney was fired after working for us for three years (instead of three months, the actual time he worked for us), which violated Haitian severance laws.

The judge awarded them $60,000 US in damages. We later found out the judge, lawyer, and plaintiffs had cooked up a deal to divide the money among themselves.

We eventually settled for $10,000, simply to resolve the matter. Joe and I paid it from our own pockets. We'd had enough. There was too much hard rain in our lives. We simply wanted a day without steel falling on our heads.

Chapter 19

One Child

*K*ETCHUP.

I even like the way it sounds. When I was little I put it on every-thing. Even the worst foods can be made palatable by ketchup. I still smother it on eggs, beans, meat, and fish—I even put it in soup.

When a young boy named Ashley first asked me for ketchup I knew we were a lot alike. Ketchup was considered a treat at the or-phanage, not a necessity. Most of our food supplies were donated in bulk from generous organizations such as the United Nations World Food Programme and the SYSCO Corporation. Almost everything could be made tastier with ketchup, and our children begged for the brightly colored condiment with every meal.

I had first met Ashley at the Port-au-Prince hospital. A small street urchin of about six, he just showed up one day and began to follow me around, helping to care for the other children. He had no guardians and soon came to live with us at the orphanage, where he quickly became everyone's favorite. Ashley loved good food, music, and learning. And the little guy loved me. He prayed for me every night, an experience I continually found humbling and beautiful. I bought him a small battery-operated radio. From then on he always wore headphones either attached to his ears or hanging around his neck. He spoke two languages, Creole and English, but rarely said anything, except to ask a question or point out something he found interesting. He kept his shoes neatly tied and his clothes compulsively clean and neat.

From day one we knew Ashley had medical problems, though we weren't exactly sure what. His belly protruded too much, even for a starving child. One old nurse examined him, raising his arms, pushing his stomach—about a gallon of fluid came up. Something was seriously wrong. Ashley was short of breath a lot, too. More medical tests were given. Ashley was found to have a severe heart defect, along with a long list of other maladies. He was on a strict diet from that day on. Among other restrictions, Ashley could not have salt of any kind because he suffered so greatly with swollen joints and water retention. That meant no ketchup.

One day he asked to talk to me privately. I knew it was something of utmost importance to him. He took me by the hand and led me to his little room, shared with several other boys. We sat down on his neatly made bed.

"You know, Mama Susie," he said, "I have worked very hard to help the house mothers with their chores."

"I've heard that," I said with a smile. I knew it was leading somewhere.

"And I have done very well in school."

"Yes," I said, "you should be very proud of yourself."

"Well"—his head bowed—"I feel I have earned the right to have ketchup with meals like all the other children."

Ashley had been with Mercy and Sharing for two years. He was eight years old now and a beautiful little man.

"Ashley, baby, please don't ask me for that." I held his hands in mine. "You know your heart is sick and that makes you special." He wiped a tear from his cheek and wouldn't look at me. "Honey, special people have to be especially strong." I rubbed the top of his hand.

"Are you special?" he asked.

"Well, I'm strong, but not like you are."

"I don't want to be special anymore," Ashley said.

This wasn't really about ketchup. It was about wanting not to be too tired to play and not having to spend time with a doctor who poked and prodded and took away his treats and told him he couldn't be overly excited about anything. Ashley looked at me with believing eyes. Surely the woman who could produce a radio could make him not "special" anymore. He had seen children at the compound get well. He had also seen some who didn't. He waited for me to tell him which fate was his.

I hugged Ashley to my chest, unplugged the headphones from his ever-present transistor radio so we could both hear, and turned up the volume. I sang along and danced a seated, rather awkward version of "Macarena"—one of his favorite songs. He laughed and tried to copy me.

> *Always at the party con las chicas que soy buena*
> *come join me, dance with me . . .*

EARLIER, THE MIAMI CHILDREN'S Hospital had honored me for their International Children's Hall of Fame. I had made good contacts there, and it dawned on me that maybe they'd be able to help

Ashley. I called the hospital's charitable branch and made a trip to Miami to discuss my plea in person. Several months later, all was a go. After providing detailed medical reports to a pediatric heart surgeon, we obtained a medical visa for Ashley, then talked to Ashley about the plan. He and I sat together outside the orphanage on a concrete bench. Overhead was a large banyan tree with leaves that fluttered faintly in rare puffs of breeze. Wind was unusual for the area around the orphanage. It was bringing in some dark weather with its gray- and indigo-colored clouds. I knew Ashley needed to be filled in.

"Ashley," I said. I spoke slowly and carefully; I wanted to make sure he understood. "We need to talk about some things, and I want to know what you think about them."

Oh, the smile on his face. He nodded deeply, then turned his radio off and slid the headphones down around his neck.

"There is a wonderful doctor in the United States who might be able to help your heart get well so you'd feel better," I said. "It means you and I would need to fly to Miami together. You would spend a lot of time with doctors in the hospital and have an operation. You'll be asleep during the operation and it won't hurt and you won't remember it. There is a family in Miami who wants to look after you while you're there."

I spoke maturely to him too—I tried to speak as if he were a young man, not knowing if he would ever live to become one. Ashley said nothing. He just took it all in.

"You also need to know," I said, "that you may not be able to have the surgery if the people at the hospital don't think you're well enough." Doctors had told us open-heart surgery would be Ashley's only chance of survival, but I didn't mention that to him. He was very, very smart, and he studied my face with his chocolate-syrup eyes.

"Do you want to do this?" I asked. It was a grown-up decision for any child, but it needed to be his.

"Will I be special anymore?" he asked.

"You will always be one of the most special people I know."

His eyes brightened. "Can I live with you?"

"We'll travel together, but the foster family will take care of you once you're in Miami."

He did not hesitate. He bounced up and down, exposing both rows of perfect white teeth. "Yes! Mama! I go to the United States with you!" He hugged me and ran to tell his friends.

I sat under the banyan tree for a long while, thinking, praying.

It began to rain.

ASHLEY PACKED HIS RADIO and his few possessions. I bought him several pairs of new underwear and clothes to wear on the plane. On the way to the airport, I watched as he looked with pride from the car window to the streets of his country. He waved excitedly to people he did not know. I patted his chest and felt his heart fluttering wildly. He took a couple of sips from my water bottle. He often threw up after drinking too much water and did not want to soil his new clothes.

I could never have anticipated the day that lay ahead of us. Ashley squeezed my hand on takeoff, asking for assurance. I showed no alarm, which seemed to satisfy him. He gazed out at the ocean that he had never touched as we drifted upward like a feather toward the sun. He told me of the gifts he would bring back to his friends at the orphanage. He laughed as we popped through a small bundle of clouds.

For me, to be flying to the United States with a little boy who had once been left to die was certainly not my doing. I tried to grasp how this might have been arranged. The odds that a former *Playboy* centerfold and this little boy would ever come together were astronomical. Who orchestrated this? Whoever it was needed to be thanked. This child got blessed, and I got redefined.

Ashley had never seen an escalator before. In the Miami airport, he clung to my hand for dear life. With my other hand I heaved our two pieces of luggage. As I stepped onto the escalator, Ashley wrenched his hand free and stopped dead in his tracks. Unable to turn around quickly with the luggage, I floated helplessly upward and away from him. "Mama!" he shouted in panic. His face began to get lost in the sea of people. I tried to run back down through the tired and irritated travelers, now standing shoulder-to-shoulder on the escalator. "Mama! Mama!" Ashley shouted again. I could just make him out now, stepping back away farther from the moving metal monster.

"Wait! Ashley! Just wait there!" I yelled. His voice grew smaller and fainter. "For bloody Pete's sake!" I'd lost him. I counted the seconds until I reached the top of the escalator and ran to the side that would carry me back. *I'm a horrible mother.* . . . I clutched our luggage, praying no one would snatch him. In front of me was a throng of slow people. Ashley was nowhere in sight. Frantic, I scanned the crowd. Against a far wall, Ashley stood. He clutched the crotch of his new britches. He was crying.

I held him.

"Baby," I said. "We'll do this together."

He pointed to the escalator and shook his head furiously.

"Honey, remember I told you that you would have to be extra strong on this trip?"

He nodded.

I picked him up and told him to hang on to my neck as I balanced him on my hip. As I hoisted the two bags and stepped onto the moving stairs I felt a warm wetness seeping through the waist of my shirt. He buried his face in my hair, embarrassed. "Don't worry," I whispered. "We're okay." When we reached the top, I took him to the ladies' room, where we both dried ourselves and changed into new clothes from our luggage.

We checked into our hotel room at the Miami airport and got ready to meet his foster family the next day. Ashley wanted to walk around and explore. The hotel elevator, he decided, was safe. We rode up and down eight times. In and out of kiosks we darted, Ashley touching all of the brightly colored fabrics and lace of scarves and hats. He scrutinized rows of candy, magazines with glossy covers, and tiny toys with shiny wrappers. He showed me every treasure. I pretended I, too, was seeing these things for the first time. We giggled and gasped at all the strange things. Ashley glided, angel-like, through shops and people and stores and faces. Any time he let go of my hand I felt a twinge inside. People turned to look at this small child, so eager, so light. His world that day, and mine, was pure joy.

The woman behind the counter in the jewelry store was from Haiti, and when Ashley spoke to her in Creole she answered him in the language of his home. He beamed and chattered as if it were the most natural thing in the world to find a woman who spoke his first language in the perfect place called America. She lifted the glittering jewelry from the case to the counter. Ashley touched every piece tenderly, carefully. The woman laughed as he put each necklace on and examined himself in the mirror. Ashley took scarves and embroidered shawls from the racks and held them to himself. He had never seen or touched such beautiful things, and they held no gender assignments for him. They were just works of art.

I asked the woman, who had now been thoroughly enchanted

by Ashley, if she had any things for young men. She produced
from the opposite side of her glass station a large display of heavy
silver and gold-plated chains. None had the shimmering rhine-
stones that Ashley liked so much, so he picked out a fake pearl-
and-diamond necklace with a garish pink rhinestone dangling
underneath. Ashley draped the necklace around his neck. He
showed me his reflection in the large stone and threw his head
back in laughter. I couldn't help laughing too.

Ashley would be entering the real world in twenty-four hours.
Things were going to be tough for him. Nobody knew quite how
long Ashley would stay in this new country. Maybe he'd go to a
new school where kids could be cruel. I couldn't bear the thought
of anyone making fun of him. I lifted a heavy silver-plated chain
from the display of men's jewelry.

"I'm not sure if I should do this," I said. I sought his face and
rubbed my chin, becoming very serious. "Naw, I better not, you're
just a little boy." I pretended to oscillate in good judgment. His
gaze left the mirror, now clouded with moisture from his breath,
and he turned his attention fully on me. "I think maybe you're
grown-up enough to wear a big man's chain." I took the fake
pearls from around his neck.

The saleslady kindly played along. "If you think he's really
ready . . .," she said with exaggerated caution.

"I'm ready! I'm ready, Mama!"

His shoulders arched backward slightly so he could see it resting on his chest. I paid nineteen dollars for the chain, and we
thanked our new Creole-speaking friend. It was nearly 8 p.m. and
the shops in the airport were pulling down their chain-link gates.

Back in our room, I ran a bath for Ashley, then took one myself.
Ashley had picked out a toy model airplane from a store and organized the parts neatly in rows. From room service I ordered him

steamed vegetables and chicken without salt. I chose for myself a rich spicy conch chowder. We both ate vanilla ice cream for dessert. I turned on the TV as Ashley looked at the pictures on the box of his new toy. He could not read the instructions but figured out the complex model from the pictures. I dozed.

"Mama. Mama." He shook my shoulder gently, wide-eyed and upset. He held his now fully assembled airplane next to its picture on the box. Tears formed in his eyes. He took my finger and put it on one wing of the model aircraft. A tiny red taillight was missing. He looked at me in complete despair. I turned the box upside down and shook it. We both crawled on hands and knees examining every visible inch of carpet. The model was simply missing a part.

"Sweetie, you need to go to sleep," I said. "We'll go back to the store when they open in the morning, okay?" Reluctantly he complied. It was 10 p.m. I tucked him in tight beside me, and we stared at each other in the dim light that came from a crack in the curtains. After a long time his eyes closed and I watched him twitch and smile while he dreamed.

At 1 a.m. Ashley woke me again. He was fully dressed and had his shoes on and tied. "It's day, Mama!" he said. He held his model plane in one hand and the box and instructions under the other arm. For some reason, he needed that plane to be perfect. I could not get him to put his pajamas back on. He dozed off next to me fully dressed, holding his airplane.

At 7:50 a.m. we sat outside the shop on the floor, legs crossed, until the lady came to work at 8:00 a.m. and lifted the gate. She opened the box of another model plane and gave him the piece that was missing. Ashley's smile illuminated the toy store. The taillight now in place, we sat on stools in a café and waited to meet his foster family. I reminded him about them—wonderful people with a little girl a couple of years older to play with and a little baby they would probably let him hold if he was extra careful. Ashley gripped his spoon full-fisted, scooped up the last of the oatmeal, and drained his glass of orange juice.

I drank an espresso and wished we had more time together. Ashley played with his airplane, pretending it was taking off into the wild blue, soaring around and around above his spinning stool. In the distance, I saw a family. I knew it was the Woodrows.

"Are you Susie?" asked the woman. An attractive person, she held her daughter's hand. A tall, husky man with brown hair stood a few steps behind holding a one-year-old boy.

"Yes. Hi! Mrs. Woodrow?"

She nodded sweetly. Ashley hid behind me, his plane now hanging at his side. "And this"—I pointed to the child clinging to the back pockets of my blue jeans—"is Ashley!"

The little girl spoke first: "Hi. I'm Sophie. I'm ten years old. Don't be afraid, Ashley. I'm gonna be your best friend." She lifted the baby from her father's arms and cuddled the child like a doll under her chin. "And this is my baby brother, Jeffrey. Ashley, we're gonna have so much fun together! I have a bicycle and you can ride it! And we can play house and go swimming!"

I felt Ashley release his grip on one of my pockets. His head came around under my right elbow to take a closer look at this gregarious little girl.

"Can we sit and talk for a while before you have to leave?" I asked Mr. and Mrs. Woodrow. Before anyone could answer, Sophie handed the baby to her father, grabbed Ashley's hand, and was halfway down the aisle to the toy shelves. She chattered away, giggling and holding tight to Ashley's hand. *That's what he needs*, I thought and smiled to myself. *A strong woman in his life.*

I sat with Melinda and Greg and talked about the surgery and

Ashley's medications, diet, and likes and dislikes. Melinda and I had spent hours on the phone together prior to this meeting. The Woodrows had hosted another child once before and were recommended to us by an organization much like our own. All was set. I had spent months talking to the staff at the Miami Children's Hospital's humanitarian department. The doctors and nurses were already like family to us. We were aware that Ashley's heart had deteriorated since beginning the process of getting him here, but we all still hoped.

When it was time for the Woodrows to leave, I asked if Melinda would call me the next day. I fumbled in my purse for my wallet to pay the bill for our coffee. My nose started to run and my eyes got red. I did not want Ashley to see me cry. Melinda appeared at the cash register with a tissue in her hand. "You know we'll take care of him like he was our own boy," she said. I liked her and knew that Ashley would soon love her too.

"Ashley, honey!" He picked up his plane and walked toward me. I straightened myself and prepared myself to perform a happy good-bye scene. "Now, baby, like we talked about, you're gonna go home with the Woodrows! They have everything ready! I'm so excited for you!" I clapped my hands together to prove it. "So . . ." I knelt down to touch his face. "Be a good boy! You're a little man now. You even have a man's chain around your neck to remind you how big and strong you are!"

I hugged him so hard he gasped.

"I love you, my son," I said, and turned to go.

I had taken only a few steps when I felt small hands around my waist. "I stay with you in the United States!" He looked up at me with tears in his eyes.

"Honey, I'm just going home," I said, holding my plane ticket in my hand. "See?" I bent down. "To Aspen."

Ashley nodded. He lifted his airplane with both arms. "It's for you," he whispered. I realized he planned to give it to me as a present all along. That's why it had to be perfect for him. Ashley ran back to Sophie, proud to have given me his perfect treasure.

I didn't cry until I got past security.

I FOUND OUT LATER THE Woodrows and their new charge walked down the corridor to the electric glass doors that opened automatically to the United States of America. But Ashley would not walk through.

"No, I stay here in United States!" he said, and backed away.

"That *is* the United States!" Sophie said, pointing through the open doors to the outside world.

Ashley thought the airport was the entirety of this new country. It had been so wonderful, so inclusive, how could anything be better?

My phone rang in Aspen the next morning at 5 a.m. Joe was already up and handed me the phone. He looked alarmed.

"The Woodrows can't find Ashley!" he said.

I swiped the hair back from my face. "What's wrong?" I asked, into the phone. "What do you mean? He can't be gone!"

Melinda's voice was shrill and high. "We're looking everywhere. I tucked him in last night after he had supper and he was fine. He was fine!" Her voice was shaky and weakening. "Oh, God—he was fine. . . ."

I heard Greg in the background. "Honey, I'm going out to look at the duck pond!" They had walked to the neighborhood duck pond the evening before, and Ashley had sat for more than an hour feeding the ducks bread.

"Melinda?" I said, suddenly terrified. "Could someone have taken him?"

I sat up in my bed with my arms around my knees, praying. *Please let him be okay.* Over and over I prayed. Each moment I grew more panicked. Half an hour passed. I rocked back and forth. The phone rang.

"Melinda?" I shrieked.

"We found him," she said. "He's fine, just fine."

"Oh God! Thank God!"

"He was sound asleep underneath Sophie's bed the whole time," Melinda said. She was laughing and crying. I could hear Greg and Sophie playing with Ashley in the background. "I think he was afraid and must have snuck out of his bedroom in the middle of the night and crawled under her bed."

We realized Ashley wasn't used to having a room all to himself. At the orphanage he slept in a big room with lots of other children and one of the house mothers. So from that day on, Sophie slept in a sleeping bag in Ashley's room beside his bed. Melinda told me they giggled and laughed every night until they both fell asleep.

Days passed before test results came in. News looked grim. Doctors advised Melinda and Greg to take Ashley home and make him as comfortable as possible. Ashley's new family responded with utter love. Greg took time off work and spent days carrying Ashley around on his shoulders after he became too weak to walk. They went for pony rides and to the park, but mostly Ashley asked to spend time at the duck pond.

Melinda phoned regularly to keep me up to date. More tests were performed in hopes that Ashley's condition might improve, but nothing looked hopeful. One night Sophie woke up her parents. "Daddy?" She shook his shoulder. "Ashley's legs hurt."

When they reached Miami Children's Hospital, a team rushed to his aid. Ashley's legs had swollen double in size and he was in great pain. Trish was able to pull every string she had and book me an immediate flight to Miami. By morning, the medical team had managed to reduce the swelling with medication, and Ashley no longer winced with pain. Ashley's main doctor sat beside Greg and Melinda while Sophie slept curled in a chair beside Ashley's bed. Melinda put Ashley's headphones on for him and adjusted the tuning knob until he smiled.

"This is hard for me to say," the doctor said, "but . . . you should let him have anything he wants to eat today." He swallowed and rubbed his eyes. "His heart is just worn out. I don't think he has more than a few hours."

When Ashley woke up, Sophie, Melinda, Greg, and several nurses were around his bed. They gave him some water, asked if he was hungry, and told him he could have anything he wanted. "Rice and beans—like at the orphanage," he answered without hesitation. But when the food came, Ashley wouldn't eat. Melinda called me while I was still on the airplane.

"Mix 'em together and mash 'em up real good," I suggested. "That's what the cook does at the orphanage. Oh—and he likes orange Kool-Aid. . . ." I thought for a moment. My voice quieted. "And ketchup, Melinda. Lots of ketchup. Please give him as much as he wants."

From the airplane I called Nolette at the orphanage. I asked her to gather all the children and have them by the phone. I called Melinda back and asked her to place a call to the orphanage.

From the hospital bed, Ashley talked to each of his friends at the orphanage, one by one. He smiled and chattered, with his favorite meal on a tray before him. Ashley told them what he was eating, and though they didn't believe him at first, he described how good it tasted. He asked Melinda for another bowl very loudly so that he could be heard all the way in Haiti. He wanted all his friends to share the experience with him—Ashley was eating beans and rice, and the ketchup was piled on high.

Later, when I arrived at the hospital, Melinda told me that when Ashley spoke to the littlest children his tone was strong and loving. When he talked to the girls his tone was shy and sweet. With the boys he was silly and goofy. He grew tired after speaking at last to Nolette, whom he told about the ducks and his new best friend, Sophie, and the little baby who sometimes cried when they played house.

Ashley handed the phone to Greg. Melinda tucked him in because he felt cold. Sophie kissed him gently on his cheek. Ashley curled up in his hospital bed.

With a peaceful orange Kool-Aid smile, Ashley drifted to heaven.

Chapter 20

One Volunteer

I N THE DAYS BEFORE 9/11, airport security was not as it is today.
The variety of policies in that era gave me a chance to bring a
friend to Haiti that some found unwelcome. My motivation was
companionship. I have a wonderful husband and amazingly sup-
portive friends. Still, there is a void that calls to me continuously.
When I find someone I love, who loves me back, I cling to that
company. When that someone is wrested away from me, I do not
let go easily.

"REMOVE YOUR *PURSE* FROM the countertop, please!"

"Okay, but just . . . can't I . . ."

She handed me my boarding pass. "Next!"

"Yes, but, you see . . ."

"Next!"

It wasn't a purse. Freud, one of my little whatevers, was dreaming happy puppy dreams inside the little bag. Denver airport throbbed, a cacophony of movement and impatience. A hurried passenger pushed me aside. I peeked inside the bag and shrugged. *Oh, well.* The airport in Aspen had closed due to a snowstorm. Joe, who had taken off work to drive me to the Denver airport, stood near the glass exit doors waiting to kiss me good-bye.

"Were you able to change your ticket?" he asked, reaching down inside Freud's bag to rub his yawning face. "Do they allow dogs? Or do I need to take him?"

"I got my ticket, but the lady was so cranky I didn't get a chance to ask about Freud. Don't worry, nobody'll notice the little guy."

"I wouldn't do that if I were you, hon," Joe said, frowning. "Why don't you just let me take him back home?"

"Honey, I'm lonely and he makes me laugh. C'mon," I whined. "I need him."

Joe rubbed the inside corner of one eye and didn't argue further. "I wouldn't take him, but I know you will." He lifted me up and kissed me, holding the back of my neck with his long fingers. "I love you. Please don't take any crazy risks!" The constant ebb and flow of Haiti's violence was at a peak just then, and kidnappings of foreigners and businesspeople were reported almost daily.

"Don't worry, I won't. I love you, precious!"

At the gate I called Trish out of boredom. "What do you mean you have Freud with you?!" she shouted. "Frontier doesn't allow dogs!"

"Well, you didn't tell me that."

"You didn't tell me you were taking the dad-blame mutt!" I was surprised she didn't curse. Maybe I was becoming a good influence on my dear friend.

"Stop yelling at me!" I spoke firmly and rationally. "They won't even know."

"Call Joe and tell him to come back to the airport and get the goddamn dog!" Trish blew cigarette smoke into the phone. I had spoken too soon.

"No!"

"Okay, but when they won't let you on the plane, don't call me crying."

I was hungry and smelled bacon nearby. *Mmmm, McDonald's.* Freud lifted one ear while the other flopped over his head like a cap. "Are ya hungry, baby?" He tilted his face. "Yes, Mommy," he said with his eyes. "I'm a poor, poor peasant puppy, hungry and naked. Please feed me!"

We sat and shared an Egg McMuffin, waiting until the final boarding call. I tucked him safely in his bag, shushed him, and told him he had to be good for a couple hours. Minutes later I sat obediently in my aisle seat. Freud reclined elegantly under the seat in front of me, licking his privates. The stewardess bobbed back and forth through economy class, pushing tray tables up and repeating, "Seat belts . . . seat belts . . . seat belts . . ." like a blind auctioneer.

A noxious bubble drifted up from the bag. It burst in midair. A dreadful fume dispersed across rows three to six. I looked toward the window seat at my fellow passenger, who had his knuckles between his nose and upper lip.

"Freud, honey—do you feel okay?" I whispered.

Again a gas leak burst forth, this time with a long slow "phfffffffffffffff" and a little "ttt" as a closing statement. I rubbed my chin and looked at my row mate with angst. "Sorry." I gave an exaggerated shrug of repentance. I'd never see these people again anyway.

The pilot asked the flight attendants to be seated. The plane plummeted down the runway and into the sky. Freud let out a tiny polite whine. I opened the zipper an inch and patted his nose. I could see one maple-syrup-colored eyeball looking up at me. Freud took it as his cue. Out he flew. He wiggled past me and ran down the aisle. I understood his discomfort now, as projectile diarrhea sprayed in every direction. "Freud! Baby!" I shouted, disconnecting my seat belt and chasing after him.

"Miss! Miss! Sit down! *Now!*" said a stewardess over the intercom. Her eyes narrowed, no longer the face of the friendly skies.

"But . . ." I said, still standing in the aisle. I pointed. Several unfortunate passengers lifted their pant legs and skirts to assess the damage. Freud sat at the back of the plane, shaking and crying helplessly.

"Miss! You must take your seat—immediately!"

I dutifully strapped myself back in. Craning my neck, I pleaded for Freud to come to me. Suddenly the plane's speed slowed considerably. The intercom crackled. "Ladies and gentleman, this is your pilot. Apparently we have contraband on board. We will be returning to the gate to await security."

Hoo boy. I had really done it now.

Freud inched his way back up the aisle. "C'mon, baby, you can do it," I said. I could almost reach him. Suddenly he stopped and arched his back. An oozing trail of egg-yolk-colored poop appeared. "Gross! Oh God!" I heard from unidentified rows. "Awww, man!"

We landed, parked at the gate, and two beefy security men began to escort Freud and me off the plane. The pilot met me at the exit and suggested we not fly again with Frontier.

"Hang on," said the stewardess. She approached me with a roll of toilet tissue. "You'll need to clean up before you leave."

◆　◆　◆

TRISH LAUGHED AT ME for ten full minutes before she hung up and found a flight that would accept a small dog. I arrived in Port-au-Prince a day late due to the small "delay."

It was a horrible time in Haiti. Many of our employees at Mercy and Sharing were afraid to go to work. Gangs had set up barricades throughout the city, and there was talk of retraining the corrupt Haitian police. Foreign soldiers and special ops security teams were being brought to Haiti from all over the world on contract jobs.

I sat on the last stool in a bar near the Visa Lodge and leaned against the counter. Freud had traveled the rest of the way without incident and happily pawed a fruit fly he had befriended. Five noisy Americans in green-and-brown fatigues sat at a nearby table hoisting bottles of Presidente beer, their dusty lace-up boots propped on the bamboo railings of the half wall to the patio. I tapped my pen on my large hardcover notebook to give the impression of deep concentration. The men's conversation pricked up my ears.

"I think this is all we got, right here, right now," said the one named Paulo. "When we die, that's it, baby."

"Not me," said another—I struggled to catch his name. . . . *Cheese?* "If I only get to scrub toilets in heaven, I hope I make the cut." He cuffed Paulo around the neck with a thick hairy arm and lifted the smaller man from his chair. Cheese gritted his teeth in a teasing smile and tousled Paulo's lanky dark hair. "C'mon, ya little sissy. I'm takin' your sorry butt with me. I ain't scrubbing no toilets by myself!"

Paulo surprised Cheese with a half-serious openhanded right jab under the chin. The two scuffled and growled like a couple of boy puppies from the same litter. "Somebody's got to teach you girls to behave in public," said one of the other men.

I ordered a bowl of pumpkin soup that came with bits of meat I could not identify. Probably goat. It was seasoned with spices from the Dominican Republic that gave it a thick, woody aroma. The men left their empty Presidente bottles on the low table and scuttled out.

"Hmmm, that smells good!" someone said. I looked up from my spoon, then quickly down at my open book. Cheese was sitting at the other end of the bar. He ordered another beer. I pulled the book closer, feigning deep study. Cheese did not move. He was built sturdily, the type of huskiness that comes from bearing a heavy load, even if it belongs to another. "Do you mind if I ask what you're doing here" he said. "You don't really look like you belong in a place like this."

"I just like it here," I said. "I try to help the children." I had learned to be cautious and not give too much information.

John Branchizio Jr. was his real name—Cheese for short. He was in Haiti on a government-contract security detail. After finishing college in Arkansas, he spent nine years as a Navy SEAL in Central and South America. An ankle injury after a parachute jump forced him to quit the military, but he was still extremely active, and swam, competed in triathlons, and ran marathons. He was the father of a young son whom he referred to as "Little B." In three weeks he would leave Port-au-Prince before heading home to San Antonio, Texas.

"I have a big ole mutt named Big Mac back in Texas," Cheese said with a nod at Freud. "I sure do miss him sometimes. Hey—do you know Jesus Christ by any chance?"

"I'm already there," I said. "You don't have to try and convert me."

"I love the Bible. I'm all Texan and all Christian. I even nicknamed my troop the God Squad. Not all of 'em like it, but I don't give a rip."

John Branchizio was the real deal. I saw him several times at the bar over the next few days. I've been mistaken about men before, but there was never a hint of flirting from him. The friendship that developed between us was different. The men in his unit, hotel employees, kids on the street—Cheese acted the same way to all. Anyone he met, he simply *loved.*

A FEW DAYS LATER I went to the government hospital to take supplies and pay employees. I spent less than an hour inside the abandoned-infant ward, then walked outside to cry and gather my thoughts. Sometimes the place has that effect on me. Now and again, when I'm completely frustrated (and even then, very rarely), I bum a smoke off someone. That day, I did.

As I alternated between taking puffs and wiping my eyes, a frail woman hobbled toward me. She was bent nearly in two and looked as if she would break if touched too firmly. She pulled my arm and spoke with authority. "Come!" I crushed my cigarette in the dust and followed. We walked into a narrow alley between two concrete buildings. On a torn piece of cardboard lay a girl, maybe four or five, with short, stiff braids held with faded plastic hair clips. The girl's legs twisted unnaturally, and her body was curled into a fetal position. Around her ankle was a string on which hung a piece of paper, a prescription for medicine.

I knelt beside the girl and touched her face. She was breathing. Her dirty blue dress was severely soiled around her pelvis area. Through a rip in the clothing I saw pus dripping out and pulled back the cloth. Her hip bone protruded through her light chocolate skin. The wound had become severely infected and was crawling with parasites. As I lifted her into my arms, her eyes opened. At most, she weighed twenty pounds. She began to shake. I held her tightly and turned to ask the child's story from the old woman.

She had disappeared.

I scanned the buildings, wondering if a parent or relative might be watching from the shadows. I was completely alone. A few passersby pointed at me, laughing at the odd sight of a woman in a clean dress and nice shoes holding a dirty rag doll who would surely die anyway. In America, you cannot simply take a child from the streets. Children must belong to *some*body. In Haiti, it is a decision I face regularly.

I held the little girl as we raced down the bumpy broken roads back to the hotel, where I hoped I could get a phone line to reach our staff doctor. I ran to the front desk, still holding the girl.

"I need a laundry basket with soft towels in it," I said to the desk clerk. "And a phone line immediately." Phone lines were sporadic that day, and I struggled to reach our doctor while the clerk took the child from me and laid her in the basket.

"Hey, Little Suz! Whatcha . . ." Cheese came toward the front desk but stopped when he saw the girl. He bent down and tightened his lips. "This poor kid." He took her hands in his. The girl's eyes fluttered open, then fixed on his and never left.

"She needs antibiotics," I said. "These phone lines are just crazy today, and she's so dehydrated. I'm not sure if she'll make—"

"Take her to your room," John said. "I'll find you a doctor." He sprinted down the steps to his vehicle.

I sat in my room with the child for more than an hour. I rocked her and sang in a low voice. She would not drink anything, but I dabbed her lips with a cloth and clean water until she began to lick them.

Finally John pounded on the door. "Suz, open up, I've got a doctor!"

He had plenty of military connections in the city and demanded action. The first five told him he needed to wait until the next day at the earliest, or bring the girl in. John refused. He kept searching until he found a military doctor who agreed to come back to the hotel.

We named the girl Vicki. Had she been born in another country she could have been a supermodel. She was that kind of beauty.

The doctor came repeatedly, working on her for several days until she had recovered enough to be transported to the orphanage. A few months later, Joe and I gave each other the best anniversary present ever—we used gift money to have a skin graft taken from Vicki's back to cover the hole where her hip bone stuck through. We learned later she has cerebral palsy, and is often more sick than the other children at the orphanage. She is there to this day and has become as dear to me as a daughter.

JOHN BRANCHIZIO BECAME ONE of our board members at Mercy and Sharing. He jumped in full force. He soon handled the storage and shipping of all donated items. In 2000 he arranged the necessary logistics for an American Airlines 757 jet to fly in 39,000 pounds of beans and rice for our feeding programs. He had trained air marshals in hand-to-hand combat techniques and was well connected with several international security firms. He often arranged for protection of children and board members who stayed in Cité Soleil. He got a new job with Dynacorp, a company that provided security for the United States in Israel, Iraq, Afghanistan, and throughout the Middle East. He was baptized in the Jordan River and was dating an Israeli girl. Still, he often found time to visit us in Haiti.

One morning a little boy wandered near the gates of the government hospital. He was about three years old and teetered on spindly legs, crying, saying, "Mama! Mama!" to all the women who sit nearby selling sugarcane, cigarettes, and mangoes. I first saw him when I went outside to purchase a bottle of water. A great pair of black eyes met mine. "Mama! Mama." The boy tottered over to me and wrapped his arms around my leg.

"He thinks you're his mama," laughed a merchant.

"For Pete's sake, what's he doing in the street alone?" I pried his little arms from around my leg and picked him up.

"His mother, she die," said the merchant. He wasn't laughing anymore. "He don't know his papa. He's been here every day for two weeks, maybe more. We give him little food. But he cannot stay here, he make pee-pee in the streets, it bring flies to food." Several others nodded and confirmed the story.

The clerk at the hotel met me with a worried look when I came through the door. "Another one, Madam Susie?" she said. "The boss don't like it. He say that this is a hotel, not an orphanage."

"I'm only keeping him here till tomorrow. Then I'll take him to our orphanage," I said. "He's just a little boy. He's scared."

"Okay, I will not tell, but you had better watch out."

I went to the restaurant and ordered rice and beans for the little guy. In the quiet of a corner table I asked his name again. He misted up and told me he didn't know. Cheese and Paulo and his team came into the restaurant for "grub," as they called it. I waved Cheese over and introduced him to my little friend, who held a big glass of water to his face without much success in getting any into his mouth.

"Hey, little man! Who are you?" John was immediately on his haunches beside him, helping tilt the glass more effectively. The little boy licked his lips with a tiny pink tongue and bounced up and down in his seat beside me. He gobbled rice and beans, using his hands. "Somebody's hungry!" John laughed, and said we should order him something more. He ordered another burger for himself and pulled out a picture. The edges were worn, as if it had been taken out of his pocket many times. "This is my little man. My son, Tyler." Cheese drew a deep breath that filled his chest. "He's into dinosaurs. He doesn't like to swim yet but he wants to be a Navy SEAL when he grows up." Cheese and the little boy both stared at the photo.

I ordered some vegetables for the boy and mashed them with a fork. John ordered a hamburger. The little boy picked up one of John's French fries and popped it into his mouth. Then another. He did not stop.

"Guess you can't eat just one, huh, little man?" John pinched off a piece of hamburger, poured some ketchup on the plate, dipped it, and gave it to the boy. The child grinned from ear to ear.

"That's probably enough food for him right now," I said. "Don't feed him too much too quickly—he won't be able to take it."

John brushed my concern aside. "What are you gonna name this little guy?" he asked as the child picked up the hamburger.

I frowned at the burger and shrugged at John's question. Naming children, a great responsibility, felt routine to me by then. I often named children after donors, board members, or friends back home. Often a special bond develops between the child and the person he or she is named after. "How about Johnny?" I said.

Cheese lifted his great hairy hand and smoothed his goatee. "Really?" His voice cracked. He looked at his namesake, his eyes misty. "Is there anywhere around here I can buy him some britches and shoes?" He swallowed hard and hugged the child.

"Yeah, but wait until I get back," I said, "and no more food for him, okay?" I excused myself and went to the front desk to see if any phone lines were available.

"Joe! Baby! You're a father again! It's a boy!" I was giddy from the sound of his voice and from fatigue. "We named him Johnny in honor of Cheese. I really need you. Talk to me forever. . . . I'm tired and feeling blue."

"You're my 'forever girl,'" Joe said. "I love you more than anything in this world. Don't you forget it." We had been married for twelve years, and he knew by now that when I was away from him for long, I soon started to feel anxious and insecure. This was one of those calls and he knew it instinctively. "Will you come home soon?"

"Yes, baby, as soon as I can," I said. "I miss you so much." Between all his responsibilities at the law office and for the foundation, Joe often worked fourteen hours a day, including Saturday and half a day on Sunday after church services. Mercy and Sharing had grown. We were caring for more than 1,800 children in our orphanages and schools. Joe, being the sole breadwinner in our house, took the responsibility of covering all expenses of Mercy and Sharing not covered by fund-raising. Over the years our personal outlay had amounted to more than $500,000. Joe and I talked until the phone lines gave out. When I got back to the table, Johnny was still eating.

"Uh, Cheese," I said, "exactly how much has he had to eat so far?"

"Ah, nothin' he wouldn't find at a Texas potluck," Cheese said.

"No, seriously," I said. "What?"

"Mmm. He's a growing boy. He was hungry. Lessee—the burger, a couple Coca-Colas, some spaghetti, fish, mangoes, a fruit punch, another side of beans, chocolate ice cream for dessert . . ."

"I get the picture," I said, shaking my head. Johnny sat on Cheese's knee, his tiny arms around John's thick neck. I reached to pick the child up. He clung tighter. I had experienced enough sensitive digestive tracts in children by then to know that our young friend was going to be okay, but things would undoubtedly get messy very soon. A smile crossed my face. Our board member would have to learn the hard way. "Well, looks like he's yours until tomorrow, Cheese."

John smiled unknowingly. "Well, little Suz, I gladly volunteer."

I reached into my bag. "I've only got six diapers." I handed them to John. "Pace yourself." I went to my room. It was still early evening, and I lay on the bed reading, listening to the fullness of night, with its mysterious sounds of howling dogs, crowing roosters, and the occasional snap of distant gunfire. Mystic fuchsia and melon colors drifted through the room, painted as though from the vanishing sun on the horizon.

The next morning I knocked on Cheese's door. He opened it, dark circles under his eyes. "Get much sleep?" I asked.

"The mangoes were probably a mistake," he said. He motioned to a cot, where Johnny lay asleep in the morning sun. The child wore a diaper fashioned from a pillowcase and John's bootlaces. "We ran out about midnight. Projectile diarrhea—all night."

OVER THE NEXT THREE years John Branchizio spent as much time as he could at our orphanage. He became a protector and father figure to all our children. He loved to pick them up and carry them on his huge shoulders, especially those who could not walk. On some of the more dangerous nights, John stood watch by our front gates, his eyes ever alert, his gun by his side.

A little boy named David came to us during those years, paralyzed, unable to leave the wheelchair we were able to get for him. John worked with David constantly. They rattled to each other in English and Creole. Neither understood the other's words, but they didn't seem to mind. About a year into David's "therapy," I walked into the courtyard one afternoon, where I heard Cheese laughing and shouting, "All right! That-a-boy! Come on, little man! You're doing it!" And there was David, halfway across the courtyard, moving his metal walker by himself, all smiles, walking toward John's outstretched arms.

Little Johnny also flourished at the orphanage. He grew into a gorgeous child, happy, smart, and constantly by Cheese's side whenever he visited.

THE NEWSPAPER REPORT WAS carried in papers around the world— Israel, France, Australia, Russia, and all across America. Some articles or pieces were lengthy, some shorter. I sat on the couch in the living room and read them all as the auburn-and-yellow aspen trees shimmered in a bone-chilling wind. I saved them in my heart, in my ocean of sorrow, in my inability to let go.

October 15, 2003 Gaza City

A roadside bomb went off beneath a convoy carrying U.S. diplomats Wednesday in Gaza, killing three American members of a security detail and injuring another, U.S. officials said.

The convoy was carrying U.S. Embassy officials to Gaza to interview Palestinian students who have applied for Fulbright scholarships in the United States.

Two Americans died at the scene, a third on his way to a hospital, and a fourth was hospitalized.

President Bush blamed Palestinian officials, saying they "should have acted long ago to fight terror in all its forms."

Among the dead was John Branchizio, who died two days after his thirty-seventh birthday. . . .

❖ ❖ ❖

WE HELD A MEMORIAL service at the orphanage.

More than two hundred mourners, mostly children, came to pay homage to their friend. On the stage at the front of the chapel, we set up a folding table covered with a white linen cloth on which we placed flowers, a Bible, and a picture of John. After three little girls sang a farewell song in Creole, all the orphanage children stood to walk across the stage to say good-bye. Many smiled as they walked by; some wept. Johnny patted Cheese's picture and touched his face as he crossed by, murmuring words of prayer and remembrance. Last to cross the platform was David. He moved his metal walker by himself. His face was bright, his smile strong.

Chapter 21

The Secret Song

FEBRUARY 2004.

Aristide and his loyalists had managed to remain in power for a decade, but his administration was dogged by charges of human rights violations, corruption, and widespread, grinding poverty among the Haitian people. Haiti erupted in violence as anti-Aristide militias sought to overthrow his government. It was as if the entire country had been doused in gasoline, and someone tossed a match.

We were not immune.

Masked gunmen with automatic weapons surrounded my orphanage. They threatened to kill all my children if not allowed to take over the compound.

Reginaud Basin, the foundation's new director in Haiti, called me first. "These are serious men," Reginaud said. "They have already stolen everything in our warehouse in Cité Soleil. They will do as they say."

Reginaud wasn't lying. Why would he lie? I knew who he was talking about—some of these gunmen were the same gang members Mark had once befriended, but times had changed. One of our children had been shot three times in the stomach as she made her way to the feeding center in Cité Soleil. She lived, but we were warned. For some reason, the gang members believed I—or anyone associated with me—needed to be taught a lesson.

"Reginaud," I said, "I'll be right down."

Trish was able to book another red-eye immediately. One of my best volunteers, Kathleen Carlson, connected with me in Miami. Reginaud picked us up at the Haitian airport. He had already proved his worth many times over. I had hired him as my in-country director after firing Poupon Pacaud. Reginaud seemed to run the foundation well. A Haitian national, he was forty-three, educated in New York, and had a business background. We talked on the phone daily. The children at the orphanage all loved him. Several times Joe and I flew him to Aspen and hosted him at our house. When I received the Rose Award at Kensington Palace in London, we flew him there as a reward for his hard work.

As we rushed to the orphanage, Reginaud and I began to compare notes.

"Things are very hot in Haiti right now," Reginaud said. "I predict Aristide will be out of here in seven days. Things are getting worse."

Gunfire crackled in the distance. We passed a barricade of smoldering tires. Black smoke oozed from the fire, cloaking a group of men who shook their fists as we passed. I caught flashes of their rifles, pistols, machetes, and sticks. Word on the street was that President Aristide had made enemies of the armed gangs called the Chimère ("ghost") by demanding more and more of their cut of the drug trade. It was a strange relationship. Aristide had hired the

Chimère in the first place as his unofficial militia. They were thugs, criminals, murderers, drug dealers, and drug lords who drove around in government vehicles wearing flak jackets and helmets. Word was he also gave them a zero-tolerance mandate, meaning: "If you see somebody doing something you think is illegal, shoot them."

"It's probably Viximar who made them all mad at you," Reginaud said.

I nodded.

Viximar, who had been with me since we began in 1994, had betrayed me in the end. He had falsified adoption papers to make money on the side. I was saddened by this, but didn't vilify Viximar. He was paid a living wage by Haitian standards, but greed can often prove overpowering. Maybe he thought he'd lose his job someday and figured he needed to take extra measures. There could have been a million reasons why he did what he did. I have many good workers within the foundation, many of whom I adore, but I have learned over the years that Haitian culture is one of desperation. A poverty-stricken country is fertile ground for corruption and greed, even for the best of us.

"How is Viximar doing?" I asked. Since our experiences with the Pacauds, we had learned not to fire anybody right away. Our new tactic was to put them on probation, where they still drew a salary until, if necessary, we could build a solid case and take the appropriate action then.

"Oh, you know," Reginaud said, "he eats, but he is very angry at you."

It would have been easy for Viximar to feed the gangs information on when I would arrive, when the orphanage wasn't completely guarded, and what were our most vulnerable times.

"By the way," Reginaud said. "I told the gangs we would have

a meeting with them today." We drove by more angry protesters.
The entire city of Port-au-Prince seemed to be on fire.

"Fine by me," I said. "When?"

"I told them no later than noon."

"Reginaud—that's in thirty minutes! We'll never make it."

Reginaud nudged the driver. "Hurry a bit," he said.

Our Isuzu hurtled on. In the distance I could just make out another barricade. The Chimère had begun routinely piling old tires
in the middle of essential thoroughfares, pouring gasoline over the
tires, and lighting them on fire. Enough room was left for one vehicle to pass, only after getting permission from the leader of each
barricade. Worthiness was often based on what you were willing to
offer.

Suddenly our SUV screeched to a halt. I could see a group of
masked men running toward our vehicle. Naked from the waist up,
all carried assault rifles. A dead body lay in the road. It must have
happened the night before, because the body was covered with
flies. About twenty men surrounded our vehicle. A haze of yelling
and screaming erupted, part English, part Creole: *Out! Out! Get
out! Get out!* We got out. *Shoot them! Shoot them!* Reginaud started
talking, talking, talking, very fast. I started going at it too—a
blather of anything I could think of: *I respect you; I'm praying for
you*—trying to sound like a missionary, thrusting my hands in front
of me where they could be seen. *Les enfants! We're taking care of
children!* On and on, pleading our case, trying to convince them
we support whatever they're doing. Reginaud's hands were in the
air; Kathleen was halfway in the car and halfway out. The men
pointed their guns at our heads. All fingers were on triggers. One
main gang member gave the order: *Shoot them now! Shoot them
now!*

For some reason—something I said, something Reginaud

said—the main gang member lowered his rifle. The others kept their guns aimed at our heads, but it sounded as if they were beginning to debate among themselves. Reginaud jumped back into the car. The head gunman yelled at him: "No! No! No!" Reginaud stuck his hands back up and nodded at us. Slowly we started to climb back into the car. "Respect! Respect!" Reginaud repeated. The head gunman began pushing the other rifles down. Another started removing rocks and tires in front of us. Reginaud hit the accelerator and we squeezed through. To this day, I don't know what turned the tide.

We raced on to the meeting with the gang members. Three minutes before twelve, we arrived. On the dark dirt floor of a vacant church, we sat on our haunches—Reginaud, Kathleen, and I. There were no lights. Twenty or thirty faces peered at us from out of the murkiness. I recognized several: Amaral, the current gang leader of Bellecourt; Blanc Mano, who works my area and Billy, leader of a different gang.

Reginaud translated for me.

"I want to make sure Mercy and Sharing is still in good favor here," I said. "I also ask that if there's any shooting, it won't happen near the children."

They all laughed. I couldn't read their minds, so I smiled. I've learned that even in the midst of heated discussions, it's good policy to smile when you say something the other finds funny. I also know gang members can kill me if they choose. There's mutual understanding—they know if they kill me, I must have powerful friends who will come after them, in some way or another. And I do. So the gang leaders are not exactly sure what I have in my pocket. And I've never shown them.

"It looks like Aristide will be leaving soon and things will get worse," I continued. Reginaud kicked me so hard I thought I would bleed. He didn't translate for me, but several gang members understood enough English to get it. I saw my faux pas. These people were guarding Aristide. If Aristide left: a) they'd have no source of income anymore; and b) whoever took over in Haiti would get rid of them because they're criminals, murderers, drug dealers, and dangerous. So that was a stupid, stupid thing for me to say. I changed direction quickly: "We're thinking of making a project in Amaral's community, and also of expanding into Billy's territory."

They seemed pleased with that suggestion and started listing projects they wanted. Billy wanted a basketball court like the one I built for Amaral. And he had visions for other projects. The list grew longer and longer. Finally I interrupted; good relations were important, but not the main reason I was here. "As you know, one of our little girls was shot, and right now my orphanage is under siege. I'm told we have a problem getting our food back and forth. I'd like to know how we can resolve this."

Amaral spoke: "We will make sure nothing happens to your kids. We really do want you to expand, and we have many ideas for projects." He pointed to Blanc Mano. "How about him? Can you do something for Blanc Mano?" Blanc Mano lifted his shirt and showed a gunshot wound. It had been treated with a homemade plaster bandage and looked infected.

"Can you get me a doctor?" Blanc Mano asked.

"You know there's no doctor that's going to come down here," I said. "I'm going to have to take you out—would you agree to that? But I can't do it right now. We've got to get to the orphanage immediately." I knew it would be tough to find a doctor who would help Blanc Mano. Everybody in Haiti knew him as a criminal and assassin.

Blanc Mano agreed.

"One more thing," Amaral said. He said it more to Reginaud than to me. Amaral cleared his throat like he had something very important to say. "It's a message: The blanc needs to talk to Patrick."

I had never met Patrick, but I had seen him from a distance and knew his reputation. He was a huge, mean, well-muscled thug who commanded a tribe of henchmen in Cité Soleil. They always seemed to be at war over turf, women, and drug money.

"I don't see Patrick anywhere here," I said.

Amaral nodded. He looked directly at me. "He'll find you."

WE WERE NOT SURE how we'd get into the orphanage compound, but we drove on anyway. It had been surrounded for several days now. Sometimes the gunmen fired into the air, Reginaud told us. Reginaud had spoken by phone to our elderly orphanage director, who said our children were frightened and crying a lot. Several times the gunmen had pounded on the gates, yelling their demands and shouting that they wanted to talk to the blanc. They had announced that if Reginaud and I didn't show up by noon the next day, they would start shooting children. The director thought he recognized Patrick as leader of the gunmen.

I had previously heard Patrick's claim that he owned my land. It didn't mean anything. We have people coming to our gate on a monthly basis claiming they own our property—that's just the way it is in Haiti. Until recently, there hasn't been a title law that could be easily enforced. We fought hard to gain clear title to the land, and received it, but if people don't know we have the title, they try familiar tactics. It's just business. Gang members often claim they own land because they've got clout. If you're a little peasant, and you're sitting on a backyard plot, and someone like Patrick comes around claiming he owns your land, you're probably going to let him have it.

So Patrick had already tried this with us. And Reginaud had spoken to one of his guys and told him to take us to court. So Patrick did, with Reginaud acting on my behalf. The judge threw the case out, encouraging Patrick to come back when his documentation was tighter.

Patrick was still after us. About a half mile before we got to the compound, I could see Reginaud start to sweat. I had no idea how we'd be able to get into the orphanage with the gunmen surrounding it, but we kept going. Beads of perspiration dotted Reginaud's forehead and rolled down his cheeks. He kept glancing from side to side. The rocky dirt roads leading to the orphanage were surprisingly bare. Things were too quiet—that's what happens when gangs of armed gunmen roam the neighborhood. *Jesus*—I closed my eyes—*I know you can do all things. . . .*

Suddenly our SUV's brakes screeched. Men surrounded us. They wore stockings over their heads and scarves over their mouths. All carried rifles. They ordered us out of the car. They spoke loudly and fast—I didn't catch half of what they were saying. Reginaud got out.

"Patrick?" Reginaud kept saying. "Where is Patrick?"

The men hollered—evil, dark, laughter. You can't just *talk* to a man as powerful as Patrick.

"Patrick," Reginaud repeated. I was so glad Reginaud was on our side.

From the shadows stepped one of the largest men I've ever seen. He shoved his henchmen aside, opened the passenger front door to our SUV, and climbed inside. Reginaud shook his head, incredulous, and climbed in the back with me. The crowd drifted away, pointing their guns down, looking for the next vehicle to come along. Another man climbed on the back bumper of our SUV. He held a U.S.-made assault rifle.

Patrick was in our car.

"Drive," Patrick said to our driver. (We often have a driver in Haiti. It helps to have someone navigate local roads, and you can seldom safely leave your car without having someone guard it.) We drove up to the orphanage. Men with guns surrounded the compound. They saw Patrick and opened the gates. Some prayers are answered in the strangest ways. The children were all inside, kept out of view. Anything could happen now.

I've learned that the minute you sit down with angry people, you need to get them to stop yelling so you can find out what they really need. I invited Patrick to one of our little buildings, where we could be alone. Reginaud came along to translate. Patrick's sidekick with the rifle came too.

"I understand there's a problem," I said. "If I've done something to offend you, please tell me now."

Patrick stood up. Out of the corner of my eye I could see Patrick's henchman fidgeting. Patrick took three steps toward me and paused. He stared directly into my face. His arms rose. Was he going to strangle me?

Suddenly Patrick lunged. He grabbed me around the neck with both arms. I felt smothered. Patrick's sidekick jumped up and threw his hands in the air: "No, no, no! We love you! We love what you do!" This was all in Creole.

"We don't have a problem with you," Patrick said. This was his "hug." He let go and sat down.

My head was spinning. "I'm so relieved. Tell me what I can do. I know there's been so much confusion."

"Water," he said. "We want water."

"To drink?"

"The well," Patrick said. "We want to use it."

We have a well that's 250 feet deep. It's one of the deepest wells near Port-au-Prince. The UN dug it. When I bought the land, the well was already there. It's secured, walled in with iron, and a real commodity.

"We tried to use the well a couple times and were sent away," Patrick continued.

"Do you mean my people sent your people away because they wanted water?" I said. "Oh, my gosh! That will never happen again! You can put one of your guards there with my guards to make sure. We have water up the ying-yang; you can take it twenty-four-seven." I figured that as long as Patrick had his own guard there too, it would give him a responsibility to protect the well.

Patrick walked toward me and hugged my neck again. In Cité Soleil, where Patrick lived, nobody hugs anybody; it's not that kind of atmosphere. But when I go there I always hug everybody I talk to. The mean guys—sometimes they back off and don't let me hug them. But I always try. Patrick knew that about me. He was honoring me.

"One more thing," I said. "What about the gunmen around the orphanage—can you get them to leave?"

Patrick looked away. "There are legions here," he said. "I will get mine to leave. But Aristide gave us all guns." He looked at me. "You are rich. I cannot help you further."

SEVERAL OF MY CHILDREN looked underweight. Most were dehydrated. The skin on their little arms hung loose, and their lips cracked when they smiled. What should have been the whites of their eyes were mustard colored.

Reginaud explained that they were recovering from measles and all of them had gone through a long bout of diarrhea. This was the first I had heard of it. Reginaud promised they were getting the nutritional supplements we had sent via ocean container from the United States. The little ones still laughed and seemed cheery, so I accepted this. Our nurse confirmed they were recovering, but gave me a grave look.

I had hired two armed guards from a security company. As it turned out, the guards were more frightened than the children. I gave orders that one watch the front gate and the other the back because we had no razor wire, and gunmen could easily scale the wall.

"But they've been shooting at us—every night," was the reply. "What do we do?"

"Shoot back!" I said. "Protect the children—they can't run!" I nodded toward the handicapped quarters, where sixty-two children lived.

"But we don't have any bullets!" said the guards.

"You're joking, right?" I said through my translator. This had to be a miscommunication. Surely the security company would not send guards with 12-gauge shotguns and no ammunition. I clenched my jaw to hold my temper and keep from scaring the children hovering nearby.

It was true. It was nearly sundown and the shooting would start soon. I was so furious I didn't have any energy left to be afraid. If I said the things I wanted to say at that moment the guards might leave us and take their empty guns with them. We would be all by ourselves—forty women and nearly a hundred orphaned children, most terminally ill or paralyzed.

"UN-BE-LIEV-ABLE! Tell me where to buy bullets, shells, whatever those things take!" I yelled to no one in particular. Everyone squirmed and shrugged and seemed to consider who they knew that had a spare bullet. Daniel, one of our workers and a good translator, snuck outside the gates to determine the whereabouts of a secure ammunition seller. It seemed to take forever. I paced around the compound. A train of children followed me. I had a tremendous headache. Each time I rubbed my forehead, fifty toddlers did the same. I walked and walked, praying, thinking, trying to plan how to protect us long enough to work out a lasting solution.

Daniel rolled the gate open several inches and squeezed back in. "We have to go to Pétionville," he said. "But we have to hurry. There is a man on Rue Grégoire who sold ammunition to rebels several days ago. If we leave now we may still catch him." He took my arm and commanded the children not to follow. We ran to the truck and tore through the compound gates. We took back alleys to avoid barricades. When we arrived at Rue Grégoire we began asking for a man named Kenson. We were sent to an alleyway near a small merchant area. At the third stall, a large, ink-colored man stood. His dreadlocks hung past his shoulders.

"Kenson?" I asked.

The man did not answer. I knew my Creole was not good and pushed Daniel to the front. Apparently, nobody told Kenson he was wearing a woman's T-shirt. His read: ALL MEN BEWARE, I'M PMSING! It was a lovely pink.

Kenson reached behind a makeshift counter and pulled out two cases of shotgun shells. They didn't come cheap.

We ran back to the truck and took off for the compound. Close to the gate we approached a roadblock with several Haitian police vehicles and five armed, uniformed officers. One waved us to the side.

"Identification," he said.

I handed him my American passport. I may as well have given

him a brick of gold because that's what I saw in his eyes as he jerked it from my fingers. I'd been stopped by Haitian police before, and as the policeman walked away with our documents I decided to get very ill very quickly. I fell over into Daniel's lap, holding my stomach and thinking of every noxious thing I had ever made contact with—the Port-au-Prince morgue, the time I got sick on rum, the mess I had to clean up when my dog Freud got diarrhea on the plane. In no time, I honestly felt ill. The officer came back, our documents tucked under his armpit. The driver and Daniel could leave, he announced, but I must go to the police station to verify the information on my passport. I knew it was a ruse.

"She is very ill," Daniel said. "She is sick. She needs to go to the hospital."

I whimpered.

"Ask him if I can meet him at the station tomorrow," I said in a low voice.

Back and forth they went, for at least fifteen minutes. Daniel's tone was pleading; the officer's, bargaining. At last, the policeman scribbled something on a ticket and waved the driver past.

"I couldn't understand a word you guys said," I said to Daniel. "You were talking so fast. What'd he write on the ticket?"

"His address. He wants you to mail him some language tapes. He wants to learn English and move to America."

"To the hospital?" asked our driver.

"No, I'm much better, thanks," I answered, and sat up.

We arrived back at the compound as the last hint of daylight vanished. I handed the boxes of shells to the guards and told each that if they heard gunfire close by to shoot in the air so the enemy would know we had protection. At least we would not appear as easy a target as they probably thought.

I sat down for a minute to play with the children. They climbed all over me. Daniel sat down beside me and I gave him a high five. Every child demanded to be high-fived also. I stood up and began to move my feet a little.

"Come on," I said to the kids, "come dance with me."

I punched the air and sang. The kids all started bouncing up and down. Every child who could walk joined in. Others in wheelchairs laughed and wiggled with us. It was the only thing I could think of—a song I learned when I was a teenager. I told Daniel later to be sure to explain to the kids that it was our secret song and never to sing it in front of other people. Unless people were familiar with the Michael Jackson album, they wouldn't get it. I didn't want them judging my kids.

"We're bad, we're bad—really, really bad. . . ."

It was our victory dance. To this day, some still do that jig when they get a new pair of shoes or do well on a school test, and especially if someone gets adopted.

DAYS PASSED AND GRADUALLY the orphanage felt safer, though the country was still crazy. Aristide was out, and it seemed all of Haiti was exploding. A lot of our employees could not get past the barriers to get to work. Any of our employees who wanted to spend nights received danger pay.

We began to run out of everything, especially food. There was still some left in our warehouse in Cité Soleil, but the guy who normally trucked our food was nowhere to be found. We enlisted one of the gang members out front to drive the truck, with another gang member, armed, in back of the truck with the food. The driver we chose was generally feared, so for some time we were able to get supplies back and forth. Anytime I went out we had him ride in the Isuzu with us because he commanded respect, which added to our

safety. We learned that certain times of the day were more dangerous than others. Mornings, everybody manned their burning tires.
But from noon to two, they seemed to be gone. After that, until
5 p.m., it was shooting again. Up and down, up and down.

Over time, we got our system down. All the employees came
back to work and everybody was able to come and go. We started
buying food on the streets, from the same gangs that stole our
food in the first place.

One day at the orphanage Reginaud cornered me. His face was
pale.

"It is time for you to leave the country," Reginaud said.

He knew me well by then. "I couldn't go even if I wanted," I
said. "The airport's closed."

"I have heard something," Reginaud said. He wasn't smiling. A
lot of journalists were getting out of the country by charter. I had
spoken to Joe about it as a possible option. Joe had also lined up a
military helicopter more than once for me.

Reginaud spoke slowly, carefully formulating his words. "There
are . . . rumors of a contract . . . ."

I stared at him, not knowing what he meant.

"A hit," Reginaud said. "A price . . . Susie . . . on you."

The gravity of what Reginaud said sank in. My life had been
threatened before, but it was always general. This was specific. For
some reason, somebody wanted me dead. They were offering a
price for anyone to do so. A hit on the streets was equal to having a
"wanted" poster tacked to every lamppost in Port-au-Prince. Every
gang member, every Chimère, every corrupt policeman, every two-
bit thug who owned a gun would be lining up for easy money.

"The border to the Dominican Republic is closed," Reginaud
said, "but sometimes you can get past. I will take you there myself.
If we get out, you can get a flight to Miami."

"What happens if we can't get out?" I asked.

Reginaud was silent.

Kathleen overheard the conversation and came close to me. She was no coward, and I trusted her judgment. "Reginaud's right, Susie," she said. "The children are okay now. It's time to leave."

I looked around at the faces: Reginaud's, Kathleen's, those of the children who were sitting with me. Then I looked at the orphanage wall. Anybody who did anything good—this country seemed designed to block it. The whole country outside the compound gate wanted me dead. I never knew whom to trust anymore. Getting a military flight might work, but it would mean arranging contacts, traveling back through the city—any number of links in the chain could be suspect. Reginaud was right. Better to risk a run to the Dominican border and take our chances.

I thought of Joe, and nodded.

"Let's get out of here," I said.

Chapter 22

A r r i v a l

IN THE CLOAK OF early morning we slipped out of the compound
and raced toward the Dominican Republic border. Creole voices
could be heard in the darkness. We were seven in all: Reginaud
drove, Kathleen sat next to me, and a few journalists who were
staying near the orphanage caught a ride. There are three entry
points between Haiti and the Dominican Republic: from Port-au-
Prince to Santo Domingo at Jimaní; from Cap-Haïtien to Santiago
at Dajabón; and a third route near the center of the island at Elías
Piña. We raced to the closest.

In two hours we reached the swishing of knee-high water that
separates Haiti from the Dominican Republic. The little bridge
that divides the two countries at this crossing is usually chaotic—a
mad rush of merchants: cockfighters importing their wares, Spanish soldiers posted from the UN, stick and charcoal gatherers with
loads high on their heads. This morning was strangely quiet and

heavily guarded. "No entry!" the guard shouted and held out his fist as we drove up.

"I have American journalists," Reginaud said in Creole. "They need to get back to Miami." He lowered his voice. "They would be interested in making a rrangements."

The guard glanced around. "Registration and passports," he said.

Reginaud motioned the guard closer and handed him our papers. "Our registration's been stolen," he said.

"Then you cannot pass," said the guard, handing the papers back.

Reginaud reached into his shirt pocket and folded some bills between the papers. "Perhaps I have found the registration now," Reginaud said.

Negotiations continued. This wasn't going to be easy. An hour slipped by, then another. Several other guards surrounded our vehicle. I heard the word *donation* many times, and *extra*. We traded everything we had—all the money in our pockets, and beers and juice. They wanted our luggage, so we kept giving them more dollars. Finally, we heard the magic word—accompanied by a quick head gesture—that needed no translation: "Okay."

We drove hard to the international airport, about an hour from the border. The Dominican Republic is considered safer than Haiti, but word of a contract can spread quickly across borders. Traffic at the airport seemed much lighter than usual.

"What did that sign say?" I yelled from the backseat.

"The airport is closed," Reginaud said. "But maybe we can arrange something here."

"Totally out of luck," said the guard at the curb. "They might be able to find you a plane inside, but they're going for about twelve thousand dollars each—cash only." Between us we had about fifty dollars left—it was our hidden emergency money. We offered that; the guard laughed. "Do you see anyone else here? We're closed! The DR has three airports. Try another."

The next airport was six hours away. Thank God, it was open. We spent the night in the terminal, bought tickets with a credit card, and got set to board the plane. I hugged Reginaud. "Thank you so much for all you do," I said.

Reginaud didn't smile. "It is time for you to leave, Susie," he said.

Reginaud drove the SUV back through the border. He was my hero.

SEVENTEEN DAYS PASSED. I phoned Reginaud at the orphanage every day, sometimes three or four times. He assured me operations were smooth and the children were healthy. I hired a former federal DEA agent turned private investigator to check out the real word about me on the streets. The PI confirmed the rumor. I was a target, and every gangster in the Haitian underworld knew it. I wasn't sure what my next move would be. Probably just hole up in Aspen for a few months and wait until the hit order passed, if it ever did. For now, Reginaud would have to run everything. I consoled myself by taking long walks with my dogs. Joe and I reconnected. I phoned my fund-raising contacts. Every morning I read long passages from Scripture.

Say to those with anxious heart, "Take courage, fear not. Behold, your God will come with vengeance; the recompense of God will come, but he will save you."
—Isaiah 35:4

I phoned a few other people too, just to keep a third eye on the orphanage and our food shipments in Haiti. They'd enter our compound at random times under the guise of bringing donated soap and toothpaste for the children. Reports trickled back. Most things looked legit, they said, but stay by the phone. It was hard to tell.

On April 5, Reginaud Basin called. He rambled into the phone, a long, strung-out barrage of words, some in Creole, some in English. Finally I understood one phrase clearly.

"I am going to kill myself," Reginaud announced.

I couldn't get a word in edgewise. Nothing I said connected. After an hour of listening to his mental meanderings I could determine nothing other than that he was "a very bad man" who had "succumbed to the siren song of corruption" and that "if this man should disappear" he would "be a missing person we should not miss." For fifteen minutes straight he mumbled almost imperceptibly a sentence where I could ascertain nothing but the word *milk*. After having him repeat it to me twice more, I heard the word *took*.

Finally I screamed into the receiver, "Reginaud! Please stop talking for a second!"

He hung up.

The phone rang again. It was one of my "spies."

"It's a clear shot," he said. "Definitely happening. I've been watching for a month. Happens most nights at your warehouse."

The call was short. I grasped its meaning—and now I was pretty sure who was behind the order to have me hit. I phoned one of my most trusted friends in Haiti, a man who runs a long-standing relief agency.

"Is it true?" I asked.

"We've been hearing the same reports," he said. "I didn't want to alarm you until I was certain. You know he spent most of yester-

day in our Port-au-Prince office, claiming you're trying to assassi-
nate him. He's lost it."

"Lost it?"

"Gone over the edge. Completely. There's no telling what he
might do."

"Do you think he'll try to have me hurt?" I asked.

"I'd say he's always been highly motivated to have you out of
the way."

REGINAUD BASIN WORE A Rolex watch. He liked the best suits. He
knew we were on to him, thus his phone call to me to "confess"
things and feign remorse. He probably hoped we would call off the
dogs already hot on his trail and allow him to keep his tidy salary.
But something would not allow me to let it go so easily. I needed
to send a message that certain behaviors were not tolerable. I
needed to hold him accountable for his crimes.

I phoned Trish and flew to Miami.

Mark Salter, a businessman and friend, met me the next morning at a little Cuban café called La Carreta on Key Biscayne. He's
an absolute soldier for relief development. Five years earlier he
had heard about the children of Mercy and Sharing, sold his
home and bought a smaller one, and sent us the difference. At
six-foot-four and about 220 pounds, he looks gruff and is miserly
with his smiles, but he has the capacity to cry over other people's
children.

I explained my plan.

"Susie, why are you doing this?" he said. "You're not going to
save the whole dang country of Haiti. Let somebody else do that!"

I didn't expect these words. Not having slept all night, I was
short with him. "Okay! I'm willing to do that," I said. "Show me

who. I'll give the job to anybody who'll take it!" I realized people in the café were noticing us, but I was on a roll. "Let's see . . . job description: Must work impossibly long hours with little sleep. Must be willing to bury friends and children. Able to maneuver through coup d'états and gang violence without losing supplies and getting shot at. Must have extraordinary personal radar to detect betrayal among friends and staff. Salary—oh, there is none."

Mark shook his head. "You can't go to Haiti, Susie. Not this time. You have to listen to me. They all want you dead."

This was unlike the Mark Salter I had known. Unshaven, wearing flip-flops and shorts, he looked as if he had been up all night and hadn't been to the office yet. "Susie," he groaned my name. "At two this morning I woke up from a violent nightmare. In it, you were . . ." He shook his head. "I feel it—you'll die if you go to Haiti this time. I just know it. Nobody can guarantee your safety down there anymore."

I put limited stock in dreams, but I trusted the wisdom of my friend. I softened my tone. "Mark," I said, "what do I do?"

"I've been thinking about it ever since I woke up," he said. "I've got a plan."

Mark waved from his truck as he peeled out of the parking lot. I sat there at the little table for a long time praying for strength. I pulled my Bible from my purse.

He is their strength in time of trouble. And the Lord helps them, and
delivers them; He delivers them from the wicked, and saves them, be-
cause they take refuge in Him.
                                                                —*Psalms 37:39–40*

◆　　◆　　◆

FIVE YEARS AGO, AFTER adding up the cost of staying in hotels every time I passed through Miami en route to Haiti, Joe decided to buy an old boat for me to use as a floating room. Our boat, the *Lord Jim*, had a few holes and the engines no longer worked, but for $14,000 it became my floating home away from home. I didn't care if it couldn't actually go anywhere. Two rooms, a head and a shower, and a refrigerator that still worked—all I needed. I could wake up and watch dolphins breaching and manatees nursing calves in the halcyon waters of the bay.

Joe agreed that Mark had a good plan and we'd try it. Joe telephoned Reginaud in Haiti instead of my doing it. We agreed Reginaud hated me but still might take a directive from Joe. Reginaud might also think that Joe would be more willing to forgive him than I would be.

It was a tricky situation all around. All Reginaud had officially done so far was confess to "something"—over the phone to me in Aspen. He never would admit any of the specifics of his crimes. So Joe invited Reginaud to Miami for the weekend to "work things out." Better to have Reginaud come to us than for us to go to him, Joe reasoned. Joe had a case pending in Aspen and couldn't actually go down, but he made it sound like he'd be there, too. We thought Reginaud might not show up if he knew it would just be me.

On the phone with Joe, Reginaud seemed excited to have a chance to clear the air. I knew he'd want to keep his job—we were paying him $4,000 per month, plus use of an SUV and other benefits. It was a fortune by Haitian standards.

Reginaud would opt to come to Miami to maintain his coveted position and for a chance to go shopping, perhaps a little for himself, because there were *many* things he always needed. Undoubtedly, he believed that we as Christians were obligated to forgive and forget whatever he had done, so all he had to do was confess and all would be made right again.

Wrong.

Reginaud agreed to take a polygraph test to verify the validity of whatever he was going to tell us. Perhaps he thought he could beat the machine and pass the test somehow.

An experienced business contact referred me to the Slattery Agency. Dr. John Palmatier, who ran the agency, was one of the few polygraph experts used by the U.S. military regularly. My contact felt certain that Dr. Palmatier was the best in Florida, if not the United States.

Dr. Palmatier asked me to be at the agency office at noon, one hour before Reginaud was scheduled to arrive. I recalled the many times I had seen Reginaud after a month or two of absence. I'd give him a hearty hug and say he looked well. His joy in seeing me had never seemed fake. Now the malignant truth would soon be unmasked. I entered the building with a heavy heart.

I had already filled Dr. Palmatier in on the situation and presented him a list of questions, part written by Mark Salter, part by Joe, with a few of my own. He refined them and explained how a polygraph works, how 65 percent of what we communicate is actually nonverbal, and how nonverbal communication is extremely accurate. By the end of our meeting I knew what to expect and that the level of accuracy according to current data and statistics would be high. I had taken a polygraph myself many years ago and found it highly accurate. He led me down the hall to a room where I could watch via a feed from a hidden camera and see the test on a computer screen. When he left I slid onto the carpeted floor and got close to the screen. I took off my sandals and sat on the floor with my head in my hands until I heard a faint *tap, tap, tap*.

On the screen in front of me I watched the door to Dr.

Palmatier's office open. Reginaud walked in. What could he be thinking, wearing that outfit—the gold chains, the audacious dark suit, with his shirt unbuttoned to reveal his oversized belly?

"Reginaud," said Dr. Palmatier. He began the interview by establishing credibility. "I'm a federal and state court–certified polygraph expert. I am the only PhD in the United States who runs these tests on a daily basis. Most people with my educational background are university professors or work for the Department of Defense at a place called DOD Polygraph Institute in Fort Jackson, South Carolina. I've taught polygraph and lie detection in Israel, Japan, England, and China since 1987."

Reginaud made an effort to seem interested. "Is that so?" he asked.

"Yes. I worked for many of those years in China, testing corrupt Chinese officials. I was the only American at that time ever to be requested to do so."

"Wow. China," Reginaud said, examining his fingernails.

"The Krabachers have prepared a number of questions they wanted me to cover with you."

"Joe mentioned something like that to me," Reginaud said.

"According to my information, you were hired as in-country director of the foundation's orphanages and properties in Haiti. You were also charged with the day-to-day care, distribution of food, clothing, and other necessities to the children under the foundation's charge. You were also responsible for delegating work to one hundred fifty employees under you."

Reginaud nodded.

"And you understand," the doctor continued, "that you are here because you have admitted to doing some things you regret and that is the reason I have been hired by the Krabachers to give you a polygraph exam. You do not have to take it. You do not have to answer any of these questions. My understanding is that Mr. and Mrs. Krabacher have discussed these issues with you and you have come here of your own free will."

Reginaud nodded again.

"Do you have any health issues that would prevent you from taking this test, Reginaud?"

"Oh, well, I have been very tired. And I have this thing in my underpants. A genital infection that comes and goes. At one point it was very bad and then it just disappeared and came back again on and off. It used to be that my testicles stuck together."

"Sounds like genital herpes," said Dr. Palmatier.

"Yes, I am a real sexual animal," replied Reginaud.

Dr. Palmatier verified Reginaud's full name, address, phone number, marital status, citizenship, and so on. Reginaud answered the questions quickly and nonchalantly. On the video screen, I began to notice that Reginaud crossed and uncrossed his legs repeatedly. He started bouncing his foot. I could see his jaw clenching and the veins in his forehead pulsing. He flexed his fingers and crunched them into a fist again and again. He coughed, then coughed again. Soon he coughed with every answer. He coughed to the point where his words became almost imperceptible.

Dr. Palmatier sat patiently as if not noticing, and continued typing general information into the computer. Finally, after a five-minute deluge of nonstop coughing, the doctor asked, "Would you like some water?"

"Oh! Yes! Thank you! That would be wonderful!" Reginaud rolled out the last three syllables. The doctor rose, and I watched him leave the room. Reginaud didn't cough once while the doctor was gone. He gulped the water when the doctor returned. Then the real questioning began.

"I don't remember stealing some of those things," Reginaud

said. "I don't remember taking diapers. The thing I really sold was milk. I took one container of milk."

"How big was the container?"

"Oh, you know," Reginaud said, "ocean freight, forty-foot, worth about forty thousand."

I could not believe Reginaud was revealing so much.

"What are some of the other things that you did or lied about to the Krabachers?" Dr. Palmatier asked, poker-faced.

"Ooooooh, there are so many!" Reginaud laughed. "Such as . . . overinvoicing for things. I remember putting names on the payroll of people who were actually not there."

More random questions came. It was a tactic, Dr. Palmatier had told me earlier. Then back to the crunch questions:

"Let's talk about the warehouse where the milk was kept," the doctor said. "The Krabachers said it was protected by armed guards and an employee they hired to keep inventory of supplies. How did you circumvent that system?"

"I fired their employee and hired someone I could get to do my things," Reginaud said. He looked almost gleeful. "They never knew. With one hundred fifty or more employees they did not check to see if the faces matched the names on the payroll. I fired the security guards and got a kickback from the new ones I hired. If they give me trouble, I fire them too. It was not hard, John!"

Reginaud rubbed his face, growing restless. He cocked his head to one side, then sat resolutely back into his chair. He closed his eyes. The silence was disturbing. Reginaud began speaking with a very different, self-possessed tone.

"John, who are you, really? I do not believe you are a polygrapher. I think you are someone else. Let me see your identification." Dr. Palmatier, without a word, opened his desk and pulled out his passport and a picture ID. He pointed to a couple of books on the shelf he had authored and several certificates framed on the office walls.

Reginaud was unconvinced. "Those are not real!" he proclaimed. "You can have all those made up anywhere, John." He had taken some kind of devious turn. The doctor wasn't put off for a minute.

"Reginaud, you have admitted to some serious things here. Why wouldn't you lie to me about doing these things?"

Reginaud grinned. "Oh, I feel cleansed to be able to say that to you, John. I want to tell you everything." His tone was almost whimsical. "Therapy is good. This is good therapy. It's liberating, talking with you, John, so liberating!"

Reginaud started coughing again and the doctor left to get him a lozenge. Dr. Palmatier opened the door to where I sat. The interview had been going for two hours.

"I can't believe he's telling you all this," I said. "Why would he confess to so much?"

"He wants to keep his job," the doctor said. "My hunch is that he needs the money to support his lifestyle. Plus, he believes you're still overly trusting of him. He wants continued access to your valuables in the warehouse so he can keep his scams going—that's where the real money is for him. Probably that's why he came here in the first place. He thinks he can either trick you into thinking he's sincerely repentant or intimidate you into leaving him alone."

The doctor returned to Reginaud.

"Yes, Joe Krabacher is a good man." Reginaud began talking without any questions. "And Susie can be good. But she is so very, very difficult, John. And so naïve."

Dr. Palmatier continued. "Why did you steal from Mercy and Sharing?"

"Women will do anything for a man if he has money," Reginaud said, a bemused smile appearing on his face. "And many women need me. When you have money, then the Haitian women love you. These women, they have needs. They all come flashing you."

"So you admit you stole milk from children to finance your affairs? And you gained, what did you say—about forty thousand dollars?"

"John, the children were fine! They did not need the milk. They had plenty."

I remembered the time I came to the orphanage when it was under siege by gunmen, how the children looked underweight and dehydrated. Reginaud said it had been measles. This devil! This small worm of a man! He had starved my children right under my nose. One of our children had died shortly after. The doctor blamed malnutrition. Reginaud had urinated on us. He had slit our throats.

I got off the floor and asked the receptionist to please have Dr. Palmatier call me when it was all over. I had seen enough.

Two hours later, back on the boat, I felt the need for a shower and a good dose of Cuban coffee. After peeling my sticky dress off I climbed into the tiny shower, leaned against the wall, and let the cold water wash away the memory of this bad dream. I attempted to shave my legs and underarms but bumped my head against the walls of the tiny shower each time I bent over. I put my foot against the wall, shaving one leg at a time. The cell rang. Balancing on one foot I opened the shower door but tipped over. Water sprayed from the open shower while the phone continued to ring. I pulled myself from between the toilet and the wall, grabbed a blanket from the futon, and ran with the phone upstairs to catch a better signal. "Hello? Hello!" It was the doctor.

"I would be very careful of Reginaud Basin if I were you," he said. "His perception of reality is skewed enough to make him dangerous."

"What would you do if you were me?" I asked.

"I'd find a lawyer and file criminal charges. Maybe you can prosecute him, get him thrown in jail. You may be able to retrieve the stolen funds. We've got his confession on tape—in some states it is admissible and can be used in court. Florida is one of them. You may want to ask your husband if he knows a good criminal attorney here in Miami."

I took a deep breath. "One more question, Dr. Palmatier." It was the question that had been on my mind for several days. "Did Reginaud Basin plan to have me killed? Did he order the hit?"

The doctor was silent for a moment. "I asked him if he ever planned to kill, harm, or frighten you, or had met with anyone to discuss having it done. Reginaud made his usual effort to distract me and sculpted a long description of what sounded like a no. Then I asked the question again, more specifically."

"What was the answer this time?" I asked.

"The answer from his mouth was no. But the technology detected a deceit. Based on my analysis of the test, and all the other relevant information, it's my professional opinion there were physiological reactions consistent with deception."

It was too much information to process. "So he was lying, then? He wanted me killed all along?" My voice cracked from fatigue and dread.

The doctor's tone lowered. "Reginaud failed the test."

I NEEDED TO CALL Joe. I got dressed and walked a couple hundred yards past the marina to a little café called Sundays at the Beach. I wanted to cry but could not give in just yet. Joe can always tell from my voice when I've been crying. I asked for an outside table and ordered a glass of frosted pinot noir and the special of the day, fresh stone crabs in butter sauce. They tasted so good. I closed my eyes and rested my chin in my hand. Jesus thanked God for the cup of wine at the Last Supper. I had to marvel at that. He knew he was about to be betrayed by a man who had been very close to him. Jesus knew he would be murdered within hours. Yet he still thanked God for the wine and bread. I bowed my head.

Thank you, God, for this wine. And thank you because I can have food when I am hungry. Please let me feed my children. Help me find an honest person to care for them when I'm not with them. And Lord, please help me love my enemy even when I'd rather hate him.

"Joe! Hi, honey. . . . Can you talk?" I asked when he picked up.

"Hold on, baby." I could hear the dogs yelping in the background. "Let me take you off speaker phone or they'll go crazy! They miss you and so do I, baby!"

I smiled and waited while he rounded them into a more manageable pile in his office. "Well? What happened?" he asked. "I've been trying to call you!"

I tried to reach beyond myself for a calm that would allow me to give the full report. Step by step, I filled Joe in. He took notes. He would call Reginaud later and tell him he was indeed fired. And Joe would call an attorney in Miami and begin to develop a case. Reginaud Basin would pay back the money he owed. We wanted him in jail.

"You okay, baby? Where are you now?" Joe asked.

"I'm at a café near the boat," I murmured. "I'm fine."

Then came the words I thought I had maneuvered safely past. "So you'll be on the five-thirty flight tomorrow? I'll pick you up in Denver."

I so wanted to be on that flight. How I wanted to go home right then.

"Honey," I said, firmly but respectfully. "You know that ain't gonna happen. We have at least three children in critical care right now. And I'm going to have to find someone we can trust to be our new director. We've got to find a way to get the supplies we have left from the warehouse to the orphanages and schools. There's no telling what else I'll find out once I get there."

"No," was all Joe said.

"Honey," I said. "You know I have to."

Joe was silent for a minute. His silence was encouraging me. "I know," he said. I knew he was planning who he would call next: a new security company, new guards, new people.

"I love you, Joe," I said.

"I love you, too, Susie," he said. "Now get some sleep."

Chapter 23

Hope

OCTOBER 2006.

There is no end zone in Haiti, no line you can run across to spike the ball or dance a jig. Not here. In fact, during the writing of this book, one of the foundation's volunteers was wounded by a gunshot, kidnapped, and held for $300,000 US ransom. Fortunately, a resolution was negotiated and our dear friend lived.

I have often imagined what it would be like to say my work is finished—what I would give for some buzzer, some whistle or checkered flag that marks the game as over and says I can run home a winner. But there is no definable end to the foundation's work.

On my desk is a ticket to return to Haiti. I will go, shortly. This time, what might I encounter? Many of my children were found in boxes or buckets, sometimes simply lying in the dirt by a gate or alleyway. Many are deformed or handicapped. Sometimes starvation, AIDS, or violence took their parents. Sometimes these little ones were deserted because the family could not or would not buy medicine or food to keep them alive, or because of a belief system that considers handicapped children a curse.

Raymonde came to us this way. He was left outside the gates of the government hospital in Port-au-Prince. For at least three days, we were told, he had sat on a piece of cardboard, rocking back and forth, back and forth, back and forth, chewing the forefinger of his right hand so that the flesh nearly fell away. He stared straight ahead most of the time, riveted. He kept on staring as he defecated and drooled, and the garbage and dust piled around him.

I named him Raymonde after the UN soldier who helped me when I found the child. Raymonde's body was crooked, his head misshapen—anyone could see right away he had some sort of developmental delay. I tried to pick him up, covered in excrement as he was, but he shrieked and scooted away. Passersby gathered and watched with interest, whispering and pointing. The guards who control the gate laughed as their shoulder straps swung loose, guns pointing haphazardly at the crowd and, far too often, in my direction. When little Raymonde screamed louder, I got on my knees, crawled behind him, and sat very still. I hummed while I swallowed and sniffed away any sign of tears—tears only scare a child and invite ridicule from bystanders. *Why would a foreigner care so much for a crazy child?*

Slowly, Raymonde began to watch me from the corner of his eye. I could see a thaw, a beginning of trust. Soon he allowed me to touch the small of his back, his little knee, his hand. I picked him up, carried him to safety, and saved my crying for a private time. I always imagine that the people who leave children behind are hopeful. Perhaps they watch from behind a shanty wall or some rooftop to see if their little package of skin and bones is taken up by anyone. I have to think so. It's too much for me to imagine that a mother or relative or friend could leave a dying child behind without so much as looking back.

There will be more children just like Raymonde.

Another one of my children, Kensen, was found in the Port-au-Prince city canal with a cinder block tied to his ankle. Kensen was trying desperately to keep his nose above the sewage-saturated rainwater. Nearly every bone from his waist down had been broken. A passerby had seen something barely moving in the sludge and gained the assistance of a Haitian national policeman to pull him up over the steep banks of the canal. The child was brought the same day to our abandoned-infant ward, located in the rear of the government hospital.

Anyone in Haiti could tell you why Kensen was in the canal. He had club feet. Practitioners of voodoo believe spirits were summoned to curse the family with this unhealthy child. Neighbors urged them to drown the child slowly.

I know these things are terrible. I pray that decades from now I will no longer wake in the deep part of the night dreaming of demons. They come to me frequently, these images of hell. I see eyes of murderers and twisted serpents, thirsty, crying against God. Maybe, at least, by my speaking out, some small portion of the undead and terrible things I've seen can be put to rest.

There will be more children like Kensen.

I don't believe we are wrestling simply with humanity's evil. If God exists, then why wouldn't a devil also exist? If Satan is real, it'd be a great benefit to him for us to believe he isn't. I have to believe there's a personality behind the horror I routinely witness. It's simply too much awfulness to pin onto chance. But I'm not afraid of the devil. I brace myself with a stronger power. "We are more than conquerors through Him who loved us. Neither death nor life, neither angels nor demons, neither the present nor the future, nor any powers, neither height nor depth, nor anything else in all creation, will be able to separate us from the love of God that is in Christ Jesus our Lord" (Romans 8:37–39).

It's often casually explained to me that these pieces of "living furniture" such as Raymonde and Kensen have nothing to offer and are a waste of good money. But each one is a person, a living soul. I have found triumph comes when I set small goals for myself, attainable, cherished prizes—for instance, when an abandoned boy, covered with diarrhea, warms to me so I'm able to pick him up. It's an entirely new definition of success. Who is not valuable when we see this new kind of value? My brother, even after he got AIDS and committed suicide, and the quadriplegics at my orphanage, and my Down syndrome children, and my cerebral palsy victims—all give me something so cherished. I have seen children unable to talk. Others unable to hear. Somehow they *all* bring me songs of my own thankfulness—thankfulness that I get to hold them, and sometimes even a strange sort of thankfulness that I am not like them. Even after all the hardships I have endured in this life, I am truly able to say I have been given so much. Can you imagine what heaven will be like for people who have never known the earth's inheritance? I mean, I expect it to be glorious and wondrous, but for those who live on this earth in constant agony . . . I hope to get a glimpse of their wonder when they first arrive.

It may be a short flight to heaven for some. I think of these words a lot: "Do not neglect to show hospitality to strangers. For some have entertained angels unaware" (Hebrews 13:2). How literally should we take these words? Could some of these street children in Haiti, particularly those who seem to live for but a moment then pass on into eternity, actually be *angels*? Maybe these little ones have been flown here only to offer us glimpses into the transcendent. They're part of the vast unseen world that becomes visible, if only for a moment.

THERE IS A POEM by Miriam Teichner I will not forget:

> *Stab my soul fiercely with others' pain,*
> *Let me walk seeing horror and stain.*
> *Let my hands, groping, find other hands.*
> *Give me the heart that divines, understands.*
> *Give me the courage, wounded, to fight.*

Why would anyone write that? Why would anyone ask to enter into suffering? I want that kind of life, crazy as it sounds. What we can suffer for another is truly the mark of love. I confess I'm not there yet, not entirely. My limits are great still. William Penn grasped it. He wrote about self-sacrifice in 1702: "Though men should not find it relish'd high enough for their finer tastes or warmer pallats, it will not, perhaps, be useless to those of lower flights." In other words, pride or loftiness will rob a soul of understanding, but meekness and humility lead to wisdom.

I understand more of that now. To enter into suffering is why I was placed on earth. From the time I was four until the moment I stepped foot in Haiti, I wondered what assignment God had in mind for me. When I took the phone call that informed me Hugh Hefner wanted to make me a *Playboy* centerfold, somehow I hoped it would lead to something greater. I hoped posing in a magazine would lead to purpose. How easy it is to seek fulfillment within the sphere of people and things that can be seen. But our souls are never satisfied with this. None of my old life offered what I was truly searching for.

Although my life's calling in Haiti is difficult, I hope I never run from it. To care for others is what I was created to do. My ability to care came from my own struggles. All the junk I went through armed me with a most incredible passion for suffering children. Suffering breaks my heart, but it doesn't break me. This isn't everybody's calling. I am only outfitted to care for these children because I felt like a monster myself when I was a kid. Today I know in the same way that these kids are not monsters either. They were born in very dysfunctional bodies, but they have thoughts and feelings and dreams. When I look into their eyes, I know why I am here. I recognize the image I saw when as a child I looked in the mirror—too much maturity for a child, old before her time, expressions children shouldn't know, feelings children should never feel. I had all those. I used to look into the mirror at home and cry. Usually, it would be after a whipping, or after my grandfather dropped me off, or maybe after somebody made fun of me in gym class for not being allowed to wear shorts. In the mirror I saw a sad, sad little girl, too old, too wise. The terrible ordeal I lived through is what equipped me for my life's calling today.

It's been many years since the night I watched that TV show— the one about the Mongolian sewer children. At last count, 3,400 Haitian children are in my care. Mercy and Sharing oversees eleven projects, ranging from feeding centers to orphanages to schools. We have new, impeccable Haitian directors, Rose Marie Martin, Gary Downey, and Dr. Manuel Castro.

And we've just bought some new property in Haiti. The land is on the mountainside along the ocean, bright, clean, and breezy. We plan to move all our handicapped and terminally ill children there, where they can see the sea and be cooled by a gentle breeze. We'll have a therapy center there to help those who can be more independent. We'll have more space—we intend to have 125 terminally ill and handicapped in residence. Orphans, of course. Plus a home for 125 healthy infants and toddlers. In time, we hope to add a trade school, a nutrition program for some 350 per day, an emergency care unit, and a primary school.

What do I wish for my children?

I hope I'm raising my kids to be extraordinary citizens, strongly educated human beings, deeply aware of what they do and don't want to have happen to themselves or their bodies. My kids are going to have dignity in their hearts and won't feel like charity cases. When these kids grow up, if they have strong guidance, maybe they can become people who affect the entire world for the better, or at least their own country.

One of my biggest obstacles in this work is sorrow. August, September, October, and the years pass away. Joe's birthday is October 13—the same day as John Branchizio's. Mark's birthday was October 15. My birthday is two weeks later. How this river races onward. The scents that lived on in the possessions of people I once knew have gradually vanished. With them, the razor sharpness of the grief that accompanied their passing has dulled, and in its place comes a new kind of sorrow—like fine dust floating in air. It sifts softly between my fingers but is never completely gone. Occasionally I pick out a shard—some still remain—and I see the reflection of people I loved so vividly again. Sometimes I pierce my soul with it, sharply again, so I do not forget they were once so very present.

Here is my peace:

There is a Love that is joy and beauty. So many of my friends, so many of my children, have found this Love. Their story is for eternity and has only just begun.

For today, my reward is in hope.

I believe that generations can be transformed by love, that the possibility of no child ever suffering does exist, that absolute good will ultimately triumph over evil, and that all will be made right one day in God's perfect timing.

Am I happy? Yes, although this world is so imperfect. I keep sight of a world where there are no more sorrows or tears, a world that we're invited to by grace. I know I will be there someday.

In the meantime, I choose to walk through the lowlands to slap away the talons of darkness that cling to my children, seemingly unloved and forgotten, but indeed the angels of a lower flight.

Acknowledgments

To my children in Haiti—the orphaned and abandoned—who never knew they were heroes. Also to the widowed, the sick, and poor who shared their country, and to those who are still with us, living to serve and heal their country. You have exemplified to all who read this book the commonality between all humanity, which is that the need of the basic elements sustaining life are equal only to the desire to be loved and cared about. In addition, deep in the eyes of the poor and abandoned, I have learned to approach the God of the Universe, and born in my soul was the desire to serve Him.

Joe, my husband, to whom this book is dedicated, thank you for never having let me feel alone through any of the events of the chapters in this book. Frank, my father, I love you and I am glad you are my father. My mother recently wrote to me asking for forgiveness and for a second chance. Thank you, Mama, and I can't wait to try.

To my friends, thank you for still being my friends, even though I tortured you all relentlessly with insecure, panicked phone calls seeking "honest" opinions, or as we all really know, assurance that each chapter should stay in the book rather than simply being ripped out due to potential embarrassment on my behalf.

Some people can't be put into a category because they are so many different things to us. Cheryl Heiberger, thanks for running the office, soothing our frazzled nerves, and solving problems often before Joe and I know we have any. You are family. We love you. The Verdeja family, for showing me what a family can be like and making me and Joe part of yours. Trish Shea, you have been a true and loyal friend to me—thank you from the heart, you are truly unique. Bob Hunnicutt, thank you for loving Trish (Why don't you ask her to marry you?). Brenda Branchizio, our bond began through a mutual tragedy and grew through love that usually only sisters share. Nancy Taylor, I thank you for your living example of true humanitarianism in Nicaragua and for your advice and willingness to pick up the phone and be a calming, sane influence during every crisis in Haiti. E. J. Christensen, I thank you for your infatigable ability to argue with me about any subject, which has kept my "verbal judo" skills competitive, at least. Joe and I consider you a brother. Thank you for all the volunteer time you have put in over the years to improve the lives of the children of Haiti. To all the children who run to hug my neck after church on Sunday, especially Megan, Marta, Christiana, and Lauren. I can't wait to see what you become. It will surely be amazing. Ingrid Gillette, Haiti will never be the same without you. We will laugh and cry together for years to come about the things you and I saw when we lived there together. Mark Salter, Ricky Hicks, Janet Hoover, Sonya Rodriguez, Carol Mason, Tonya Youngling, Linda Helmick and the Woodrow family, I love and thank you all for every prayer, every call, and every ounce of trustworthy advice. I would never forget the precious Patch Adams. Your dreams for the children and poor of the world have renewed my spirit every time I talk to you. As you always say, "Whoopie!" Derek Brown, for writing the song that describes my most secret doubts and then puts them all to rest: "When will you comfort me?" Our extraordinary board of directors: Jeffrey Leck, Ken deLaski, Frank Scott, Richard and Karen Taylor, E. J. Christensen, Mike Lypka, Dave and Carol Anderson, and Jean Dany Pierre-Francois.

Organizations that have literally put profit and commercial gain aside to save lives and feed thousands, and others who have shared so generously cannot go without mention: American Airlines; Bridgeway Charitable Foundation; Cargo Express; Compagnie Des Tabacs, Comme Il Faut; Crossroads Church of Aspen; Cure International; deLaski Family Foundation; Galambos Architects Inc.; Gift of Life; Kids Against Hunger; LDS Humanitarian Services; Miami Children's Hospital; Montefiore Medical Center; Seaboard Marine; Stop Hunger Now; Sysco Foods; (and many more that I have not mentioned to protect your privacy).

To our faithful donors who never have forgotten the children of Haiti, Mercy and Sharing thanks you from the heart on behalf of all of these children.

And last but not least, thank you does not express my gratitude to my ever faithful editor Marcus Brotherton. I know without you on my side I would have gone insane. You were a calming voice in every circumstance. You helped me defend my words and thoughts. Also, my agent, Barret Neville, thank you for your guidance. Trish Grader, my editor at Simon & Schuster, thanks for your patience; and Meghan Stevenson, thank you for keeping me on schedule.

About the Mercy and Sharing Foundation

THE MERCY AND SHARING Foundation is a private, nonprofit relief organization founded by Susie and Joe Krabacher in 1994.

Projects include an abandoned-baby unit at the public hospital, a school in the slums of Cité Soleil, an orphanage for terminally ill and handicapped children, an orphanage for healthy infants and toddlers, and a number of new feeding centers, including our recently opened health center. We have about 150 employees, mostly Haitian nationals, who help provide a loving, caring, and nurturing environment for our children.

Mercy and Sharing does not believe in charity. In all of our projects there is a common thread: opportunity. We teach our children to learn and to teach others, to learn a trade in their adolescence and to later provide for themselves and their families, and to better their country.

It is our goal to help alleviate the suffering in Haiti, for this generation and the generations to come. Your generosity, either corporate or individual, can greatly benefit the people of Haiti by developing educational programs to combat illiteracy, providing medical facilities to heal the sick and the malnourished, and supporting social programs to create hope and promote the ethical treatment of people. Mercy and Sharing is a 501(c)(3) organization.

For more information, or to become involved, please contact:

MERCY AND SHARING
201 N. Mill Street, Suite 201
Aspen, CO 81611-1557

1-877-HAITI-KIDS
1-877-424-8454
Fax: 1-970-925-1181

Susan Scott Krabacher
susie@haitichildren.com

www.haitichildren.com

ABOUT THE AUTHOR

SUSIE SCOTT KRABACHER IS founder and president of the Mercy
and Sharing Foundation, an international relief organization
dedicated to providing a safe haven for abandoned, malnourished,
and impoverished children in Haiti.

Prior to her current work, Susie worked extensively as a model
and actress, appearing in the centerfold spread of *Playboy* magazine
as Miss May 1983. She credits her renewed Christian faith and the
purpose she found in caring for Haiti's poor as the factors that led
to her life's transformation.

Susie's work as a dedicated humanitarian has been featured on
shows such as *Good Morning America, Inside Edition,* and *The
Oprah Winfrey Show,* and in periodicals such as *People, Marie
Claire, The Wall Street Journal, Los Angeles Times, Chicago Tribune,
The Denver Post, The Globe and Mail, San Francisco Chronicle,* and
more.

In 2006, Susie was honored by World of Children, Inc., an international children's advocacy group dedicated to honoring ex-
ceptional child advocates from around the world. In 2004, Susie

was granted London's Rose Award, presented by the People's Princess Charitable Foundation, which was established by Princess Diana's son Prince William to further his mother's commitment to helping the needy. Susie has received the International Humanitarian Award from the National Association for the Advancement of Haitians, the National Achievement Award from E-Town Radio, the Citizen Cool Award from the Ben & Jerry's Corporation, and the Gift of Life Award from Rotary International. She is a member of the Miami Children's Hospital Hall of Fame and has been awarded honorary citizenship in Haiti.

Susie spends nearly every waking hour working for the children of Haiti and draws no salary. All expenses of the foundation are contributed by private donations, corporate sponsorships, and by Susie and her husband, Joe Krabacher, an Aspen attorney and real estate developer.